{Between the Lines}

master the *subtle* elements
of fiction writing

JESSICA PAGE MORRELL

WRITER'S DIGEST BOOKS
Cincinnati, Ohio
www.writersdigest.com

Visit our Web site at www.writersdigest.com for information on more resources for writers.

To receive a free weekly e-mail newsletter delivering tips and updates about writing and about Writer's Digest products, register directly at our Web site at http://newsletters.fwpublications.com.

10 09 08 07 06   5 4 3 2 1

Distributed in Canada by Fraser Direct, 100 Armstrong Avenue, Georgetown, ON, Canada L7G 5S4, Tel: (905) 877-4411. Distributed in the U.K. and Europe by David & Charles, Brunel House, Newton Abbot, Devon, TQ12 4PU, England, Tel: (+44) 1626 323200, Fax: (+44) 1626 323319, E-mail: mail@davidandcharles.co.uk. Distributed in Australia by Capricorn Link, P.O. Box 704, Windsor, NSW 2756 Australia, Tel: (02) 4577-3555.

Library of Congress Cataloging-in-Publication Data

Morrell, Jessica Page
  Between the lines : master the subtle elements of fiction writing / by Jessica Page Morrell.
      p. cm.
  Includes index.
  ISBN-13: 978-1-58297-392-0 (pbk. : alk. paper)
  ISBN-10: 1-58297-392-X (pbk. : alk. paper)
  ISBN-13: 978-1-58297-393-7 (hardcover : alk. paper)
  ISBN-10: 1-58297-393-8 (hardcover : alk. paper)
  1. Fiction—Authorship. I. Title.   2005035160
  PN3355.M67 2006

  808.3--dc22

Edited by Kelly Nickell
Designed by Grace Ring
Production coordinated by Robin Richie

DEDICATION

To storytellers everywhere …

ACKNOWLEDGMENTS

A large thank you to Jane Friedman of Writer's Digest Books, who suggested that I transform my workshop into this book.

Another big thanks to Kelly Nickell, my talented editor, for her insights, patience, and special help with the structure.

Gratitude to Clark Kohanek for his friendship, generosity, and vast knowledge about all things story related.

Thanks to Bill Johnson for his support and information on films, as well as all he does for writers.

Many thanks to all the writers whose work has illuminated the craft of fiction, especially Nancy Kress, Donald Mass, William Noble, Sol Stein, James Frey, Oakley Hall, Gary Provost, and John Gardner.

Finally, thanks to my students and clients for writing their stories, which have taught me so much.

Table of Contents

Preface

*I*ve been thinking about something that Thomas E. Kennedy wrote. He said, "There's no doubt that teaching is the best way to learn because it forces you to test your assumptions and see if they're really true." I've been teaching fiction and nonfiction writers for fifteen years now, editing for about nine years. Much of what I've learned has come from analyzing what succeeds and fails in my students' and clients' stories, paragraphs, and sentences. What I've learned, working with writers on all sorts of manuscripts and in all my classes, is that fiction requires a profound depth, a lasting resonance.

I've layered my understanding of fiction like a mason constructing a stone wall. My wall has taken years to build, but it's sturdy, and what I've learned I'm happy to reveal here. Like a mason I began with a foundation, a love of books, and then, awkwardly at first, I laid down my first level of stones and smoothed in the mortar. Over the years my wall grew; my mortar became stronger. This is a book about mortar, but also about the humble ingredients of mortar: water, sand, lime, gravel, cement.

I live in Portland, Oregon, about twenty miles from the scenic Columbia River Gorge. The Columbia River, tamed by dams, spans wide as a lake and dumps into the Pacific at a dangerous stretch of water. As you drive east on Highway 84 following the Columbia, you head into high desert. The river plunges through the Cascade Mountains, which are blue hued and mysterious, changeable with the seasons. A series of waterfalls tumble downward; sometimes mist rises off the mountains like a dream.

Parts of the highway parallel the Historic Columbia River Highway, finished in 1913. An engineering feat in its day, it wound past waterfalls, blasted through mountains, and was carved on steep bluffs over the wind-tossed river. In many places these old walls—some simple, some graceful and intricate—ribbon along the road and at scenic overlooks. Italian masons built much of this stonework. I

1

like to imagine these immigrants working amid the wild lands in the early 1900s. I imagine what they ate for lunch, how they kept off the rain. But this I know: They built for permanence. Their work holds true almost one hundred years later. And it's a beauty of simplicity and elegance and strength.

Writing fiction is a craft that we apply, stone by stone, smoothing the jagged places in between.

When I'm working with a client's manuscript, I first read through it, jotting notes on problems that I spot. Then I start asking myself what is missing in the story, what depths have not been plumbed. (I'm afraid something is always missing or neglected.) And, feeling like a detective, I often go for walks with my client's manuscript in my thoughts. I'm searching for the mortar and pieces that create a world that is evocative, brimming with life, complicated, and true.

Between the Lines is an accumulation of the many suggestions I've made to students and clients over the years. My students have heard me say, "Put weather in this scene," or, "You need to slow down here so we can really feel this scene," and other exhortations many times, so I'm grateful for an opportunity to gather my recommendations in one place.

I'm also grateful to be putting all these ideas into one volume, because a compelling narrative often lies between the lines, in the quiet moments and the subtlest techniques, where fiction lifts off the page and settles into the veins of the reader. This soaring isn't mere rhetoric; it is part of the "fictional dream" that John Gardner so aptly described in *The Art of Fiction*, and it also implies a level of technique that separates polished writers from hacks.

I'm assuming that you're reading this book because you want to become a published writer, that you have dreams and aspirations. I wish I could offer you a magic spell, a whispered incantation that would whisk you from unpublished writer to the status of published author. But instead I can offer my hands and nails, calloused and cracked from years of fixing stories, along with my hard-won understanding of this craft of writing fiction. And in these pages I can show you how to build permanence and grace.

A Deep, Deep World

> Though the literary dabbler may write a fine story now and then, the true writer is one for whom technique has become, as it is for the concert pianist, second nature.
> —John Gardner

The best fiction touches the deep layers in us. A writer achieves this effect by embedding dozens of techniques into his story. The process is artful, and, I'm sorry to report, often sly. In fact, fiction writers employ the sort of sleight of hand used by a magician: They distract with patter; whisper so that we lean in to hear their low, confiding tone; surprise us when we least expect to be surprised, produce flourishes that awe with their boldness. And somehow they make it look easy, although often the techniques are invisible.

But of course, writing fiction is not easy or merely a matter of employing tricks. Fiction writing means applying craft and artifice, and, like a conjurer's lightning-speed maneuvers, it can be learned. You look beyond the magician's charming grin and focus on his ever-moving fingers, the devices tucked up his sleeves, and his bag of gadgets. You start by mastering a few card tricks and then move on to a more difficult step: disassembling the magician's contraptions, applying them to your understanding, and finally adding them to your stories.

Let's begin with this understanding: Stories explore how interesting people act while dealing with significant problems at an important time in their lives. They explore human vulnerabilities and strengths and are usually focused on a character's goals and dilemmas. Stories inquire into why people act, react, struggle and change as they do. Stories are shaped from techniques that make the narrative lifelike, involved, complicated, and tense. And these fundamentals, which saturate the story with meaning, result in a deep, deep world.

It seems that there are as many types of fiction configured into novels, novellas, and short stories as there are stars in a shimmering summer sky. There are comedies, tragedies, happily-ever-after stories, horror stories, historical re-creations, fantasies, young adult stories, and novels that roller coaster along with pathos, black humor, and grim portrayals of humanity. Some novels track the affairs of the heart; others track a murderer to his hideout or a monster to his lair. Fiction can be of a serious or literary bent or can be as fluffy as marshmallows. Short stories come in all sizes, and novels weigh in at a mere 60,000 words or ramble on to 200,000 words.

So the first choice of a would-be fiction writer is to choose the type and scope of the story; then comes the reality of crafting it. That's when a word-slinger discovers that creating a compelling narrative is complex and difficult. Or, that the idea that seemed so dazzling and original when first imagined becomes flat and predictable when translated onto the page.

Adding to this reality, beginning writers are often daunted by rules and advice about how fiction is constructed. I've noticed that writers tackle fiction in several ways. Some writers simply ignore advice, preferring to wing it or write guided by instinct and intuition, claiming that guidelines are a straightjacket to plotting and creativity.

Then there are writers who take the opposite path and slavishly read every book written on the topic, outline obsessively, and work with archetypes and mythic structures. The writers in the second group often spend five, six, ten years on a manuscript, revising it so many times that it bears little resemblance to their original concept.

Perhaps the healthiest approach to writing fiction lies somewhere in between.

You see, it's impossible to write fiction without understanding its underpinnings: conflict, scene structure, and character development. Without this understanding, you might write two or three or four hundred pages, but you won't end up with a story; instead you'll produce a lot of words on a lot of pages or a haphazard pile of scenes loosely clustered around characters that never quite come to life.

A story of any length can never be haphazard or based on predictable characters. Readers want to be haunted by characters and specific scenes. They want

4

to carry the story within as they go about daily activities. They want to be transported to another time and place.

Let's begin by adding to our understanding, so that you too can create a haunting story.

INGREDIENTS FOR SUCCESS

Writing fiction means you'll be entering another realm, because fiction writing requires an intense immersion into your characters' lives and your story world. Because a novel is the sum of many parts, you must first master how these parts work together before you can add the delicate layers of techniques covered in these chapters.

It's difficult to find the perfect analogy for writing fiction, but you can compare it to another kind of artistry, an elaborate meal prepared with precision by a master chef. Every element of the meal will entice, and there will be an array of flavors, textures, and colors, all meant to beguile and satisfy.

While a magician's tricks happen at lighting speed and thus are difficult to discern, you can witness a chef at work and learn from his practiced approach. You can take note of the ingredients he works with—extra-virgin olive oil and aged balsamic vinegar, fresh oregano, finely minced garlic or ginger. You can witness how he sears the flank steak to seal in flavors and deglazes the pan to create a sauce. You may suspect that his seemingly effortless approach took years to acquire, and you'd be right. But luckily, his recipe can be followed and his techniques emulated.

When it comes to fiction, think of these elements as your ingredients, not as formulas. Remember, too, that cooking is a physical activity and requires forethought and analysis, as does fiction writing. When you cook a dish such as paella, you use a whole list of ingredients, but if you don't add the correct ones at the correct time and allow them to simmer until the flavors have melded, the dish will fail. Or, if you omit a crucial ingredient like saffron, it won't taste authentic.

Similarly, the ingredients in fiction combine to create a finished product, but they don't necessarily create an involving story. Good stories come from the vibrancy of your characters, along with the subtler aspects found between the lines.

Let's start with nine ingredients that you'll find in any successful piece of fiction.

1. BALANCE

Balance is the notion that every element in the story exists in its proper proportion. Each scene is orchestrated for its heft and potency, never used as filler; secondary characters are not more interesting than the stars, and the climax must be allowed its full weight. Every word a fiction writer uses telegraphs to readers what is important to his story and what is not.

Thus, if you spend three paragraphs on describing an altar in a boy's school, this suggests that the altar is important, perhaps the scene of a crime or an indiscretion. If the altar never appears again in the story, the reader is left with a vague unease from an unfulfilled promised. When you lavish a person, place, or object with descriptive details, readers expect them to have a corresponding importance. Keep this in mind when you invent a minor character who twirls into scene after scene, dropping funny one-liners or profound truths while the protagonist seems to shrink in her shadow, or when you create an incident that you find amusing, but has nothing to do with the story.

In fiction, three main elements tend to have the most influence over the balance of a story: character development, plotting, and setting. Characterization is the observable layers of your character, such as dialogue, appearance, and personality. Character development is about the inner world of your characters and includes their backstories, conflicts, desires, and character arcs. These depths of character are your main ingredients. Plotting means that you're dramatizing the character arc through a series of events, reversals, and problems, while keeping the pacing (the speed at which the story unfolds) firmly in check. Setting includes the locale for each scene as well as information needed to understand the story events. Each component must be aligned so that the story doesn't tilt too far in one direction.

If the characters never change or grow, the story will be unbalanced. If we never hear the characters speak or if they chitchat endlessly, the story will be unbalanced. Likewise, it will be unbalanced if the setting is barely discernible, if the middle bogs down, if there is never a pause or reflection after major events, if not enough happens in the story, or if events have no consequences.

Usually the story is designed around a central problem with a series of complicating factors that make solving the problem difficult. If the protagonist's problem is not difficult to overcome, if it is solved too quickly, or if the solution is never in doubt, the story will lack suspense and seem flat.

6

It's also important to consider balance as an inherent part of reader's emotional experience. Many novels are written to reestablish symmetry in a chaotic world, to set things right by suggesting endings and resolution that don't always occur in the real world.

Fiction opens with a lack of balance. An inciting incident upsets an already dynamic, simmering world and throws the protagonist into a situation he might not have entered willingly. The story then progresses with an urgent need to reinstate equilibrium. Balance comes into play as the fictional world and its characters strain toward stability.

Balance is fairly easy to analyze in your work. First, keep track of the word count that you allot to characters, scenes, and exposition to determine if these elements are proportional. Notice when you're showing and when you're telling and make certain that the most important moments are staged, not summarized or told secondhand. Second, make certain that you're portraying a world and characters that are unbalanced, even suffering, and then struggle to restore order.

2. READER EMPATHY

Your reader wants to be lured from his daily life into your story. He wants to forget about his bank balance, bad back, and upcoming dentist appointment. He wants to travel somewhere, be someone else, feel what your characters feel, and know what your characters know.

This emotional involvement comes from the reader believing in your story world from the opening lines. Your job is to create a world that is so brilliant that when the reader begins turning the pages of your opening chapter, reality falls away. Robert McKee, in *Story: Substance, Structure, Style and the Principles of Screenwriting* explains the dynamic this way:

> Through empathy, the vicarious linking of ourselves to a fictional human being, we test and stretch our humanity. The gift of story is the opportunity to live lives beyond our own, to desire and struggle in a myriad of worlds and times, at all the various depths of our being.

Thus, reading involves developing empathy for characters living in a realistic place and dealing with relatable problems. As you work your fictional magic, you'll tap into the reader's reservoirs of emotions, but it won't be easy. Too much

7

tugging at the emotions and you'll create melodrama; not enough and you'll end up with a report. In many of us, emotions are not lying along the surface; they are deeply felt and sometimes buried. With a surgeon's care, a fiction writer works to extricate these feelings and tap into the reader's emotional core. This is achieved by exposing characters' core feelings: As the reader comes to know your characters, usually in the midst of their suffering, the reader experiences moments of recognition and self-discovery.

3. DRAMATIC QUESTION

Your next ingredient is the single, powerful question around which your story is based. This question will be dramatized chiefly via action in a series of events or scenes. If you are writing a romance, the question always involves whether the couple will resolve their differences and declare their love. In a mystery, the dramatic question might be *Will Detective Smith find the serial killer in time to prevent another senseless death?* In *The Old Man and the Sea*, the dramatic question is *Will Santiago catch the big fish and thus restore his pride and reputation?* In *To Kill a Mockingbird*, the dramatic question is *Can Atticus Finch defend his client against the trumped-up charges and face down the racism of the community?*

Practice writing your story's dramatic question. Better yet, post it near your work space so you're constantly reminded of its focus.

4. THE *WHY?* FACTOR

The sciences of psychology and psychiatry delve into why people act as they do. These sciences categorize people's healthy, erratic, dysfunctional, or destructive behaviors into organic illnesses, genetic factors, environmental influences, learned behaviors, maladaptive influences, and the like. But at the core of all this peering into the human psyche lies the big question of *why?*

This compelling question also lies at the core of fiction. If you do not know why your characters act as they do, you do not know your characters and, sadly, neither will your readers. If you've created a group of characters who move around with the abandon of ping pong balls, you'll merely make your reader dizzy. Motivation, the *why?* of fiction, is at the heart of every scene, fueling your character's desires and driving him to accomplish goals. It provides a solid foun-

8

dation for the often complicated reasons for your character's choices, actions, and blunders. Motivating factors provide trajectories for character development, as a character's past inevitably intersects with his present. Your character's motivations must be in sync with his core personality traits and realistically linked to goals so that readers can take on these goals as their own.

Let's look further at desire, because it is the lifeblood of fictional characters. Not only do your characters want something, they want something badly. Santiago, in *The Old Man and the Sea*, desperately wants to restore his reputation and resume his friendship and partnership with the boy. And in the lonely hours when he is far out at sea, desperately struggling to hang on to the fish and fighting off sharks, we see his fierce desire acted out and the price he pays for it.

You can bestow on your character flaming red hair, an endearing, crooked grin, and a penchant for chocolate and noir movies, but if she doesn't want something badly, she's merely a prop in your story, not a driving force. But if she wants to win the Miss Florida contest, take over her boss's job, or become the first female shortstop for the Atlanta Braves, then you've got a character who will make things happen and a story that will be propelled by desire.

5. INTIMACY

Not to be confused with empathy, intimacy speaks to the level of specificity and a pulsating reality in the fictional world. Intimate fiction is populated with characters that readers know by their physicality, intense desires, emotional scars, and other factors from their pasts, along with their limitations and inner conflicts. But intimacy is not only about physicality or a character's goals; it's about a deep experience that the reader feels while living amid the story. In an intimate novel, the reader knows what he'll find in the protagonist's refrigerator because the writer takes time to create homey and practical details.

In a story rendered with intimacy, the reader knows that the kitchen and front hallway of your character's house smells of lavender or mildew or wet dog or bacon. If the bathroom is tidy or messy. If the den is crowded with family photos and keepsakes or as sterile as a laboratory. She imagines what she'll find in the glove box of the protagonist's car, and knows if your character is the sort who gets regular oil changes or lets the car limp along, neglected or abused. The reader knows how characters live and think and eat and even make love.

An intimate world isn't created by merely piling on details. It has the resonance of childhood memories, the vividness of a dream, and the power of a movie. It's filled in with shadows and corners and dogs and ice cubes and the sounds and smells of a dryer humming on wash day, and a car blaring past, rap music shaking the windows. These details lend it authority, potency, and a palpable physical existence.

An intimate story takes us to a specific place and coaxes us to remain there. It feels as real and complicated as the world the reader inhabits. When the reader finishes the final pages and leaves the story world, she should feel the satisfaction of the ending, but also a huge sense of loss, like a friend has moved to another town just when the friendship had reached a high level of closeness and trust.

6. OBSTACLES AND LAYERED CONFLICT

Many books written about fiction techniques cover the importance of conflict and obstacles, so we'll discuss these components only briefly. Conflict is not so much a single ingredient as it is linked to every element used to write fiction. Obstacles create conflict and conflict is the engine of fiction. No conflict, no story.

Well-written fiction includes ever-growing dilemmas, adversities, and pressures as the story progresses. These pressures are layered into the story and exist as outward obstacles (such as antagonists) as well as inner conflicts.

While obstacles can be physical, such as a mountain to be crossed or starvation overcome, they most often take the shape of another person or a group of people. An antagonist or villain makes a story worrisome, especially when he appears on stage with the protagonist. Antagonists come in all sizes and shapes, from the villagers in Shirley Jackson's "The Lottery," to the Nazis in *The African Queen*, to Hannibal Lecter and Buffalo Bill in *The Silence of the Lambs*. Place a bad guy on the stage and the reader pays attention, wondering what dastardly deed he'll try next, especially as, bit by bit, you reveal what evil he's capable of. And as your reader's growing concern about the villain's capabilities blooms, it flowers alongside the protagonist's flaws, weaknesses, and doubts.

Thus, your task as a fiction writer is to create a dramatic and interesting conflict that operates in the outside world, but also draws from a deep vein within the protagonist, possibly based on his greatest fear.

7. RESONANCE

There is no easy definition for resonance, but you know when the novel you're reading has it. It stems from a careful writer making careful choices at every turn and creating a story that both persists in the reader's memory and contains layers of meaning and subtle effects. Resonance is achieved by using elements of flow, language, imagery, and theme to maximize the drama, while invoking a subtle or not-so-subtle lingering presence. It is about emotions that underscore scenes and dialogue, and setting that breathes rather than exists as a backdrop.

The easiest way to achieve resonance might be to ask yourself a simple question as you craft each page and scene. As you make word-by-word choices and layer in descriptions via the senses, ask yourself, "What emotion do I want my reader to feel here?" If you understand your intent, you can choose words, descriptions, and dialogue that accomplish that aim.

8. UNITY

An effective story or novel has a single, unified purpose, mood, and voice that sweeps the reader toward an inevitable and satisfying resolution. Along the way, the writer uses devices such as tone, atmosphere, description, and action to articulate his singular vision.

This type of unity, from style choices to scene details to character development, also pushes the reader to understand themes and thus deepens his experience. A unified story unfolds seamlessly without needless digressions, extraneous characters, and unnecessary scenes, and leads to an inevitable conclusion and an enduring sense of reality.

9. SATISFYING ENDING

Finally, every story needs an ending that satisfies the reader while concluding the plot. Some endings are quiet, some ambivalent, some a dramatic or violent clash of wills. But there is always a sense that all of the tension that has been operating in your story world has finally come to a head.

John Updike, the Pulitzer-winning author of novels and short stories, described fictional endings in *The Best American Short Stories, 1984*:

> The good ending dismisses us with a touch of ceremony and throws a backward light of significance over the story just read. It makes it, as they say, or unmakes it. A

weak beginning is forgettable, but the end of a story bulks in the reader's mind like the giant foot in a foreshortened photograph.

A novel can start out slow or limp occasionally, but still be judged as well written. However, when an ending falls short, it kills off all the pleasures that came before it and leaves a sour taste in the reader's mouth. So craft your endings with the greatest care and make certain that the loose ends and issues in the story are wrapped up or explained.

{ * }

When I first began teaching, I explained to students that reading is the foundation for writing and that writers must analyze an author's techniques, track plot structures and devices, deconstruct character development, and notice places where the prose fails or dazzles.

In this book, I've included references to many of the novels I've read in the last few years, and to several that I read years ago. I've also sprinkled in a number of films as examples. My reason for including films is simple: During my years of teaching and lecturing, I've discovered that, in a classroom of twenty or in an audience of two hundred, it's difficult to find a single novel that most of the people in the room have read. On the other hand, many people have seen classic films like *The Wizard of Oz*, *To Kill a Mockingbird*, or *The African Queen*, as well as current films like *Saving Private Ryan* or *Sideways*, so it often works to use films to illustrate certain points.

Now that we've covered the basic ingredients necessary for a story's success, let's move on to the subtle and nuanced effects that we achieve by slipping delicate seasonings into fiction, those elements that often lie between the lines.

chapter **1**

Art & Artifice: Keeping Readers Spellbound

{ *Drama—what literature does at night.*

—George Jean Nathan

iction stems from the human need to recall our past, relate our daily experiences, explain how the world works, and speak to our hopes and futures. Fiction is also artifice, made up of elements woven together to engage a reader's imagination, and grows out of a need to find meaning in the happenings of our lives. While this book is about layering your writing with intricacy and resonance, it is important to note that this layering cannot happen without understanding the origins and purposes of storytelling. Let's begin with exploring fiction's origins and how stories keep readers spellbound.

Yes, spellbound, because before you can incorporate the finer elements of craft, you must recognize that fiction evolved from an oral and visual tradition. Storytelling has enraptured mankind since we began talking about 500,000 years ago and continues whenever two or more people gather. We are a species with a deep longing to pass along stories. Stories were part of ceremonies, as in the elaborate potlatch ceremonies of the Pacific Northwest natives, and exist in the oral traditions of the Celts, Germanic tribes, and Australian Aborigines. Story is at the heart of the dramas of ancient Greece and Rome. Ghost stories were told in the great castles of Europe as the nobility gathered at hearths to while away the long winter nights. Stories have been preserved on tapestries, cave walls, petroglyphs, totem poles, and the teepees of Native Americans. Storytelling evolved into Homer's epic poems, fables, fairy tales, creation stories, ghost stories, myths and legends, the contemporary novel, and even into the moving pictures of television and film.

So what does this all mean to the modern-day fiction writer? Since fiction stems from this oral and visual tradition, we attempt to make the writing physical, visceral, and potent. This physicality is achieved by using powerful charms and tapping into timeless themes.

THE READER'S JOURNEY

Two things happen when people read. First, they subvocalize, meaning they hear the words and the story told inside their heads. Second, a reader's vast array of images and memories comes into play on a sort of inner movie screen, where your words are transformed into moving pictures.

A reader's movie begins unfolding when he opens your novel, as the images of your story start flickering across the screen of his imagination. As the scenes and images appear, the reader draws on a vast storehouse of memories and experiences to incorporate what he knows about life into the story he's reading. All the birthday parties, museum trips, Fourth of July parades and fireworks, and days spent in chalk-smelling classrooms are drawn on to keep the movie running. Your job then, is to *remind* him of this storehouse of images. Reminders are best relayed through the senses, through vivid verbs and specific nouns that paint a picture, and through drama—action, dialogue, and movements on a stage.

While the brain translates marks on a page, the only sense engaged is sight. This means that the artifice of fiction comes from stimulating senses that are not actually involved while reading. You can relate that your character's kitchen smells like banana bread baking, that it is warm from the oven, and that rain is rattling against the steamy window over the sink as she moves about, chopping walnuts and stirring the batter. You can reveal how she burns her hand when taking the bread from the oven. While reading, the brain elicits the smells and other senses of the kitchen and imagines the burned flesh and the cooling relief as she runs cold water over her fingers and applies an ointment. All these imaginings are rendered from a single sense, sight.

14

THE ORIGINS OF STORYTELLING

Travel back in time and find your ancestors, primitive people frightened of the night, startled by sudden noises, and troubled by the mysteries of birth and death. To be human has always meant needing answers and solace. And ever since a fire was built and a circle of people hunkered around its warmth, stories were spun to retell the day's triumphs and tragedies, to keep away the roving beasts, cold, and darkness, and to explain birth, death, love, loss, and other human mysteries.

Stories were told by shamans and elders but also by ordinary people. But no matter the topic or who was speaking, once spoken language evolved, so did stories. Stories became part of the human existence, and since those first tales, some bathed in firelight, stories have transported listeners from their ordinary concerns into the world created by the storyteller and their own imaginings.

THE PHYSICALITY OF STORYTELLING

Imagine the evening fire where Urgg, a respected hunter, recounts the day's mammoth hunt, exhausted by the toll of the day. Some of Urgg's listeners might have been part of his hunting party, still feeling the after-effects of adrenaline, wearing skins still damp from fording a river. Or the whole clan or tribe might have gathered, including a woman with nerves raw from caring for a colicky baby. In other words, the listeners' bodies were keenly felt and their physicality was part of the listening experience and ultimately could distract them from the story being told.

Today's listener or reader has a similar physicality and exists in two worlds during the reading experience: the world of your story and the real world. Interestingly, he wants to experience the novel as an event or a series of events, like those that happen in his daily world, such as sipping a latte at Starbucks or playing touch football.

When you read about a character cooking, in essence you're extrapolating your own lifetime of cooking experiences into the character's behaviors. Or, if characters are making love, you can be physically stimulated by the scene on the page as a result of your emotional and sexual responses, which are also linked to memory.

Furthermore, while reading fiction, the reader is moving in and out of time, traveling between real time (glancing up at the clock to see if it's time to pick up her toddler at preschool) and story time (where Duncan, the head of a Scottish clan, is about to charge the enemy clan). Thus, her daily existence seeps into the story, and then she filters it out again as she slips back into the story.

The point to remember here is that a specific, sensory, and evocative writing style, blended into techniques such as creating complicated characters, potent conflict, and simmering suspense, helps your reader block out the real world in favor of your fictional world. This happens because your story has the same sensory characteristics as life and elicits the same feelings from readers that they experience in everyday life.

BACK TO THE FIRE RING

Let us return to our ancestors gathered around the fire, listening rapt as Urgg describes his near-deadly encounter with a leopard. Not only is Urgg a storyteller, he is also one of the first thespians to grace a stage. When Urgg reaches the point in the story where the leopard attacks, he leaps to his feet, pantomiming how the animal sprang from the tree, catching him off guard. His eyes widen to indicate his fright; he bares his teeth to imitate the leopard's gleaming incisors; and he crouches to imitate its feline grace. He growls and roars, slashes and parries to depict his defensive gestures. If his listeners seem to be nodding off, he turns up the volume, adding more sound effects or a twist to worry the listeners.

Since you cannot see your audience sitting around the fire, you must imagine them and borrow Urgg's techniques. Urgg discovered that, once his listeners were experiencing the story, they looked ahead, imagining what might befall the protagonist. As he began his recitation, they fell into the story, just like at night you fall into a dream. It is helpful to remember that readers are dreaming the dream along with you and want to remain in dreamland as long as possible.

Now notice the listeners: When you sit near a fire, your front or extremities become warm while your backside grows cold. So from time to time, the listeners must shift around, trying for uniform warmth. While toasting another body part, they notice that outside the fire's ring eyes gleam in the dark; from time to time the lonely howl of a wolf or coyote sends shivers down their spines; bats circle and dart; and an owl's hoot shatters a pause in the story.

16

The world and all its realities and dangers surrounds the fire ring, a compounding reality filtering through the story. By melding the real world with the story world, listeners not only identified with Urgg, with his booming laugh and frail youngest child tucked next to him, but also felt like participants in the tale because as they listened they could also smell, hear, and feel their dangerous and mysterious surroundings.

Listening to a story was an experience, like hunting, wading in a stream, or making love.

Thousands of years later, we still sit rapt in the fire's glow. And in the flickering firelight, your reader wants to be part of the story world, which can be as real as the fire ring with all its sounds, smells, and crackling flames. Look hard at your writing and create an intensely sensory world. In fiction we don't write to emote or lecture; we are seeking to revitalize an ancient form. Make certain that your story contains the timeless charms of Urgg's fireside tales—movement, sound effects, and sensory involvement.

{ * }

Storytelling endures and will continue to do so, no matter how technology changes its form. We pay attention to the ancient art of storytelling because modern fiction writers have descended from a long tribe of masters and because storytelling is a physical experience that expresses enduring themes. When we write based on mythic structure and incorporate the physical aspects of storytelling, we can bring fresh and endless interpretations to storytelling and keep this valued and necessary tradition alive.

ries

ory

ont

ory

vers

mes

the

age

ing

the

ent

chapter 2
Backstory

Prose is architecture, not interior decorating.

—Ernest Hemingway

 story can be divided into two categories: backstory and front story. Front story covers the scenes on the page that are happening in the present and pressing forward. Backstory reflects the influences from the past.

Backstory has two main jobs to fulfill in your story: (1) to reveal important information about the main characters, and (2) to help depict a fully realized story world. A character's backstory comprises all the data of his history, revealing how he became who he is, and why he acts as he does and thinks as he thinks. It also reveals influences of an era, family history, and world events (such as wars) that affect the story and its inhabitants. Backstory illuminates the origins of behaviors and motives, especially those tied into the main conflict.

Because fiction requires a mighty engine to thrust it ahead—and take the reader along for the ride—backstory, if used incorrectly, can stall a story. A novel with too little backstory can be thin and is likely to be confusing. By the same token, a novel with too much backstory can lack suspense.

So here's the problem: A constant civil war wages within a fiction writer over the how, how much, and when of slipping in backstory. It must be cleverly inserted so that it's unobtrusive and allows the front story to press ahead. Perhaps the biggest problem with weaving in backstory revolves around this simple fact:

The reader doesn't need to know as much as the writer does. If you've crafted biographies of your major players, outlined and perhaps sketched your fictional town, you'll be itching to impart all this detail. Or, if you've crafted a complicated history for planet Xenus, complete with a thousand years of wars, interplanetary travel, and ruling dynasties, you'll long to include it all. Or, if you're writing a historical novel and have spent months researching Victorian England, you'll want to pass on all your research notes.

Remember this: The fantasy world of your story will loom larger in your imagination than it will on the page. Some authors can get away with including exhaustive details (these authors are usually under contract with a publisher), but most writers make careful choices about what to reveal and what to leave out.

When deciding when and where to use backstory in your work, it can help to think about what you're trying to accomplish within a given scene. To do this, however, you need to understand the many functions of backstory.

What Backstory Can Do for Your Story

A well-told story is substantive, the opposite of a PowerPoint presentation because it teems with the lives of the characters. Backstory is the means to fill in the gaps, supply a character's motivation and depth, and clarify how a world works. Let's take a closer look at four of the most crucial functions backstory can fulfill: (1) raising the stakes, (2) revealing motivations, (3) expressing innermost fears, and (4) revealing obstacles.

1. RAISING THE STAKES

Something is always at stake in fiction. Not only do readers come to care about the protagonist, they recognize that what's at stake matters. Every story cannot be depicted as a life-or-death struggle, yet the outcome means happiness or misery, health or disease, peace or discord for the protagonist. And the stakes, which are tied to outcome, always pulse with the potential for disaster. This escalating possibility for doom is essential to create suspense and tension, and, in fact, the protagonist's life should always be depicted as deliciously precarious. Finally, the outcome of a novel, whatever its genre or plot, must always matter desperately to the protagonist and usually to other characters, particularly the antagonist, as well.

19

In the film version of Thomas Harris's *The Silence of the Lambs,* which follows the novel closely, we learn that Buffalo Bill has murdered and mutilated his previous victims. When Agent Starling first visits the investigation headquarters, Buffalo Bill's victims are displayed in graphic crime scene photos so that the reader foresees the horrible fate of his next victim. Thus, when Catherine, the senator's daughter, is captured, we're aware of the gruesome torments that await her. Further, because backstory reveals that Buffalo Bill keeps his victims alive for a certain number of days, the stakes are increased because time is running out for Catherine.

The Dogs of Babel, by Carolyn Parkhurst, offers an illustration of how to personalize and increase the stakes in a novel. The protagonist, Paul Iverson, changes in a moment when his wife, Lexy, dies under odd circumstances. His grief turns into obsession as he puzzles out the facts of his wife's death.

Paul's sanity is what's at stake in this story. In his own words, he has slipped "off the deep end" and is in danger of losing everything. It appears that Paul is forever marked by Lexy's death, unable to recover and return to his former life or forge a new one.

Parkhurst uses backstory to contrast Paul's loving marriage to Lexy with his failed marriage to Maura, his first wife:

> … whose voice filled our house like a thick mortar, sealing every crack and corner. Maura, this first wife of mine, spoke so much while saying so little that I sometimes felt as if I were drowning in the heavy paste of her words.

Maura, an anxious, controlling woman, became increasingly hostile until the marriage ended. The introduction of this backstory increases our sympathy for Paul and sharply contrasts his first and second wives:

> I met Lexy less than a year later, and I knew from our first conversation that when she talked it was an easy thing, plain and open, with none of the Byzantine turns and traps I found myself caught in when I talked to Maura.

More details told via backstory increase the reader's empathy for Paul. After Paul meets Lexy at her garage sale, he drives away "with a feeling of laughter caught in my chest. I felt happier than I had felt in a long time."

Contrasting the two women and marriages works in the story: In fact, whenever you can contrast people, events, or objects in fiction, do so. Maura is angry and obsessive; Lexy is funny, artistic, and whimsical. Anyone who has ever left a relationship with a difficult person and then found a new beloved will understand. But showing Lexy's personality and her marriage with Paul also raises the stakes because the reader feels Paul's loss and heartbreak, and is drawn into the mystery of Lexy's death. This unanswered question looms over the story, causing suspense and worry.

In your own stories, contrast is a powerful tool, as when you describe a character before and after a trauma, or involved in a happy and unhappy relationship. As in Parkhurst's story, when a stable character becomes unstable, readers worry. Backstory can also reveal that a character has a tendency toward self-destruction, depression, or rash actions, all of which raise the stakes.

2. REVEALING MOTIVATIONS

Motivation provides reasons why characters do the things they do. In fact, almost every action and choice a character makes stems from motivation. Since backstory reflects the influences of the past, it's also the source for motivations. A protagonist is a person with a burning desire, and backstory reveals where this desire stems from.

One of the great difficulties in providing motivation is making it consistent with the character's values and personality. Backstory provides a window into how a character came to be who he is. Let's say you're writing a story set during the Vietnam War, and your character, Randall, was raised in a small Oklahoma town and was the fourth generation of his family to join the army. He's idolized his father, a retired army captain who was a tough but loving parent and passed on a code of conduct that stressed honor, loyalty, and serving your country.

Now twenty-two and a sergeant, Randall's backstory motivates him to believe in his mission as he capably leads his men through the sultry Vietnamese jungle with his nerves straining at every sound. But meanwhile, his girlfriend, Kelly, has joined the anti-war movement and has been writing to him about her new anti-war views. After making love during Randall's last leave in Hawaii, she suggests they don't have a future together if he stays in the army.

Meanwhile, the senseless killing of the war, along with the uncertainty, drug use, and persistent heat and craziness is making Randall question everything he learned before he landed so far from home. He wants to be a good soldier like his father, he wants to marry Kelly, but mostly he just wants to get the heck out of Vietnam and put the stench of rotting bodies and napalm behind him. Randall's

21

dilemma would not be as dramatic if we didn't know about his heritage and Kelly and if his past and the present weren't on a collision course.

It can be helpful to keep a Post-It note near your computer that briefly states your protagonist's desire, such as "Howard Perry wants to take over the family business," "Genevieve Sanders wants to escape her painful past," or, "Michele Bronson wants to have a family." Use your character's desire as your North Star, and then ask yourself how you've proven this desire through backstory.

3. EXPRESSING INNERMOST FEARS

Backstory also helps define your protagonist's greatest fears, which naturally play a key role in the overall story. Use your protagonist's fears as a shorthand method for shaping a story line, and then turn her fear into a looming reality. If Deborah, the protagonist in your suspense novel, is a young single mother whose adorable three-year-old daughter, Bethany, means everything to her, then Bethany's safety will be jeopardized by a disease, an accident, a child molester, an unstable ex-husband, or a kidnapper.

The backstory reveals why Deborah is raising Bethany on her own (her ex-husband was a violent alcoholic), how tenuous her circumstances are (she works for low wages in a day care center but dreams of having her own day care business), information about the child's father (he was once arrested for drunk driving with Bethany in her infant seat), and information about why Deborah's family cannot help. By putting what Deborah loves most in jeopardy, fears are put into play. By validating those fears through backstory, you also raise the stakes.

In Michael Crichton's *Disclosure*, for example, the protagonist fears losing his family, career, and security. The story is set in the computer industry in Seattle, where Tom Sanders and his family are living the good life. Tom, an executive at Digicom, is in the midst of a corporate merger and expecting a promotion and a raise. Then the rug is pulled out from under him when his ex-lover, Meredith Johnson, is hired as his boss. Worried about his standing in the company, he agrees to an after-hours meeting with Johnson. But instead of discussing work matters, she makes it clear that she expects to resume their sexual relationship, and threatens to ruin him if he doesn't acquiesce.

In most stories, backstory explains the main conflict between the antagonist and protagonist, especially if they have met before. In *Disclosure*, the conflict between Sanders and Johnson would not have been plausible if they hadn't been former lovers and if her fond memories of their lovemaking didn't fuel her demands.

As you begin to express your protagonist's fears through backstory, be sure you have a clear understanding of exactly what those fears are. It can be helpful to create another Post-It that articulates your protagonist's fears, such as "Howard Perry fears that his younger brother Justin, his father's favorite, will be awarded the CEO position of the family business although he hasn't earned it." Or, "Genevieve Sanders is afraid that her past will always haunt her, especially when her abusive ex-husband moves into town." Or, "Michele Bronson, thirty-six, is afraid that time is running out on her chances for love and a family."

4. REVEALING OBSTACLES

In literary and genre fiction, all stories are built around conflict, the mighty engine that keeps the plot simmering. Conflict stems from the obstacles, large and small, placed in each scene, blocking or stalling the protagonist's progress and desires. Placing obstacles that stem from your protagonist's backstory ups the ante, because these obstacles will push the protagonist's buttons.

For example, in a romance novel, readers need to know aspects from the hero's and heroine's pasts that will create barriers to love. If the heroine is a widow and her husband, a policeman, died on the job, she'll vow never to be involved with a man in a dangerous profession again. This means that it's likely that the hero will be a fireman or involved in some life-threatening profession.

Fiction is a constantly changing world of unease, much of it subtle. Conflict must permeate every aspect of the story, and large and small obstacles are ideal for doing this, with the most potent obstacles having dark tendrils creeping in from the past.

CREATING A CHARACTER'S BIO

Newspaper editors keep a file of biographies, or bios, on hand for thousands of celebrities and politicians. This information is used to flesh out news stories or craft a quick obituary. A bio reflects the most important facts of a person's life, highlighting achievements and influences.

Before you begin writing your novel, craft bios or dossiers for your main characters. Then expand on them as the stories progress. These detailed descriptions and backstories help you shape characters who are consistent, fully realized, and compelling. If your characters exist as shadowy figures in your imagination, they will also exist as shadowy figures for your readers. Besides, writing a bio is a fun method of delving into backstory.

In each character's bio, note pertinent details and influences and think about how these can ultimately be used to shape story events and conflicts. Focus on a character's socio-economic background—if she was raised in a large or small family, in a rural or urban town, in a religious family or among atheists. Note if her parents were conservative or liberal, politically active or not involved, happily married or divorced. Of course, all these examples have endless permutations and possibilities.

Keep in mind this quote from Henry James: "We care what happens to people only in proportion as we know what people are." And don't worry if your character bio is dry and factual, such as:

Edward Simmons, 58, is a Manhattan-based lawyer specializing in estate taxes. He's married to Samantha and father to Benjamin, 28, and Rebecca, 24. He was born in Brooklyn the oldest son of Martha and Edwin Simmons, and has three younger sisters, all who live in the New York area. Simmons attended Columbia University and Harvard Law School, where he graduated in 1973.

After you establish these basics, delve into more detail and include your character's physical characteristics, influences, interests, achievements, and the like. The bottom line is that backstory begins with a character biography, a tool that can be enormously helpful. A bio helps to keep track of details so that you don't make mistakes, and shapes three-dimensional characters whose pasts cast a shadow over the story and shape motivation.

Here is a paragraph you can fill in to supplement your character's bio.

_____(character's name) is the sort of person who describes himself/herself as _____ (descriptive phrase). If called on to use a single adjective to describe himself/herself, he/she'd use _____. Friends, family and co-workers say he's best known for _____. When people first meet him/her, they notice his/her_____

_____(physical traits and personality), then they notice that _____

24

_____ (traits that add or possibly contradict dominant traits). Because of his/her past, he/she needs to prove that_____
_____(emotional need in the story). Also because of the past, he/she fears that _____(dreaded alternative) and will _____(plan of action, goals) to prevent it.

Just for fun, you might want to fill in this paragraph for famous fictional characters like Sherlock Holmes or any of your favorites.

Backstory Influences

Knowing your protagonist's or antagonist's past is the key to creating fiction where his motivation and stakes are credible. Here are some factors to consider:

- What major childhood influences, traumas, events, and emotional wounds have shaped your character?
- Where does he stand in the family birth order?
- What era, historical period, or events influenced him?
- Have any significant people in your character's circle died? If so, how did he react?
- Who was the most significant person in his childhood?
- What past relationship most influenced him?
- How did the last relationship end?
- Is his occupation what his parents or family hoped he would pursue?
- What occurrence from his past will affect the plot?
- What regrets does your character have?
- What is his worst fear?
- What is the darkest secret or shame from his past?
- Which events from the past still influence him?
- What emotions will your character feel/display/hide when under fire?

THE CASE OF ANTAGONISTS

Backstory forms antagonists and villains who scare the bejesus out of the reader and push the conflict. The antagonist's main role is to force the protagonist to triumph over his real or perceived flaws to win the prize and accomplish the story goal. The best antagonists are complex and unforgettable, like Stephen King's Annie Wilkes in *Misery*, who dubs herself Paul Sheldon's "Number One Fan," but treats him like a caged pet. Sheldon slips into her clutches after she rescues him from a car accident during a snowstorm, and because of his injuries and pain medication, he is helpless as she cares for him. Annie drives him mad with her mood swings from nursery talk to psychotic rage; from coy to cunning; from fawning and star-struck to murderously vengeful. King fleshes her out with rolls of fat and bad breath, gives her an arsenal of medications and tools of the trade, and settles her in a conveniently remote house that whispers dangerous secrets.

While King has created a powerful and frightful antagonist, it is her backstory that worries the reader. Wilkes's mental and emotional states stem from her past and place the crippled, drugged, and terrified Sheldon in a vulnerable position. Why doesn't she work? Why does she have no friends or outlets besides Sheldon's romance series?

The answers are revealed in a grisly scrapbook of newspaper articles revealing a trail of death that has followed her since she was eleven. The latest articles are about a trial in which Annie, called the Dragon Lady, was accused of murdering patients at hospitals where she had worked. The more the reader becomes aware of Annie's dark past, the more she begins to worry about Paul's uncertain future.

26

Backstory Vehicles

The world of the story and the people who populate it must have connections to the past, or the present-day story will seem undeveloped. Generally, readers like to get their bearings in a story within the first pages before being hit with backstory, which is most often introduced via summary, dialogue, and flashbacks. To a lesser degree, it's also presented through introspection, dreams and nightmares, and prologues. Let's look more closely at these vehicles and their variations.

SUMMARIES

Summaries are a quick way to explain as much information as possible with as few words as possible. Summary is an indispensable tool in a writer's repertoire and is especially helpful in creating backstory that doesn't bog down the forward march of the story. However, too much summary can weaken the overall level of suspense and make a story read more like a report.

In Jane Hamilton's *The Book of Ruth*, the narrator looks back on childhood events, "trying to see through into the past," so that she can understand how and why things have happened to her while living in the small town of Honey Creek, Illinois. The opening paragraph describes how she is grown now and searching for meaning and for understanding of "the kernel of meanness in people's hearts." A great deal of summary woven into the first chapter settles the reader into the fictional world, suggests its mores, and suggests how the protagonist was shaped by the larger influences of place.

To set the past and present in context, the narrator describes the world of Honey Creek in eight paragraphs of summary that quickly sketch a typical Midwestern town.

> You will miss the town if you drive through listening to your favorite song on the radio or telling a story about your neighbor. The two blocks of white clapboard houses with black trim will look like nothing more than a cloudy morning. Only Mrs. Crawford's house is blue, like the color eyeshadow my friend Daisy wears, and she has a red barn in the back. She had her place painted blue after her husband, Bub, died, and everyone figured she'd gone crazy with grief. Then for Christmas she put lights all over the trees in her yard, colored lights which flashed on and off.

The summary describes Memorial Day parades and takes us past the post office, grocery story, church, and more houses.

The river comes next. Our town is named after it. It isn't deep or long, but it has water and bloodsuckers and fish.

Perhaps Honey Creek isn't as peaceful or idyllic as the town name implies. The narrator describes how, when crossing the bridge, you'll see a factory, then takes the reader along toward the edge of town:

About a half mile out of town is where we live, on a farm. We live in a wooden house, but I wouldn't exactly call it white. It hasn't been painted since May got married the second time, which would take me a long time to calculate, because I'm not, as anyone within twenty miles could tell you, a wizard in math. There are pink granite stone steps up to the porch, similar to palace steps. We go around back to the kitchen door, where the trash and tin cans could trip and kill you if you weren't paying strict attention. May plants purple and red petunias in the planters each year. That's when the washed-out gray house looks drab, compared to the flowers.

And again, with a few deft strokes, the narrator suggests that all is not quite right at the homestead. There are several techniques that you can borrow from Hamilton's summary. The narrator uses a wide-angle approach to introduce the town, then draws closer and closer to the house she lived in, where much of the pain and drama in the story occurs. This method of starting wide then narrowing down appeals to readers, who are familiar with it from films and landing in an airplane with the earth growing larger and larger.

The protagonist also manages to slip specifics of her own backstory into the summary, as when she says she's not a math whiz. In the example below, we get a glimpse of her childhood as she describes her girlhood longing to march in the Memorial Day parade wearing a Red Cross uniform, and her mother's response:

She cut a paper plate in half and pinned it in my hair, drew a cross on her white apron, and set me walking.

With this brief anecdote, the reader is alerted that May is perhaps not a doting mother.

The summary also sets up important places in the unfolding story, such as the church, which the family attends each Sunday, but receive little solace and guidance from the Reverend's words.

A few details about the parade—which doesn't have a marching band or fire truck, but rather features three horses, five old men in uniform, and the Kraut

Queen—also paint a quick sketch of small-town life. The parade summary explains the town's size, sophistication, and resources. It also creates a backdrop for a story about abuse, implying there will likely be little interference from authorities or officials.

FLASHBACKS

Flashbacks are brief scenes of events that took place before the main action of the novel. They're used to explain motivations, character histories, background influences, or information that cannot be told during the linear sequence of a story. Backstory delivered via flashbacks will span back in time at varying intervals so that readers meet characters at various ages under varying circumstances. The best flashbacks are small scenes, whole and sensory.

Writers are generally advised to use flashbacks judiciously, because they must cast a light of significance onto the front story. While the subject of flashbacks is covered in depth in chapter six, the main thing to remember when planning your backstory is that flashbacks are a flexible and useful device that need to be handled with care.

DIALOGUE

Dialogue is a quick means to insert backstory, as when one character tells another character about his past. However, there are a few caveats to keep in mind. First, the past must always add or enhance the present action. Second, in our daily lives we learn about each other's pasts through conversation, so there is a natural tendency to mimic this method. Fictional dialogue revealing backstory must be handled with kid gloves because it's an abbreviated and intensified form of real speech often containing tension and conflict. It's difficult to talk about the past and maintain that undertow effect.

If Janice is revealing a trauma or some troubling history and Brenda is clucking sympathetically and handing her tissues, you dilute the tension in the scene. On the other hand, if Brenda doesn't believe Janice, or if she is unsympathetic, then the tension works. This makes the scene difficult to write unless Brenda is an antagonist. You need to tread carefully to create tension—perhaps Janice is reluctant to reveal her past and must be coaxed by Brenda to divulge details. Or, Janice can break down or be visibly upset so her emotions create the necessary tension.

Or, the recitation can be interrupted by another character coming into the scene, which will keep the tension and suspense brewing until the past is revealed.

Make sure that at least one character in the conversation is learning the information for the first time in order to make the disclosure realistic. When both characters know the information, novelist, writing instructor, and columnist Nancy Kress calls this "As You Know, Bob," dialogue. This sort of story talk sounds like this:

> "As you know, Bob, before mom and dad died and when we lived on the farm, life was pretty good. But then once they died and we needed to sell the farm to pay the back taxes and you ended up working at the button factory, well, it seemed like things went downhill from there."

Another dialogue exchange that must be handled carefully is when one character gives another character a history lesson about a place. That type of information may work better in summary form, as we saw in the earlier examples from *The Book of Ruth*.

One final tip: Diction and grammar are easily used to reveal a character's background and education. Sprinkled in rather than liberally applied, a few colloquialisms and expressions are a quick, yet rich means to create backstory. A helpful example of this method is found in the narrator's voice in *The Book of Ruth*. It reveals that, while she's not sophisticated or highly educated, she has a keen awareness.

INTROSPECTION

Backstory can also be introduced as introspection, but most stories work best when introspection is proportionate to action. Thoughts are not as compelling as actions. If you spend too much time inside your character's thoughts, the story becomes boxed in and static. However, many novels are rich with introspection, such as J.D. Salinger's *The Catcher in the Rye*, which features blow-by-blow doses of introspection after the main character is kicked out of prep school. Salinger's method was deliberate because his character, Holden Caulfield, is in the process of a mental breakdown and the reader needs to be inside of his thoughts often for the whole impact to be felt. Holden also has a unique view of the world—part innocence, part cynicism—and a complicated personality that is self-destructive, hopeful, and rebellious, all wrapped up in the sort of narcissism that teenagers are prone to. Novels with first-person viewpoints obviously work best for using intro-spection to reveal backstory.

Consider introspection as a tool of last resort to reveal backstory. Also, keep in mind that the thoughts from the past must always be triggered by something that happens in the present. Further, the events or memory must be inherently dra-matic or emotional, connected somehow to the present, and must illuminate the character and his motivations.

There are also natural places in the story, as in real life, in which introspection makes the most sense in a scene. These moments might come after a dramatic scene, as when a character sorts out what has just happened. Introspection also works when your character's right brain has a chance to roam free because she's occupied with familiar tasks, such as highway driving, showering, gardening, or walking, or when the mind is not quite awake—immediately before falling asleep or upon awakening.

NIGHTMARES AND DREAMS

Most of us lead rich and complicated lives once we fall asleep, and it seems natu-ral to use dreams and nightmares as a device for revealing characters and their pasts, especially their traumas. Dreams can also provide a sort of shorthand for events and influences because they are naturally vivid and metaphoric. Some au-thors use a recurring dream or nightmare to signify a particularly important event or worry. If a character has been traumatized by a rape, assault, violence, or death of a loved one, these events can cause nightmares. When your character wakes up in a cold sweat with his heart racing, this can show the depth of his pain or that he has unresolved issues from his past.

However, like many techniques, dreams must be used carefully. The first rea-son for this caution is simple—the dream has been used by too many writers too often and has become rather clichéd. Also, the actual dream is often much more meaningful and dramatic than its retelling. Finally, writers have a tendency to depict long, complicated dreams. If you're using a dream, use the most arresting images from it, not a complex re-creation of the dream sequence.

PROLOGUES

Backstory is sometimes woven into a prologue, as when the writer needs to con-vey the history of a character or story world because the historical influences are considerable. Using prologues is dangerous because there are facts from the past that are pertinent to understanding the story and then there are facts that exist because the writer is fascinated with them.

The best prologues are depicted as a scene, contain tension, and raise questions. A big lump of exposition is difficult to digest and can water down the prologue. Try this: After you've written the entire manuscript, snip off the prologue and then give the abbreviated manuscript to readers. After they've finished reading your story, ask them specific questions about the backstory that was contained in the missing prologue. If they've caught on to the information without it, you can dump it. (Prologues are covered in more depth in chapter ten.)

PLACEMENT AND STRUCTURE

I wish that I could offer you a neat list of rules about how and when to include backstory. It might dictate that you don't insert backstory until page 8 or after page 323, or that most of the backstory must be relegated to the first half of the book. However, no such guidelines exist. The reason is simple: There are thousands of story types, needs, and structures, and guidelines cannot possibly apply to all these diverse situations.

However, I can offer a few suggestions for placement and structure to keep in mind as you craft your first fifty pages.

The opening chapter is your story's threshold, through which the reader enters the story world, leaving the regular world behind. The reader doesn't want to wander past the threshold; he wants to be tugged by the hand. So, in those first crucial moments, a writer introduces the protagonist, setting, point of view, voice, and story question.

Most of the opening must be spent on these elements and the inciting incident—the action the starts the story in motion and introduces change. Since the opening has so many things to accomplish and the reader needs to cross the threshold and understand where he has arrived, don't launch prematurely into backstory before the front story has been established.

Your structure requires weighing the backstory information with this in mind: It should only be included if the events that follow cannot be understood without it and if the reader cannot care about the characters without it. Remember, caring about the characters doesn't require knowing their whole life history. Making readers care about story people in your opening can be as simple as showing an elderly woman struggling to catch a train, as Agatha Christie does in *What Mrs. McGillicuddy Saw!*, or by having a waitress trip while carrying a heavy tray. Sympathy does not necessarily equal backstory; a few evocative details will suffice.

Read through your first fifty pages and highlight wherever you've used backstory information. If it's a mostly chronologically structured story, and you discover that one third or more of your pages contain backstory, it's time to ask hard questions about your structure. You also might want to find a published novel with a similar structure and analyze when and how often the author included backstory. Again, highlighting the author's backstory information can give a quick visual assessment. How do your pages measure up to the other novel?

Finally, when it comes to backstory and structure, you should strategically *withhold* information until the last moment, even as you tease readers with tidbits of information and minor skirmishes. This withholding creates suspense and intrigue and is especially important in the opening chapters. Also, keep in mind Hemingway's iceberg metaphor, echoed by James Scott Bell in *Plot & Structure*. Bell explains that nothing slows down a story more than an exposition dump. He writes:

> Don't tell us everything about a character's past history or current situation. Give us the 10 percent above the surface that is necessary to understand what's going on, and leave 90 percent hidden and mysterious below the surface. Later in the story, you can reveal more of that information. Until the right time, however, withhold it.

If you think about an iceberg, its danger lies in the giant mass beneath the surface. In a sense, many aspects of fiction work with the iceberg method of revelation. What lies above the surface often only hints at a more dangerous core, and this is particularly true in the first fifty pages.

The iceberg method is also helpful to keep in mind when you introduce characters in your story. Readers want to know the essential details about a character—male or female, approximate age, attractive or unattractive. If your character is acting and talking, the reader will believe that he is real, so reveal only the tip.

BACKSTORY IN COMMERCIAL AND
LITERARY FICTION, AND IN SHORT STORIES

Backstory is especially necessary in horror, historical fiction, fantasy, and science fiction. In a horror story, it provides clues about supernatural elements and causes the reader to fear the adversary, whether it's a zombie, a psychotic nurse, or technology that is taking over characters' brains. In fantasy and science fiction, backstory explains how the world of the story came to be and how events from the past are influencing the present.

Literary fiction most often focuses on the contemporary world or the recent past, with excursions into the deeper past. It generally requires less backstory about the story world because most readers have a fairly sophisticated understanding of how the world works. This comes back to the helpful notion that it is the writer's job to remind the reader what he knows about the world, not spoon feed him. If you're writing a novel set in Manhattan, you won't need to list all the skyscrapers or landmarks and how they came to be. But you will need to depict the level of energy, noise, and diverse humanity that exists in New York.

Backstory is also needed to prove the world of a short story. Short stories are fiction on a budget. They will always feature a smaller cast of characters, fewer scenes, a single plot, fewer settings, and usually, but not always, they will cover a short period of time. Simply defined, a short story is a story that you can read in a single sitting. The maximum word length for short stories varies, but most people agree that it is at least 1,000 words and not more than 20,000 words, although some define 7,500 words as the maximum.

Because of budgetary constraints, short stories will have less backstory than novels, but it is still needed. Ethan Canin's short story "Emperor of the Air" is a terrific example of how backstory provides details that create veracity and motivation in the story. The story revolves around two neighbors who are feuding over a diseased and magnificent elm tree. A flashback to the protagonist's boyhood illustrates his attachment to the two-hundred-year-old tree, which in turn exacerbates the conflict. The neighbor's personal history and the protagonist's relationship to his parents are also touched on through backstory.

Shirley Jackson's famously disturbing short story "The Lottery" follows a ritual public lottery that involves a New England village choosing a sacrificial victim. Much of the backstory in this pared down short story must be surmised

34

through the exposition, and the details Jackson chooses to include slyly suggest her themes of scapegoatism and violence. Because there is so little room for backstory in short stories, every detail should be suggestive or important.

By explaining the backstory of a mysterious box used for the gruesome yearly ritual, Jackson suggests that people can become attached to the history of their town and repeat and re-create a violent aspect of history without fully understanding it.

COMMON BACKSTORY PITFALLS AND HOW TO AVOID THEM

There are many pitfalls in creating backstory that amplifies rather than stalls the story. Here are some common pitfalls and how to sidestep them:

- **In your final editing pass, look for places where you've dumped backstory.** Suspect any places where backstory runs for several pages and is used strictly to catch up the reader on past events and influence. Parcel the information into small bits if possible, and weave it into the fabric of the story so that it doesn't overshadow the front story, particularly the first chapters.

- **Look for places where you're teaching seminars.** These lessons might be about fifteenth-century architecture, judging at dog shows, or the Aborigines of Australia. Although these are topics about which your reader might not be knowledgeable, pare your lesson down to the most essential information, and stop showing off to prove you've done your research.

- **Examine your manuscript for places where you've gift-wrapped the backstory.** Backstory shouldn't be calling too much attention to itself. Sneak it into the story by spreading it around, withholding the most intriguing information until the last possible moment to create suspense.

- **Take the long view.** If you're not a person blessed with patience, writing fiction will teach it to you. A novel is a complicated and protracted unveiling of character and events, so don't be in a hurry to explain all you know about a character or situation in the opening chapters.

- **Tread carefully when using a viewpoint character to explain how your story world works.** It's common for writers to use an adult looking back on

35

childhood, or some other viewpoint person who now has the benefit of a sort of bird's-eye view of the world that he didn't have previously. In science fiction, fantasy, or historical fiction it's difficult to use a viewpoint character to explain the world he lives in because the character would assume that the society he lives in is normal. So when you're using a viewpoint character, always respect his bias and blindness to his everyday reality. Sometimes you can use a newcomer, time traveler, or child to explain unusual aspects of the story world.

- **When introducing backstory, analyze whether you're simply inserting it into scenes or chapters, or using a trigger.** A trigger can be an event, a memory, or dialogue that reveals previously unknown information. As in a gun firing, it sets off change and causes ramifications. For example, places function as triggers in John Knowles's *A Separate Peace*. When the protagonist, Gene Forester, visits the campus of the school he had attended fifteen years earlier, two specific locations, a marble staircase and a tree growing near the Devon River, hold special significance. After these triggers fire, time slips into the past and Gene relives the events of those school days. Not every bit of backstory can be instigated by a trigger, but this device is used whenever possible.

{ * }

Writers are attracted to fiction writing for many reasons, but often because it gives them an opportunity to comment on some aspect of humanity while using a make-believe world and make-believe people. Also, fiction writing is just plain fun.

That said, it requires intense analysis and planning to impart important information at just the right moment. Relating backstory requires not only playing God with your characters and story world, but strategizing, scheming, and worrying over each element.

chapter 3
Cliffhangers & Thrusters

{
This suspense is terrible. I hope it will last.

—Oscar Wilde

*N*o matter if your story has quiet themes and a languid pace; it still must be a gripping, irresistible, page-turner. Creating a page-turner involves using devices that drive the story ahead so that your novel is unputdownable. Everything in this chapter is about page-turning. Devices in other chapters, such as suspense and tension, cause narrative drive, but the devices in this chapter illustrate structural elements and how the placement of words, scenes, and interrupted action can press the story ahead. Techniques like foreshadowing, tension, and suspense prickle the reader's nerves. A nervous reader is an involved reader, and an involved reader keeps turning the pages.

Involvement begins when you create a realistic story world, implant an issue that demands to be resolved, and introduce a character or group of characters who are intensely interesting to readers. These are the broader strokes of fiction writing, but many of the techniques that create a page turner are delicate and are designed to be unobtrusive, yet still powerful.

The techniques and devices that press the story ahead create narrative drive. The sometimes subtle and sometimes bold brush strokes of narrative drive are called thrusters and cliffhangers. Thrusters are structural devices (meaning they can be seen in the story) that push the story ahead, move the action forward, and raise questions or cause curiosity about unanswered issues or things to come. They can occur at any place in a scene or story, but are most often in the opening or closing paragraph of a scene or chapter, and they can consist of a single sentence or several paragraphs.

Cliffhangers, which are a specific type of thruster, occur at a scene or chapter ending and interrupt the action so that it must be continued in the next scene or chapter. Since cliffhangers always appear at the end of a scene or chapter and leave the events unresolved, the reader is propelled forward to see what happens next.

Remember that all thrusters (including cliffhangers) cause curiosity and heightened interest in the reader. Note, too, that while both thrusters and cliffhangers push the story ahead, only cliffhangers interrupt the action and, thus, force the reader to proceed for completion.

MEETING READER EXPECTATIONS

When reading fiction, there's a natural expectation that "Once upon a time" will lead to "and they lived happily ever after." It's also natural for the reader to expect rising and falling action and tension to exist between these two points. And these hills and valleys are greatly influenced by using cliffhangers and thrusters. In fact, when suspense is all-important, as it is in mysteries, crime stories, and thrillers, thrusters and cliffhangers are built in to the story's framework through clues, red herrings, and unanswered questions.

When fiction is diagrammed, it is often shown as a scalene triangle with the opening scenes or rising action leading to the sharp peak of the climax, followed by a quick drop-off of falling action.

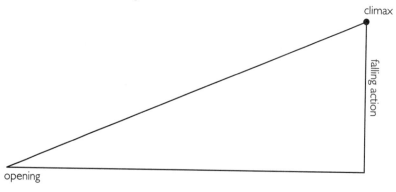

But the structure is actually more of a roller coaster or a series of zigzags. The rising and falling action within the scenes rewards the reader like a thrill ride and gives him a reason to cling to the car, elated and terrified, as it plunges ahead into the unknown.

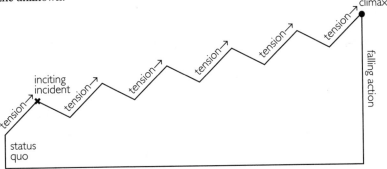

OPENINGS AND THRUSTERS

All beginnings matter. Stories, scenes, and chapters cannot simply commence; they must create a tingle in the reader, pique curiosity, and *thrust* the story and readers ahead with potency and punch. Think of beginnings like a summer thunderstorm. In many portions of the country, a thunderstorm begins with an ominous, sultry thickness in the air, sometimes days before the actual storm hits. Often the sky is tinged with a queer yellow or green before murderous clouds cluster like black mountains overhead, and then finally unleash torrents and thunder, tearing apart the sky with lightning bolts.

Some openings plunge immediately into action, while others start in the middle of action with thunder crashing. Most usually start with the conditions preceding the storm—the unbearable humidity, the strange colorations of sky, the air as thick as a sauna. Often openings suggest actions to come and lay the groundwork. If you don't open with action, you can compensate by using setting, exposition, or some other element to thrust a reader ahead.

Dating Dead Men, by Harley Jane Kozak, begins with this short paragraph:

It was a cigarette burn.

Now, at first glance that opening might not seem profound, but if you think about it, it catches the reader's attention and demands that he move ahead. Thus these five words are considered a thruster. After all, the burn might be on someone's skin, on a corpse, or on a priceless antique. It piques curiosity, as beginnings are designed to do.

Me & Emma, written by Elizabeth Flock, plunges right into the central conflict with the first sentence, and also announces the theme of the novel, abuse:

> The first time Richard hit me I saw stars in front of my eyes just like they do in cartoons. It was just a backhand, though—not like when I saw Tommy Bucksmith's dad wallop him so hard that when he hit the pavement his head actually bounced.

After this dramatic opening, which is also a thruster, the reader wants to know more about Richard and the child who has been hit so hard she sees stars. Also, because children are prone to dramatic statements and hyperbole, a bold opening sentence or paragraph draws the reader in, because the reader wonders if the child is stating facts or exaggerating. The opening also creates sympathy for the narrator and heightens the reader's awareness of her vulnerability, which in turn creates a hook.

You have more than one sentence or paragraph to create a thruster in your openings, but notice the power and immediacy of short statements. You've also got plenty of options for your story and chapter openings—sometimes jump right into action, sometimes drop a bombshell, sometimes raise a question, and at other times proceed more slowly.

While openings must drive forward, they don't need to shock, titillate, or manipulate readers to press ahead. You can push ahead without shrieking at the reader or trying too hard. Openings are seductive, not strained or melodramatic.

ENDINGS AND CLIFFHANGERS

Endings often *are* the thunderstorm described above, shrieking from the wrath-filled sky, shaking the world and leaving it unsettled. But then again, not every climax results in a storm. Scene or chapter endings can be handled in many ways and can serve a number of purposes. They can ratchet up emotion, pause for significance or in the midst of action, hint at upcoming conflict, prepare the reader for action, or slow things down a bit. But no matter your aim, your scene and chapter endings shouldn't wind down like a dying clock ticking away its last seconds. To impel the story and your reader forward, the majority of endings must close with a bang, uncertainty, or a change in direction.

Scene and chapter closings designed as cliffhangers are made up of interrupted drama and unfinished business. Such "to be continued" endings leave characters and readers dangling amid unfinished business. Scenes and chapters can also end with thrusters—for example, a question that's raised but not answered—but the action is not paused mid-scene to accomplish this. Keep in mind that all thrusters are designed to tease and torment the reader, and the best thrusters and cliffhangers cause an emotional response in the spirit of "Oh dear! Now what?"

Why leave your readers in such distress? Because the unknown is deliciously tantalizing. In our ordinary lives, most of us don't like mysteries, we want instant answers and solutions. This desire for results translates to the page as well—the less we know, the faster we read. When an outcome is left hanging, we naturally fill the gap with our imaginings, which is just the sort of involvement that writers hope for.

In the mystery genre, this participation is heightened. The writer is a tease, dropping clues and red herrings to mislead, while the reader notes the clues and formulates opinions about the murderer's identity and motivation. The game baits and then rewards the reader, especially when the surprises are dropped in toward the end of an action, keeping the reader on edge. Surprises, which usually come in the form of action, new developments, and revelations, are often the opposite of what readers expected.

It's helpful to keep in mind that the drama is often weighted at the end of sections for emphasis. In the theater the most drama is located at the end of an act; in television action rises right before the commercial break; and in fiction the largest dose of drama often lands at the close of a scene or chapter. Readers naturally remember beginnings and endings most clearly, and drama naturally picks up steam as it rolls forward, with the reader expecting culminating events and outcomes. So as you write, look for ways to emphasize your endings with action, emotion, and significance.

Let's look again at *Me & Emma* for an example of a thruster at the end of a scene that accomplishes what I've just described. In this scene in chapter three, Richard abuses Emma, and although the reader is never taken blow-by-blow through the scene, we are shown the aftereffects. The scene ends on this note:

I look back at the bed and I see that Emma's curled up like a little baby wanting to get back into her mother's stomach. She's trying to be really small, hugging her legs up to her chest like she is.

I hate Richard.

You can see that this final image and statement packs an emotional wallop and impels the reader forward.

When using cliffhangers, remember that they are unanticipated, just as any action stopped midway in real life is unanticipated. They should never be presented as silly, cheap gimmicks. Cliffhangers, especially those connected to disasters, must be linked to the scene goal. So forget about bullets flying and bombs exploding unless they are organic to the action, built from the raw materials of the scene. For example, at the end of chapter eight in Harley Jane Kozak's *Dating Dead Men*, Wollie is at work in her shop, cleaning with a Dustbuster. Take a look at this chapter-ending cliffhanger:

A *shadow* stepped in front of me.

A hand reached down and switched off my Dustbuster.

Naturally the reader is wondering who is interrupting her cleaning and is worried, since *shadow* implies an ominous presence. The next chapter plunks us into the moment with this thruster:

He wasn't a customer. This was not a person who went card shopping. I was backed up against the Birthday rack, Dustbuster pointed like a *gun*.

He had several inches on me, a big man, and not a young one—sixty, at least. His hair was white and the rest of him was tan, and not just a living-in-southern-California-without-sunscreen tan. His tan was like a vocation.

Because the cliffhanger and the opening thruster are intricately connected to the stream of the story, the actions are plausible and intriguing. The reader cannot help himself—he's got to discover the identity of the leathery guy who doesn't belong in a card shop.

While it would be helpful if a certain formula existed to delineate just how many endings need thrusters (including cliffhangers) and how many do not, alas, no such formula exists. Every story has unique pacing requirements and sometimes needs to chug along, sometimes needs to slow down, and sometimes needs to speed along like a runaway train. Over time, you'll develop an ear for adjusting the speed. The more you write, the more your instincts will take over.

CLIFFHANGERS EMBEDDED IN CULTURE

While all stories need thrusters woven throughout them, cliffhangers, a subsidiary of this device, must be handled carefully so that they're not gimmicky. Readers have been weaned on cliffhangers since the early 1900s, when serial radio programs left listeners dangling from day to day and week to week with unresolved outcomes. Serials were popularized in nineteenth-century magazines and newspapers, when writers such as Arthur Conan Doyle and Charles Dickens wrote stories that ended at a high point of drama, only to be continued in the following issue. In the silent film era, movie serials of the *Perils of Pauline* ilk ended with the heroine tied to the railroad tracks with a steam engine bearing down on her. When the succeeding episode began, moviegoers would discover how the plucky heroine had escaped and moved on to her new adventure.

Daytime soap operas have always teased their viewers with unresolved conflicts, and most television programs insert cliffhangers before every commercial break. Television programming capitalized on the cliffhanger formula when one of the biggest viewerships in history tuned in to find out who gunned down J.R. Ewing on *Dallas*. Contemporary television programs from *Buffy the Vampire Slayer* to *The West Wing* to *Law and Order* have made the cliffhanger a staple. Television writers often devise the season finale as a cliffhanger to guarantee that viewers will return the following season. And reality television is based on the cliffhanger factor, as viewers tune in each week to discover if people they've come to admire or loathe have been voted off *Survivor*, *The Apprentice*, or *American Idol*.

CREATING MOVEMENT WITH THRUSTERS AND CLIFFHANGERS

Writers of fast-paced genres such as mysteries, adventures, and thrillers often employ intercuts, or scene cuts, to move back and forth quickly between two time frames, settings, or viewpoints. Intercuts are also considered thrusters, since they move the reader from scene to scene, viewpoint to viewpoint, and place to place without using a transition, causing excitement, interest, and forward movement. It works like this: When scene one ends at the dock, scene two opens with an argument aboard the ship without showing the characters boarding. Or when scene four—featuring buddies Ben and Al at the football game—ends, the story jumps to scene five with Janice and Sally, their wives, stepping into a lingerie store. Notice that the same characters don't need to be in the scene that follows. Whisking a reader abruptly to a new locale builds suspense and intrigue, and keeps the pace sizzling. This back-and-forth can be dizzying, so be careful not to overuse this device.

In *Dating Dead Men*, the viewpoint is that of the protagonist, Mary Wollstonecraft Shelley, called Wollie by her friends. The story is nonstop action, and Kozak's thrusters, cliffhangers, and scene cuts work particularly well to keep the action zipping along as Wollie dates forty men in a sixty-day marathon and becomes entangled with a slew of bad guys after meeting the mysterious Doc at a mental hospital, where she's visiting her brother.

In the middle of chapter nine, Wollie receives a phone message from Doc, who has gone missing. The next scene cuts to a new locale, leaving the reader to wonder about Doc's message and his feelings toward Wollie. Because these issues are left unresolved, and because there was no interruption, the closing scene is a thruster, but not a cliffhanger.

The next scene starts with Wollie and her friend Joey in Pet Planet shopping for ferret food. This is an example of a scene cut, because the previous scene ended in Wollie's apartment.

The pet store scene ends with Joey asking this question, a classic chapter-ending cliffhanger device:

"Wollie," she asked, "is there any reason someone might be following you?"

Naturally readers want to know who is following her and why, but then another scene cut occurs, and chapter ten is launched in a new locale and with another mood.

Because the reader doesn't know why he's moved to this new location, his curiosity is increased—the goal of every thruster. You can see how these jumps from place to place and mood to mood keep the reader locked into the action. You don't need to begin scenes exactly where you have left off in the previous scene. Better yet, from time to time, take the reader where he least expects to go. If the story is well crafted, the reader will be able to make these leaps with you.

JANET EVANOVICH: QUEEN OF THE CLIFFHANGER

Janet Evanovich is the creator of the comic suspense series based on Stephanie Plum, a New Jersey bounty hunter. While crafting her zany plots, Evanovich takes the element of the cliffhanger to new heights. In the series, she depicts Stephanie as torn between two men—Joe Morelli, a sexy cop and trustworthy sort, and Ranger, a mysterious and dangerously attractive hunk. She ended *High Five*, the fifth book in the series, on a cliffhanger, with readers wondering which man, Ranger or Morelli, issued this final line:

"Nice dress. Take it off."

As expected, this cliffhanger created a lot of buzz. When the sequel, *Hot Six*, appeared, it blasted to the top of the best-seller list. Since romantic tension is a major subplot in the series, Evanovich developed a pattern where one book features Stephanie in good standing with Morelli, seemingly heading for marriage and stability of sorts, and then in the next book their relationship is tenuous. Ranger, with his simmering brand of sexuality and possible criminal proclivities, is the device that accomplishes this push-pull, thus creating a series based on cliffhanger outcomes.

Evanovich also inserts cliffhangers within the books to end scenes and chapters, but is careful to conclude some of them. After all, the reader needs to put the book down from time to time.

Alternating Viewpoints and Narrative Drive

When a story features multiple or alternating viewpoints, the reader jumps regularly from character to character, often chapter by chapter, with each shift acting as a natural thruster. Why? Because the outcome from Character One's situation is left unresolved as we jump into Character Two's situation. Both viewpoints, with their unfinished business, will linger in the reader's mind if you choose to include a third character's viewpoint. This approach leaves plenty of unresolved endings from which your story can grow.

A provocative example of alternating viewpoints is Kaye Gibbons's *A Virtuous Woman*, which tracks the story of Jack Ernest "Blinking Jack" Stokes and Ruby Pitt Woodrow Stokes. The story opens in Jack's viewpoint after Ruby has been dead for four months. Learning that she died of lung cancer at forty-five, the reader is pulled in, wondering how her husband is working through his grief. The story then switches back in time to Ruby's viewpoint. She's busy cooking and filling the freezer with food for Jack to eat after she dies. The story keeps switching back and forth, revealing the history of their complicated marriage, their differences, and their devotion. Since a reader is rarely privileged to hear both sides of a relationship, the structure is especially powerful and enticing.

Two of Barbara Kingsolver's novels, *The Poisonwood Bible* and *Prodigal Summer*, also employ multiple viewpoints that thrust the reader forward from head to head and location to location until the story merges in the climatic scenes. Borrowing from Kingsolver's framework, string together scene after scene with little exposition or filler to impede the reader's leap. Be sure your thrusters keep the suspense humming.

Utilizing High-Octane Devices

Let's recap for a moment: Thrusters plunge the story ahead, sometimes depriving the reader of something he wants to know. Cliffhangers, a subset of thrusters, interrupt important action, forcing the reader to await an outcome in the next scene or chapter. Thrusters are especially important in crafting contemporary fiction because stories set in the ordinary world require a major dose of suspense and movement. In science fiction and fantasy, the nature of the genre supplies unknowns. Mysteries naturally create suspense because they are based on characters puzzling over terrible events and motivations. In realistic fiction, the unknown factors come from other sources, such as the protagonist's character arc, and are linked to structure.

When you're working with your plot structure, look for places where you can torment the reader with uncertainty. Let's look closer at specific devices that, when skillfully interwoven with thrusters and cliffhangers, work to power fiction forward.

CHASES

Many suspense novels and thrillers are based on the drama of the hunter and the hunted. Often a chase requires a one step forward, two steps backward approach. For example, after chasing down many false leads, a police detective finally discovers the suspect's hideout and hurries to secure a search warrant. The scene could end on his assistant rushing into the room with the warrant, and the detective grabbing his keys and heading for the car. Naturally the reader will be curious about where the villain lives and will keep reading. Or the scene might end with the detective arriving at the warehouse/hideout to discover that the villain has vanished along with all traces of his illegal operations. The question is not only where he has gone, but who tipped him off.

Dennis Lehane's suspense series with Boston private investigators Angie Gennaro and Patrick Kenzie is based on chasing down a criminal in each novel. In *Prayers for Rain*, the fifth in his series, upscale predator Cody Falk toys with his victim's minds by inventing torments that drive them to suicide. Since there is no murder weapon, the chase involves a dangerous battle of wits with plenty of cliffhangers keeping the reader plugged in.

DANGER

Horror fiction capitalizes on danger in all its nightmare modes. Danger can come from a sinister killer, a supernatural phantom, a monster, or a force of nature that has become monstrous. In most horror tales, there comes a point where the protagonist is isolated and weakened by the events of the story and must face the danger alone.

For example, a rapist with an appetite for teenage girls has eluded capture and is stalking a beach community. Alicia, the protagonist, is baby-sitting at a home on a heavily wooded lot, far off the main road. After playing Monopoly with her charges and settling them into bed, she returns to the living room and her geometry homework. The reader appreciates how Alicia patiently played with the kids, coaxed them into brushing their teeth, and tenderly tucked them into their bunk beds. Alicia comes from a troubled family and is dyslexic, so school is difficult for her. So when she hears the sound of tinkling glass coming from an upstairs window, we're terrified for her, not just because danger is imminent, but because she's a sympathetic character. When she reaches for the phone to dial 911, the reader is pressing the buttons along with her. But then, as the chapter ends, we learn that the phone line has been cut, and our worst fears are about to explode.

If the story you're writing doesn't include physical danger, you can still make your protagonist's situation perilous. As you craft scenes and events, focus on your protagonist's fears and vulnerabilities, then make certain that the story events capitalize on them. Also, in each scene ask yourself, "What is the worst thing that can happen now?" and then determine if that outcome might work. Danger comes from arguments where the words are so vicious or heated that the pain will never be forgotten. It can stem from trust destroyed; innocence violated; passions quenched; and hopes shattered. The point is that, after these events, the protagonist's situation worsens.

FLASHBACKS

Flashbacks are part of the roller coaster ride of structure because traveling back and forth in time can be dizzying and thrilling. Try inserting your flashbacks at different points in the scene. A flashback is typically not positioned midway in a scene, but if you can justify its presence, consider using it there as a way of prolonging the scene's outcome. Or experiment with placing it near the end of the scene, but make certain that a profound trigger causes the character to remember the past. Once the trigger occurs, slip into the past for a brief visit, then bring the character and reader back to the present. With this return, make certain that a shift occurs in the character. Flashbacks create subtle or not-so-subtle shifts of mood or emotion, and also cause delays in the scenes where they are inserted. You can also use flashbacks in the emotional moments after dramatic scenes (called the sequel) when your characters are taking stock of things and possibly deciding on a future course of action.

The Deep End of the Ocean, by Jacquelyn Mitchard, is about the far-reaching repercussions of a child's kidnapping. The kidnapping occurs in a crowded hotel lobby as Beth Cappadora and her three children are checking in for a class reunion weekend. Chapter three depicts how chaos reigns after three-year-old Ben's disappearance and how Beth is so raw and hysterical that she's tranquilized. Waking in the middle of the night, she leaves the hotel and drives to the high school.

Details of the school setting are woven amid memories of Ben during the family's recent trip to Florida. In this flashback, we learn of Ben's fear of the deep end of the ocean and sharks. After this memory of her son's vulnerability washes over her, Beth climbs to the top of the bleachers and "emptied herself of tears." The flashback works to create sympathy for the protagonist and the missing child.

In *Riding With the Queen,* Jennie Shortridge uses a series of flashbacks to illustrate the downward character arc of down-and-out singer Tallie Beck, who has returned to her hometown out of desperation and must come to terms with her past. The flashbacks depict moments in her adult life when she messed up or numbed herself with drugs and alcohol, along with childhood traumas that illuminate her adult behaviors and complex relationships.

Much of the conflict in the story stems from Tallie trying to come to terms with her mother's mental illness. Her mother is now stabilized by medication and is enjoying a flourishing art career, but Tallie has a hard time reconciling her memories with the accomplished woman with whom she now lives. As Thanksgiving approaches, Tallie's memories of a long-ago Thanksgiving, when her mother ended up in an emergency room because of a psychotic episode, cause a bitter argument. Tallie leaves, then returns to find a note from her sister directing her to the hospital (a thruster device). She drives there, heavy with guilt, believing that she sparked her mother's relapse.

> "It's all my fault," I say to Jane and we clutch each other, pulling into a hug, much more emotional about all this than we ever were as kids. It feels good to hold on to someone, though, and I wish I would have known that then.
>
> "How could it be your fault?" Jane pulls back and looks at me.
>
> "I … I just lost it," I say, feeling queasy, not wanting to tell her, but I have to. "I yelled at her, Janie, so bad. I was really mean."
>
> Jane looks confused. "But—"
>
> "Tallie, honey," Audra interrupts. "Your mother had a heart attack."

49

The chapter ends with this information, thrusting the reader ahead to discover the seriousness of her mother's condition. The scene would not have been as powerful without the flashback from a long-ago Thanksgiving, escalating all the emotions in the present time.

Borrowing from Shortridge's techniques, look for places in the story where you can stage a scene that echoes or mirrors the past. A holiday or special occasion, a specific setting, a reunion, or any event linked to powerful memories and emotions can work. These moments in two different times not only mirror each other but reveal how the characters are similar or changed. Make certain that the present-day event contains a new wrinkle, conflict, or problem, or stirs emotions in the protagonist, which in turn press the story ahead.

EMOTIONAL BOMBSHELLS, SURPRISES, AND INTERRUPTIONS

Surprises staged in fiction work best when they cause or are linked to powerful emotions in the characters, especially the protagonist. These bombshells have extra impact when staged as scene thrusters or cliffhangers because the reader needs to find out what happens after the explosion. And because these emotional moments are staged at the beginnings and endings of scenes, the impact is greater because the reader is paying special attention at these points.

Returning to our earlier discussion of *The Deep End of the Ocean*, after a poignant flashback leaves Beth weeping in the high school over her son's disappearance, the chapter ends with the discovery of a new clue that confirms Beth's worst fears and powers the story ahead:

> When she looked up, not at a sound, but at something else, a disturbance of the air, Candy Bliss was standing at the foot of the bleachers. She held a plastic zip bag, small enough for a sandwich. In it was Ben's high-topped shoe, so clean and new the red parrot still glowed in the dark.

This new discovery, structured as a cliffhanger, tugs at the reader's emotions. After all, what is more precious than the tiny items worn by small children? The shoe implies innocence, and its appearance deepens the mystery and Beth's sense of loss.

Then a thruster kicks off the next chapter:

Finding the tennis shoe changed everything.

    It was the shoe that made Ben kidnapped. It proved for Candy Bliss that Ben had not wandered away on his own.

After a reader scans this first sentence, he'll naturally want to know why Ben was kidnapped and by whom. Mitchard inserts thrusters throughout the opening moments of chapters and scenes, and these thrusters create emotional bombshells that require further reading to discover their implications and impact. In your own stories, look for ways to create intrigue with opening and closing sentences that create urgency laced with emotion.

Bombshells aren't the only ways to manipulate thrusters and cliffhangers into emotional high points. Keep your characters—and your readers—from getting too comfortable by interrupting or prolonging climactic moments. If you've set the stage for a romantic interlude complete with candles, a cozy fire, and a good Cabernet, interrupt the happy couple by sending them into a sick child's bedroom, staging a disagreement, or causing the fireplace to belch out so much smoke that the smoke alarm shrills and the fire department arrives. Once romance is disrupted, the unanswered question is whether they'll return to their former intimacy or let the child's fever, the argument, or the flaming chimney drive a wedge between them? And because the reader is rooting for them to consummate the romantic relationship that has been building, she'll keep reading to find out if the relationship can withstand the interruption.

Story events are never predictable. Unanticipated events sideswipe your characters, and insights come at the last moment but are not acted on. You must bushwhack your characters at intervals, changing directions or shifting gears when it is least expected. Here are some possible cliffhangers or thrusters that can catch your reader (and characters) unaware:

- weather suddenly changes
- the doorbell rings, the phone rings, someone arrives at the party
- the protagonist is not believed
- the protagonist is deserted by his friends
- a trust is betrayed
- the protagonist arrives at a new setting

- the protagonist's past swoops into the story to influence the present
- the villain arrives on the scene
- the villain threatens the protagonist

NOVELS WITH GREAT CLIFFHANGERS AND THRUSTERS

Ellen Foster, Kaye Gibbons

Peace Like a River, Leif Enger

A Sight for Sore Eyes, Ruth Rendell

Black and Blue, Anna Quindlen

Housekeeping, Marilynne Robinson

She's Come Undone, Wally Lamb

Cities of the Plain, Cormac McCarthy

The Memory of Running, Ron McLarty

Sea Glass and *Light on Snow*, Anita Shreve

The Dive From Clausen's Pier, Ann Packer

TRAPS

In fiction, a protagonist is generally in a precarious situation, but walking into a cleverly set trap is the worst. A trap can be deadly and literal, like in Alice Sebold's *The Lovely Bones*, when fourteen-year-old Susie Salmon follows her killer, a neighbor, into a cornfield where he's built an underground room.

The trap succeeds best when the reader realizes that it is indeed a trap while the protagonist is in the dark. In the film version of Thomas Harris's *The Silence of the Lambs*, Agent Starling knocks on the door of the serial killer's home believing she's making a routine call to collect background information. The viewer, who has already visited Buffalo Bill's chamber of horrors, knows differently and longs to shout at the screen, "Don't go in there!" as she steps inside, ramping up the suspense to near unbearable levels.

If you're writing a novel where you are not springing an actual physical trap on your protagonist, think about other less dangerous entrapments. They can be benign, like staging a surprise party for a notoriously shy protagonist; sending a character who is inappropriately dressed to a fancy party or dangerously cold environment; or sending him into a room where another character is fuming with anger. Or it can be a situation in which an antagonist wrests information, a promise, or a concession from your protagonist, who gives in against his better judgment.

TICKING CLOCKS

A ticking clock pushes at the reader's nerves and causes her to turn pages because the time to stop a possible disaster is running out. Ticking clocks can be found in so many scenarios: a deadly storm is brewing on the horizon, a serial killer will strike again, or a ship must arrive to rescue the shipwrecked victims before it is too late.

A famous ticking clock occurs in Frederick Forsyth's political thriller *The Day of the Jackal.* The plot evolves around an assassin, the Jackal, hired by a secret terrorist group to murder Charles de Gaulle. However, when the Jackal's mission is leaked to government officials, an investigator, Claude Lebel, is given the task of stopping him. With a bounty of half a million dollars in the equation and the Jackal's complicated and meticulous preparations, the reader wonders if the murder can really be prevented. As the minutes count down to the Jackal's plan, it seems that there is no power on earth that can stop him.

Your task when planting your own ticking clock is to add an element of desperation or jeopardy to time slipping away. A character fighting a fatal disease gets sicker and sicker. A character tossed into an icy ocean fights off hypothermia. A character trapped on a mountain staves off hunger, wild animals, and injury. A character in the late stages of an addiction tries to make one last big buy. A character tries to reach the church to stop her true love from marrying another. You get the idea.

REVERSALS

A reversal occurs when a scene or chapter ending is the opposite of the beginning. Reversals create narrative drive and suspense because mood shifts, switcheroos, and the like cause the reader to flip pages.

Reversals showcase the ups and the downs of a character's life. For example, a protagonist can be destitute and end up winning the lottery, a happily married couple can separate, or a celebrated detective can be forced to resign in disgrace. Interspersed throughout a story, such reversals heighten the zigzag effect we've been discussing. But the best reversals aren't merely surprises or blips in the action; they haunt the story or characters.

Reversals play a large roll in Laura Moriarty's coming-of-age story *The Center of Everything*, featuring Evelyn Bucknow and her single mother, Tina. They live in a small apartment outside of a small town in Kansas during the 1980s, and Tina makes one bad decision after another, like having an affair with her married boss. Moriarty plants a series of reversals in the novel, such as when Tina's lover impregnates her and leaves town, and when Evelyn turns to her grandmother's church for stability and discovers that their fundamentalist beliefs are strange and illogical.

In another traumatic reversal, Tina, pregnant and unemployed, tries to apply for welfare, but ends up in a confrontation with a caseworker and collapses outdoors from heat and despair. The reversal in this incident is chiefly tied to emotion: In the opening of the scene, Tina is grim, determined, and in charge, and in the closing of the scene, she is near hysteria. The next chapter begins with another, more far-reaching reversal, showing how the incident causes a decisive shift in how Evelyn views her mother and their relationship:

> My mother knows I don't like her anymore. She has stopped trying to get me to smile at her, and when I say I want to eat dinner in front of the television instead of with her at the table, she shrugs and says fine. But she is still my mother, she says, still the boss around here, and when she goes across the highway to the Kwikshop, she makes me come with her, holding my hand tight in hers.

As in this case of Evelyn and Tina, reversals can drive a wedge between characters while proving that life can be uncertain or capricious. The author also uses this reversal to propel Evelyn into her character arc as a person more stable and ambitious than her mother, but ultimately this arc will include compassion for her mother also.

In your own stories, suspect every scene and chapter where your protagonist is unchanged by the events. Emotional reversals are a constant in fiction, occurring within every scene along with obstacles or conflict.

{ * }

We began this chapter talking about enhancing narrative drive, but by now you might be thinking that your job as fiction writer might more accurately be titled Chief Torturer. After all, you're denying readers what they most want to discover, often inflicting this torment at the end of a scene or chapter. Or, you're asking questions but not providing answers, jumping from place to place, and demanding that the reader hang on for the ride, all while teasing him with potential disasters.

Not every scene can appropriately end on a cliffhanger, but when possible, end in the midst of an action, or with an unanswered question. If you're noticing that few of your scenes end on a cliffhanger, try trimming the final paragraphs to determine if the scenes work better shortened. Keep cliffhangers spare by ridding sentences of modifiers, using short sentences, and honing in on the most crucial information.

And because scene openings must also drive the story, when you continue after a cliffhanger, don't always resume exactly where you left off. Start scenes with a provocative statement, moment, or tease. Remember that scenes don't start off slow and they rarely end slowly, although at times you'll need to allow a reader to catch his breath.

chapter 4

Epilogues

> An epilogue is more than a body count. An epilogue, in the disguise of wrapping up the past, is really a way of warning us about the future.
>
> —John Irving

ictional endings are written with a lingering potency. They must fulfill the promise of the story and answer the story question. In addition, they must address all the large and small questions created by the plot events and subplots. Ultimately, the success of a story hinges on the ending. In *The Art of Fiction*, John Gardner offers this assessment:

> A novel is like a symphony in that its closing movement echoes and resounds with all that has gone before. ... It is this closing orchestration that the novel exists for. If such a close does not come, for whatever theoretically good reason, we shut the book with feelings of dissatisfaction, as if cheated.

Gardner's point, that your ending must be carefully crafted so that a reader never feels cheated, is one worth remembering. In fact, as you write your novel, you might want to create a checklist of all the questions, subplots, actions, and secrets that must be resolved by the climax. Once you've checked off all the tasks the climax and ending must accomplish, you'll be able to assess if the final moments have packed a proper emotional wallop and then pointed toward the future.

If possible, you also should allow readers to inject their own meaning or surmising into the ending. But remember that while endings can sometimes be ambiguous, they are never confusing. In most genres, like horror, thrillers, and suspense, the novel will not hold up if the ending is spelled out clearly. Horror stories often end soon after or at the moment the conflict ends, because carrying on will appear anticlimactic. If your story has featured a monster of some sort, it's natural for your story to end when the monster is destroyed. In a romance, the ending features the satisfaction of a love affair launched, hinting that the future will bring more bliss than disappointment.

The climax often depicts the gathering and collision of forces, such as the protagonist and antagonist meeting for a showdown. The events that follow the climax are called falling action or denouement and end with the plot's resolution. These events contrast with the rising action, which leads up to the climax. *Denouement* is a French word meaning "the unknotting" and describes how the ending must untangle all the threads of the plot, subplots, and complications.

As the action winds down, there are often tasks that remain to be accomplished. Sometimes subplots are left dangling, or the aftermath of the climax is so intense that if the story were to stop there, the ending would seem too abrupt. Sometimes the closing pages must carry the reader along for a while, so that the implications of the ending can be sorted out. It is also in the falling action that you, as a writer, have a final opportunity to reveal the emotional depths of your protagonist and reflect the themes of the novel. It's crucial that the ending wind down on just the right note—without flatness or overkill, yet with perhaps an echo or final whisper of enchantment.

UNDERSTANDING THE EPILOGUE

The word *epilogue* comes from the Greek and means "to say in addition." Positioned after the story has concluded, an epilogue serves the distinct purpose of suggesting the impact of the story's climactic events. It's interesting to note that epilogues were common before the twentieth century but are used less often in contemporary fiction. In ancient Greek and Roman dramas, an actor would step to the front of the stage and comment on the events of the play. Over time, however, this sort of commentary was seen as extraneous and artificial, which is why it remains risky to use an epilogue without a concrete reason for doing so.

A true epilogue is separated from the story by time and place, and usually comments on it from a different perspective. For example, the epilogue to Michael

Crichton's *Jurassic Park* comments on the events after all hell breaks loose at a dinosaur theme park. The book is essentially a cautionary tale about a small group of people, including Alan Grant, a paleontologist, who gather on a Pacific island to prove that a dinosaur theme park is a viable and safe environment. However, human greed and nature intercede, proving instead that interfering with natural selection can lead to disaster.

Since the best epilogues offer some new insight or information that hasn't yet been provided in the story or ending, the epilogue in the novel happens in San Jose where, for several days, Grant is questioned by the authorities. While there, he learns that animals of unknown origin are traveling through a rural region, devouring crops. Although the animals are not found, it is hinted that they might be the fear-inspiring raptors. Thus, in *Jurassic Park*'s epilogue, Crichton is laying the foundation for his sequel, *The Lost World*, which is set six years later and follows up on unanswered questions.

Reasons for Using an Epilogue

You need a clear reason for writing an epilogue, and it cannot be used to simply tie up loose ends, which you should do during your falling action. Without a proper purpose for including one, an epilogue might come across as anti-climatic deadweight, inadvertently signaling to your reader that you're afraid your ending is so weak that he won't be able extrapolate meaning from it without help. To avoid such potential problems, make sure your epilogue is enhancing your story in one or more of the following ways.

- **Wrapping up story events after a traumatic or violent climax.** This is an especially important technique when the ending is abrupt or surprising, as when a major character dies, or when the fate of the characters is not clearly depicted. If your ending raises more questions than it answers, you will need to rewrite it or create an epilogue to resolve this problem.

- **Highlighting consequences and results of story events.** Perhaps you've written a comeuppance story, or the ending features a major revelation. The epilogue will serve to assure the reader that justice has been dispensed.

58

- **Providing important information that wasn't covered in the climax or denouement.** If a character was ailing in the story, you might want to explain his fate. Or, if a character becomes pregnant, the epilogue can explain the birth of the child. This can work especially well if the father dies or the child has special significance to the story.

- **Suggesting the future for the protagonist and other characters.** This is an important consideration in series fiction or if you're planning a sequel. An epilogue might also be appropriate if a character undergoes severe physical, emotional, or psychological trauma, to assure the readers of his full or partial recovery.

- **Making the story seem realistic.** For example, if you've killed off a character, the epilogue can be written by another character to explain how things went down. Or, if you're writing a story and the ending was literally explosive, the epilogue assures readers that the protagonist has survived.

- **Providing data on your large cast of characters, especially if you've written a sweeping historical or epic.** Often, with a large cast, it's difficult to suggest the fate of every character. In *Vanity Fair*, William Thackeray wrote an epilogue titled "Which Contains Births, Marriages, and Deaths." While this may seem old-fashioned to some readers, in a highly complex novel you can sometimes justify following the cast into the future.

GUIDELINES FOR CREATING EPILOGUES

Writers are sometimes cautioned from using epilogues because they create two endings, just as a prologue creates two beginnings. Here is the bottom line: The information and words spent on an epilogue need to be justified and not covered earlier in the story. All endings need to engage the reader's imagination, but too much information makes it difficult for the reader to imagine possibilities and futures, and will dilute the drama of the ending. Here are a few more tips to keep in mind when crafting an epilogue:

- **Write from a fresh location, perspective, and time frame.** An epilogue written moments after the climax will seem silly and unnecessary.

- **Don't linger.** No matter how interesting the information, the epilogue is still the aftermath and must be written concisely. Most epilogues are fairly short, a few paragraphs or a few pages. The longer the epilogue lingers, the greater the chance that it will be judged as anticlimactic.

- **Keep proportions in mind.** Shorter novels often don't need an epilogue or a long denouement. The longer and more complicated your novel, the more difficult it is to tie up all the loose ends. Thus you're justified in writing a longer epilogue, but remember that it's impossible to tie up every factor in the story.

- **Beware of self-indulgence.** An epilogue is not an excuse to experiment or play cute. While it is usually written from another perspective or vantage, it also must be clearly linked to the story and not create a jarring end note.

- **Offer fresh insights that can only occur after the results of the climax are known.** Don't use the epilogue to rehash events. It is also not advisable to comment on major plot events or issues—allow them their own weight and importance, with the reader sorting out the meaning. Epilogues are not like journalism or other forms of literature—they do not "spin" the plot events like the commentators who appear on *Meet the Press* or other talking-head shows.

- **Epilogues are not catchalls.** If you discover that you have too many unresolved issues or loose ends in the story, fix them in the ending, not in the epilogue.

- **If possible, give your reader a take-away moment.** It can be a laugh, a smile, a whimsical glimpse of a character's or narrator's thoughts, or a scene or visual moment such as the game of catch and the cars heading toward the baseball field in *Field of Dreams*.

- **Be flexible in your structural approach.** Since there is no fixed structure for epilogues, find a creative format for these final words. Consider using a device such as Sue Grafton's case reports or Margaret Atwood's lecture, both of which we'll discuss shortly.

NOVELS WITH MEMORABLE EPILOGUES

Bel Canto, Ann Patchett

Moby Dick, Herman Melville

The Last Thing He Wanted, Joan Didion

The Feast of Love, Charles Baxter

Keeping Watch, Laurie R. King

Horse Heaven, Jane Smiley

The Sky Fisherman, Craig Lesley

Cold Mountain, Charles Frazier

The Moonstone, Wilkie Collins

War and Peace, Leo Tolstoy

The Fountains of Paradise, Arthur C. Clarke

Dark Tower VII: The Dark Tower, Stephen King

The Jane Austen Book Club, Karen Joy Fowler

EPILOGUES IN ACTION

Epilogues function differently depending on the author's needs and intentions. In the examples that follow you'll notice that Sue Grafton and Margaret Atwood created epilogues because their story endings involved dramatic final actions likely to leave readers unsettled.

SUE GRAFTON AND THE MILLHONE SERIES

Sue Grafton is the author of a suspense series featuring Kinsey Millhone, a private investigator living in mythical Santa Theresa, California. In each novel, Kinsey reflects back on past events, recounting a case that is already over. Then, to lend a note of credibility, the epilogue is created as a case follow-up or report several

61

months after the ending, finalizing legal details, explaining the ramifications of the arrests and murders, and noting Kinsey's personal involvement. One reason Grafton's epilogues work is that they're written in the same first-person voice that the reader has come to trust and recognize, and they're dense with details.

In *R Is for Ricochet*, the case begins when Kinsey is hired by the elderly Nord Lafferty to keep an eye on his daughter, Reba, after she's released from the California Institute for Women, where she was incarcerated for embezzlement. Like most of Kinsey's cases, what appears to be a straightforward assignment soon leads to a tangled web of deceit, cover-ups, and ultimately murder, as the epilogue indicates.

Because Grafton has created a series, the epilogues add to the sense of time marching forward, connect the dots in Kinsey's personal life, and add a layer of veracity so that Kinsey seems like a real person. Because the endings of detective stories restore the world balance, Grafton's epilogues serve to assure the reader that justice has been served.

In a series, the reader builds a special connection to the protagonist, following him for years through ups and downs, good times and bad. A series writer carries a special burden to produce an ending that assures that the protagonist will continue on, yet the character must be emotionally (and sometimes physically) roughed up by the plot. Since most series are plot-driven, not character-driven, they also suggest that despite the protagonist's bruises or angst, he is essentially the same. An epilogue can help assure readers not only of the protagonist's survival, but also that his essential nature is still intact.

MARGARET ATWOOD AND *THE HANDMAID'S TALE*

Margaret Atwood's *The Handmaid's Tale* has one of the cleverest epilogues in literature. Its cleverness lies in its format and level of specificity. The novel imagines a dark future when America has been taken over by ultra-conservatives who assassinate the president and Congress and form the Republic of Gilead. In the wars that occurred during the overthrow, nuclear arms were used and the world that exists is a nightmare landscape with a toxic environment, scarce food supplies, and a low birth rate because of widespread sterility. The government is based on religious doctrines that subjugate women into narrow roles, with handmaids designated strictly for breeding purposes. Portraying a world where women are not even allowed to read, Atwood paints a gloomy picture of the nature of humankind.

The epilogue, titled "Historical Notes," is written two hundred years after the events of the book, and softens the blow of the dark world created in Gilead. Or does it? It answers some questions about Gilead, since the reader is assured that the society did not survive, but then, cleverly, Atwood suggests that the regime that exists now is also misogynistic. Thus we learn that Gilead has morphed into a similarly repressive culture.

The epilogue is deftly presented as a lecture that parodies an academic symposium. A Professor Pieixoto, known for his study, "Iran and Gilead: Two Late-Twentieth-Century Monotheocracies, as Seen Through Diaries," gives a talk entitled "Problems of Authentication in Reference to *The Handmaid's Tale*." The reader learns that the information found in *The Handmaid's Tale* came from transcribed tapes found in a footlocker near the former Underground Femaleroad used by women to escape their tyranny. Offred, the protagonist, is not identified as the narrator of the tapes (although the readers know she is), nor is her fate known, though the professor thinks it probable that she escaped. Atwood's epilogue serves to answer lingering questions about the story and to suggest Offred's fate, since the actual ending, with people arriving to seize her, is both abrupt and ambiguous.

Like Atwood, you might want to use an epilogue to answer questions left dangling in the ending and to comment on the story's themes. Writers of science fiction or fantasy have a lot of leeway in creating plots, themes, and the individual elements in a story. An epilogue might be a space ship's log, a scientific document, an excerpt from a history book, or another character commenting on what has happened in the ending. Because science fiction and fantasy plots are naturally fantastical, your epilogue provides a final opportunity for veracity. Your readers want to believe in the world and characters you've created, so you can offer up proofs in your ending notes. These proofs should supply specific information about the ending, complete with telling details and ramifications of the ending action.

{ * }

Writers hear a lot of rules about constructing fiction, some of them helpful, some of them distracting. When it comes to epilogues, ignore well-meaning advice that they are the sign of an amateur. If you've written a captivating story, especially one that a reader can scarcely bear to leave behind, your epilogue will be a welcome addition. If you've crafted it as a meaningful and informative final glance at the story, the reader will also thank you for wrapping up the story with a final grace note.

chapter 4

EPILOGUES

chapter 5
Epiphanies & Revelations

> {
> My task which I am trying to achieve is, by the power of the written word, to make you hear, to make you feel—it is before all to make you see. That—and no more, and it is everything.
>
> —Joseph Conrad

*S*tories explore the lives and hearts of characters. While different genres place varying emphasis on character arc, most fiction is about a character's transformation. If your protagonist is the same person at the end of the story as she was at the beginning, you often have no story. In genre fiction, such as thrillers and suspense novels, action is the focus, not character transformation, yet even a detective or super spy makes for a dull read if unmoved or unchanged by the story events. In a series, the character transformation happens in smaller increments within each book because the character arc (how a character changes as a result of the major events and turning points she experiences throughout the course of the story), spans the length of the series.

An epiphany, the luminous moment when a character, usually the protagonist, realizes something she has not known previously, can be a powerful and electrifying pinnacle of character development. A character's moment of profound understanding can greatly enhance her growth, and is sometimes the turning point moment that the story hinges on. Epiphanies deepen characters, provide the high notes in a plot, trigger events, and cause, worsen, or resolve conflict. Epiphanies are often found in everyday or ordinary events.

Like epiphanies, revelations provide profound and satisfying moments in fiction, but they are not necessarily tied to the protagonist's character arc. Instead, a revelation is tied to the reader's need to know something. A revelation can come in many shapes, ranging from a nugget of crucial information in a character's backstory, to the underlying aspects of a shady business deal, to a murderer's motivation, to a character's sexual proclivities, etc. However, a revelation doesn't need to be tied to your novel's characters. It can come in the form of a clue to a murderer's identity, the location of a hideout, or the discovery of a treasure map. Ultimately, revelations are used to capitalize on the reader's need to know, which keeps him turning the pages.

EPIPHANIES VS. REVELATIONS: WHAT'S THE *REAL* DIFFERENCE?

You might be wondering what the differences are between epiphanies and revelations. After all, both have to do with new insights and their aftereffects. Subtle and not-so-subtle differences separate the two tools.

The word *epiphany* is Greek and means "manifestation"—a sudden intuitive realization that comes shining forth. I like to imagine that an epiphany shines a brilliant light into a previously dark place in a character's soul or consciousness. This new understanding is often the opposite of the truth that was previously known, and therefore provides a stunning contrast. In order for an epiphany to cause a profound change, however, it must be centered around a sudden insight concerning the *essential* nature of something, not a random or mundane recognition. This new understanding is linked to character arc and affects the story's end. Here are the key aspects of epiphanies:

- In an epiphany, a character usually reaches the new conclusions by connecting the dots, allowing his subconscious its voice.

- Often an epiphany is a direct reversal of what the character knew previously and is usually a difficult or painful truth. His views and attitudes toward events and often other characters will be forever changed by the epiphany.

- An epiphany is *earned* by the protagonist, not volunteered by another character, meaning that it must occur through a character's solitary search.

- Epiphanies are usually, but not always, assigned to a protagonist, who, as determined by the story line, lacks some crucial understanding or information before the epiphany. Secondary characters can also have epiphanies, but they must somehow affect or alter the plot and influence the protagonist.

Revelations, on the other hand, can occur in many aspects of the story, and can involve secondary characters, subplots, and backstory. And, while a revelation can provide profound insight, it doesn't necessarily need to *change* the protagonist. Revelations cause twists and reversals in the plot, and the lead-up to their unveiling causes tension. As mentioned earlier, revelations also can be about the antagonist, or can involve scientific or technical information, such as a seemingly unsolvable murder method, a family secret, or a hidden passageway in an old house.

The Importance of a Strong Epiphany

Like most things of value, epiphanies come at a price, and usually this price is in a character's suffering. In romances there is often a crucial misunderstanding between the lovers that keeps them apart until an epiphany clears up the matter and they can acknowledge their true feelings.

When an epiphany solves a mystery or problem, especially the central problem of the story, it is especially important that the road to enlightenment is fraught with suffering. In life we often learn our most important lessons with our faces ground in the mud, not while singing gaily on a mountaintop. In fiction, such understanding also exacts a cost, and often happens when the situation is bleakest and the character is drawing on his reserves to survive.

The enlightenment can happen after the character has pursued dead-end leads and is humbled by the situation. Coincidences, another character leaning over and whispering a solution, help from a stronger character, or a flash of intuition all spoil the impact of the epiphany. When you plan your character's epiphanies, make certain that you've exacted a price.

The Structure of an Epiphany

An epiphany usually slams the protagonist into a crossroad and forces him to make a decision or to somehow change. This change does not need to be an about-face, such as being politically conservative one day and marching in an antiwar rally the next. But perhaps he sees his family in a new light and realizes how his childhood years are still affecting him. Or, maybe he comprehends the dynamic in an intimate relationship that he previously didn't understand.

To set up this dramatic switcheroo, lay the groundwork to ensure that the reader sees it as a natural and organic progression of the story events. If you take care to imbue it with intricacy, the results will pay off.

There are three parts to an epiphany: (1) the setup, (2) the trigger, and (3) the realization. The setup, which can vary in length, shows readers who the protagonist is before the epiphany. The trigger is the catalyst that applies pressure to the protagonist's old way of thinking and causes it to crumble. The realization, then, is when the protagonist consciously recognizes something she had not previously understood and, as a result, undergoes profound change.

In her novel *Talk Before Sleep*, Elizabeth Berg captures the friendship that develops between Ruth, beautiful, arty, and flamboyant, and Ann, a married homemaker and mother. This friendship of opposites has a deep meaning for Ann, a shy woman for whom friendship doesn't come easily. As the story progresses, Ruth leaves her husband and moves into a charming apartment, while Ann remains married.

A series of scenes reveal how Ann and Ruth are vastly different, with two of these scenes supplying epiphanies. For the epiphanies to work, the reader needs to know that Ann's marriage is in jeopardy:

> I'd begun to hate the sound of his chewing, the sight of his shoes, one lying over the other in the corner of the bedroom. … I resented his shaver next to the bathroom sink; I wanted a bouquet of pansies there, I wanted a clear Lucite container holding all my makeup. … I knew that Ruth didn't have to even look when she pulled something to drink out of her refrigerator—she'd picked everything for herself, so how could she not like it? … She could leave the light on to read until late into the night, or she could turn it off early and go to sleep without explanation.

Clearly Ann is frustrated with her life and envious of the lifestyle she imagines Ruth enjoys. Her desire to be free and spontaneous—to be like Ruth—comes through in a series of scenes and via introspection. When the two travel to New York, where Ruth has arranged a date for the still-married Ann, it's a chance for

chapter 5

EPIPHANIES & REVELATIONS

Ann to finally take a huge risk and act out-of-character. But will she? The trigger occurs at a restaurant when Ann attempts to be the flirtatious and spontaneous woman she longs to be:

> "Been a long time since you've, uh … had Chinese?" he asked.
>
> "It's been a very long time."
>
> He waited. I crossed my legs, swung my foot a little. "Tell you what," I said. "I'm going to point to something on the Chinese side, and then I'm going to eat it, no matter what it is. I need a new experience." I held my face in a way I hoped made my cheekbones prominent.
>
> "Delivery man," Ron said, in an oily voice. Then he licked his lips. I uncrossed my legs, ordered garlic chicken from the English side, requested a fork to eat with. Something had evaporated, almost instantly. That's what I told Ruth when we got back to our hotel.

Ann goes on to explain that she had suddenly remembered who she was, the kind of person who doesn't cheat on her spouse, which is the realization. Despite believing that she wanted to be wild like Ruth, Ann recognizes that her values and her loyalty to her family are undeniable.

Another major epiphany in the story occurs when Ann spends a night in Ruth's empty apartment. She tells her husband that she's there to keep an eye on things, but they both know she's actually trying on a single lifestyle.

The setup occurs as Ann settles into Ruth's apartment, reveling in the quiet and the beauty of her friend's artwork and possessions. She cooks dinner in copper pans, and tops off the meal with apple pie and ice cream eaten off a pottery plate so lovely she keeps picking it up to inspect it while she eats. After dinner she walks through the apartment examining things, then goes into the bathroom to take a bubble bath. Ann discovers that the boxes of bubble bath above the tub are mostly empty—an illusion of richness that is a metaphor for Ruth's situation. Notice how the trigger in the example below leads right into the realization:

> It was distressingly quiet in the apartment. Even the music I'd put on radio seemed unable to penetrate a kind of bubble that had formed around me.
>
> I opened Ruth's top dresser drawer. I felt guilty looking in it, but I suddenly needed to know something, though I didn't know what. Ruth's socks were rolled

up and organized according to color. She had underpants stacked up in two piles, one pair directly on top of the other. There was a stack of the tiny cotton T-shirts she wore, folded precisely into fours. I thought, why are these like this? Who has time to do this? And then I realized that what I was seeing was not an obsessive kind of neatness, but loneliness.

After this discovery and realization, Ann returns home instead of spending the night. Later that evening, she's lying beside her husband watching the news, and although the couple don't talk, she and her husband both know that everything has changed since her epiphany at Ruth's apartment.

Notice how the triggers—the discovery of the bath products and the neatly arranged dresser drawers—are visual and easily imagined. Since the triggers are constructed from ordinary objects, a reader can easily relate to the situation. Notice too that Ann's experience fills in missing information about the truth of Ruth's life, helping her see both Ruth's situation and her own marriage in a new light. Ann is changed from this moment forward—her restlessness in her marriage and her longing for Ruth's way of life evaporate.

As you read your favorite novelists, take note of their epiphany structures and the ramifications that come with them. Apply this knowledge to your own stories, asking yourself what the new understanding will mean to your character, how she will be changed after the epiphany occurs, and how these changes will affect her future actions.

THE SUSPENSEFUL REVELATION

Imagine a revelation as a hidden gem buried deep in your story. If you don't have a murder investigation, the discovery of a valuable object, or a long-buried secret at the heart of your story, ask yourself if there is some valuable information that can be withheld for as long as possible. Withholding such information causes suspense and tension, and creates the layers of intrigue that a reader wants to encounter in a story. When you create biographies for your protagonist and antagonist, note what they fear the most, what they're hiding, and what lengths they'll go to to protect their secrets or fears from being exposed.

Dorothy Allison's *Bastard Out of Carolina* is a novel about abuse and its terrible effects on the abused child. The protagonist, Ruth Anne "Bone" Boatwright, becomes embroiled in an untenable situation when her mother, Anney, an uneducated waitress, marries Glen Waddell. Anney marries Glen because she's desperate for stability and a father for her two daughters, but the marriage exposes Bone to physical and sexual abuse at the hands of Daddy Glen.

The abuse plays out against the backdrop of the Boatwright clan, a sprawling cast that includes hard-drinking men who shoot up each other's trucks, and spirited women who marry young and age quickly. The Boatwrights supply a large portion of the story's suspense, especially as revelations about the family, particularly Bone's uncles, come to light. Their introduction early in the story isn't a revelation in and of itself, but it does provide color and context upon which future revelations are based:

> I worshipped my uncles—Earle, Beau, and Nevil. They were all big men with wide shoulders, broken teeth, and sunken features. …
>
> Though half the county went in terror of them, my uncles were invariably gentle and affectionate with me and my cousins. Only when they were drunk or fighting with each other did they seem as dangerous as they were supposed to be. The knives they carried were bright, sharp, and fascinating, their toolboxes were massive, full of every imaginable metal implement. …

The reader keeps wondering what will happen if Bone's uncles find out about Glen's abuse. When a secret such as physical and sexual abuse is at the heart of a story, the repercussions are enormous. Revelations also compel the readers to discover how far Glen will go, if Anney's desperate need for love will be overshadowed by her need to protect her daughter, and if Bone will be permanently scarred from the abuse. These questions are deeply felt because readers witness the abuse and Bone's deterioration.

Writers can also take a cue from Allison and use a cast of secondary characters to provide a realistic milieu, subplots, a secondary source of conflict, and a means to make things happen in the story. Allison also imbues her large cast with secrets, desires, and complicated lives that can all be explored through a series of revelations. In your own stories, imagine the character traits shown in the opening scenes as the tip of the iceberg, with the oh-so-satisfying revelations lying below the icy water, providing the real danger and potency.

WEAVING REVELATIONS INTO EPIPHANIES

Revelations exist at the heart of most plots, supplying the undercurrent to the larger, story-shaping epiphanies. Important revelations are foreshadowed or hinted at, and are carefully crafted, layer upon layer. In Harper Lee's classic *To Kill a Mockingbird*, Boo Radley's transformation from town boogeyman to hero illustrates how a revelation can foreshadow, be woven into, and even be used to fuel an epiphany.

When the novel begins, the Finch children, Jem and Scout, imagine their neighbor, Boo, to be a monster and his house haunted. (If you're thinking setup, you're on the right track.) The trigger, then, develops over the course of the story with a number of small incidents (such as when they discover presents in a tree), as well as larger ones (like when the children are attacked by Bob Ewell on Halloween night and rescued by a stranger). It's later revealed that the children were saved by Boo and that Ewell fell on his own knife during the attack and died.

So where's the realization, the climax of the epiphany? Well, you need to dig a little deeper. Take a look at the following excerpt, in which Scout sees Boo—literally and figuratively—for the first time, and see if you can spot it:

> He was leaning against the wall. He had been leaning against the wall when I came into the room, his arms folded across his chest. As I pointed he brought his arms down and pressed the palms of his hands against the wall. They were white hands, sickly white hands that had never seen the sun, so white they stood out garishly against the dull cream wall in the dim light of Jem's room.
>
> I looked from his hand to his sand-stained khaki pants; my eyes traveled up his thin frame to his torn denim shirt. His face was a white as his hands, but for a shadow on his jutting chin. His cheeks were thin to hollowness; his mouth was wide; there were shallow, almost delicate indentations at his temples, and his gray eyes were so colorless I thought he was blind. His hair was dead and thin, almost feathery on top of his head.
>
> When I pointed to him his palms slipped slightly, leaving greasy sweat streaks on the wall, and he hooked his thumbs in his belt. A strange small spasm shook him, as if he heard fingernails scrape slate, but as I gazed at him in wonder the tension slowly drained from his face. His lips parted into a timid smile and our neighbor's image blurred with my sudden tears.
>
> "Hey, Boo," I said.

Where you able to distinguish the revelation from the epiphany? The children's understanding that Boo rescued them on Halloween is a revelation, while their understanding about Boo's true nature as a fragile, good-natured man is an epiphany. It's an epiphany because, in this coming-of-age story, the Finch children are learning important lessons about fairness and justice, and all these understandings are tied to their character arcs.

The sheriff also delivers a revelation about the attack that also plays an important role in the story's plot. For example, if the sheriff hadn't figured out that Ewell fell on his knife and that Boo helped in the scuffle, Jem would have been held responsible for Ewell's death. Jem's fate hangs on these revelations, and they have a far-reaching effect on the story line, just as the best revelations should.

If you're wondering how to incorporate revelations into your story, try this: Before you begin writing your novel, create a simple list of the major events in the story. Eventually this list will be structured into scenes. As you create scenes, ask yourself if some of the events or scenes are based on a revelation. Do your characters have secrets? Is some crucial fact going to come to light? Is someone's past going to cause a major development in the story? If your short story does not contain at least one revelation that somehow affects the protagonist, or if your novel contains only one or two, it will likely lack adequate narrative drive and suspense because revelations drive the story forward.

NOVELS AND FILMS WITH IMPORTANT EPIPHANIES AND REVELATIONS

The Dive From Clausen's Pier, Ann Packer

The Cider House Rules, John Irving

The Havana Room, Colin Harrison

Divine Secrets of the Ya-Ya Sisterhood, Rebecca Wells

Snow Falling on Cedars, David Guterson

Amy and Isabelle, Elizabeth Strout

Harry Potter and the Sorcerer's Stone, J.K. Rowling

72

> *The Mermaid Chair*, Sue Monk Kidd
>
> *Songs in Ordinary Time*, Mary McGarry Morris
>
> *Crow Lake*, Mary Lawson
>
> *The Hours*, Michael Cunningham
>
> *The Dogs of Babel*, Carolyn Parkhurst
>
> *American Beauty*
>
> *Memento*
>
> *The Sixth Sense*

EPIPHANIES, REVELATIONS, THEMES, AND PREMISES

Tying your character's epiphany or revelation to your novel's theme or premise is a sure way to bolster tension. Since theme and premise are the subject of chapter seventeen, let's pause only briefly to define the terms. Both theme and premise provide foundations for building your story. Theme is the central unifying idea or concern of your story, and it's usually a relatively simple concept, such as justice, belonging, or greed. Your theme pulses throughout the story and helps connect ideas and events. For example, the theme of Steven Spielberg's *E.T.* is abandonment. If E.T. hadn't been left behind by his space comrades and didn't desperately need to return to his home planet, the film's events would have lacked meaning and momentum. Also, if Elliot, E.T's human friend, hadn't felt lonely and abandoned by his father, then his friendship with E.T. wouldn't have been so meaningful.

Premise is linked to the story's conflict and to the truth that is proved by the story's ending and the protagonist's journey of understanding. The premise is usually an unmasking of or a truth about human nature and operates similarly to a proof in mathematics. That is, the premise is demonstrated by the climatic scenes and other accumulated evidence throughout the story. All major scenes and details contribute to proving the premise, such as true love comes at a cost, the scars of war can never truly heal, or, in the case of *E.T.*, friendship heals a broken heart.

In Ken Kesey's *One Flew Over the Cuckoo's Nest*, both the theme and premise are linked to revelations and epiphanies. The story tracks an asylum ward in

73

the 1960s. The inciting incident is the arrival of Randle Patrick McMurphy, a trouble-making, fun-loving type who joins the ward to avoid serving time on a work farm. McMurphy immediately butts heads with the controlling and sadistic Big Nurse Ratched.

The story is told from the viewpoint of a patient, Chief Bromden, and there are revelations sprinkled throughout, such as that Chief, who poses as a deaf mute, can actually hear and speak, and that his father sold his tribe's legacy to the white man. Big Nurse is also revealed during group therapy sessions, where she picks at the men's insecurities and sexual inadequacies. These sessions expose her true nature and also work to reveal why the men are in the asylum.

The premise of the story asks how a free spirit can exist in a society that prefers conformity. The underlying themes concern courage and freedom as it comes from within. The premise and themes are underlined by an epiphany when McMurphy discovers his fellow patients are hospitalized voluntarily. He's astounded and baffled as to why the men relinquished an ordinary life for a wretched and medicated existence in an institution. The discovery happens during a group therapy session:

> McMurphy doesn't say a word. He's got the same puzzled look on his face like there's something isn't right, something he can't put his finger on. He just sits there looking at Harding, and Harding's rearing smile fades and he goes to fidgeting around from McMurphy staring at him so funny. He swallows and says, "As a matter of fact, there are only a few men on the ward who *are* committed. Only Scanlon and—well, I guess some of the Chronics. And you. Not many commitments in the whole hospital. No, not many at all."
>
> Then he stops, his voice dribbling away under McMurphy's eyes. After a bit of silence McMurphy says softly, "Are you bullshitting me?" Harding shakes his head. He looks frightened. McMurphy stands up in the hall and says, "Are you guys *bullshitting* me!"
>
> Nobody'll say anything. McMurphy walks up and down in front of that bench, running his hand around in that thick hair. He walks all the way to the back of the line, then all the way to the front, to the X-ray machine. It hisses and spits at him.

The scene continues with McMurphy confronting the men about their reasons for staying—issues at the heart of the theme and premise. He asks Billy, the youngest of the group:

74

"Then *why? Why?* You're just a young guy! You oughta be out running around in a convertible, bird-dogging girls. All of this"—he sweeps his hand around him again—"why do you stand for it?"

Billy voices the fears that prevent him from leaving the ward, that make him passively accept Big Nurse Ratched's abuse:

"You think I wuh-wuh-wuh-*want* to stay in here? You think I wouldn't like a con-convertible and a guh-guh-girl friend? But did you ever have people l-l-laughing at you? No, because you're so b-big and so *tough!* Well, I'm not big and tough. Neither is Harding. Neither is F-Frederickson. Neither is Suh-Sefelt."

In this scene, Kesey emphasizes the theme that survival and happiness aren't always a question of sanity, but of courage. This information is an epiphany because it informs McMurphy's essential understanding of other people. It also brings understanding of Big Nurse Ratched's agenda, her abuse of power, and the hold she has over the men in her charge. As any good epiphany should, this one intensifies the conflict, affects the protagonist's character arc, and alters the story line.

Re-read the excerpts, noticing that the epiphany develops in the three stages outlined earlier. There is the setup—the therapy session as well as the sessions previous to it; the trigger—Big Nurse tormenting the men; and the realization—that the men are living there voluntarily. Notice, too, how the exposés in the therapy session reveal the men's deep longing for a normal existence, which points to the theme.

Theme and premise create boundary lines in a story and often express universal truths. While writing, you can keep asking yourself if your subplots, secondary characters, epiphanies, and revelations all tie back to theme and premise. If they seem random or are added for color or diversity, it's likely that you don't need them. Also, unless your protagonist is a child, if he encounters a revelation in every chapter or undergoes a long string of epiphanies, the story might come off as gimmicky.

THE CHARACTER ARC CONNECTION

In fiction, major events and turning points force a character to change, and the range of these changes is called the character arc. Character arc is a journey of understanding, and epiphanies and revelations are important ingredients that facilitate change. A character who does not change is called a static character. For example, in *To Kill a Mockingbird*, Atticus Finch is a static character because he's the same patient, decent, and intelligent sort at the end of the novel as he was at the beginning. His son, Jem, on the other hand, puzzles out the meaning of family, justice, fairness, and racism and is transformed by all that happens. His character arc takes him from innocence to a more developed and realistic sense of fairness and humanity.

Charles Dickens's *A Christmas Carol* is built on a series of revelations and epiphanies whereby Ebenezer Scrooge transforms his miserly and bitter heart to become open and generous. These changes don't come about until Scrooge travels back in time and comes to terms with how he became so embittered, admits to his missed opportunities and regrets, and then visits the future where he's horrified to discover that he's reviled after his death.

Stephen King's *Rita Hayworth and Shawshank Redemption* is a novella about a character undergoing a profound change by learning how to embrace life and opportunity instead of acting out of fear and limitations. The theme is about hope, and the premise is that hope overcomes fear and creates resiliency. The premise is proven by the characters undergoing a series of revelations and epiphanies.

Here is a thumbnail sketch of the plot: Banker Andrew Dufresne is wrongly convicted of murdering his wife and is incarcerated in Shawshank Prison, a place of brutality and danger. Over the years, even though jailed, he clings to his dreams and earns the respect of inmates, especially the convicted murderer "Red" Redding. After discovering that the crooked warden won't help him overturn his conviction, Dufresne escapes. Then Red is paroled and faces a difficult choice.

It would appear that, as the main character, Andy has the most dramatic arc. He is, after all, an innocent man brutalized in prison. But Andy actually is little changed by the story events and carefully plots his escape to Zihuatanejo, Mexico, where he leaves his past behind.

The most dramatic transformation belongs to Red, who runs a prison black market and, after years in prison, has become "institutionalized"—so comfortable with life in prison he can't imagine life outside its walls. (Brooks, another long-time convict, foreshadows Red's release when he is paroled and commits suicide when he can't make it in the real world.)

76

Prior to his escape, Andy describes to Red in a series of revelations that he has hidden money and a false identity for his life after Shawshank. (This scene is also the setup for Red's epiphany, which comes later.) He describes the lifestyle he envisions for himself and a rock wall where something is hidden, and then Andy offers Red a job. Red immediately claims that he couldn't make it in the outer world. Andy disagrees:

"You underestimate yourself," he said. "You're a self-educated man, a self-made man. A rather remarkable man, I think."

"Hell, I don't even have a high school diploma."

"I know that," he said. "But it isn't just a piece of paper that makes a man. And it isn't just prison that breaks one, either."

Red dismisses Andy's dreams until he gets paroled. When Red leaves prison, life on the outside is demeaning, bewildering, and frightening, and he considers committing a crime so that he can return to prison. But then he searches for the wall and finds it. The moment holds a powerful revelation and is a setup for the epiphany that follows:

Black glass and as smooth as silk. A rock with no earthly business in a Maine hayfield. For a long time I just looked at it, feeling that I might cry, for whatever reason.

With his heart beating madly, Red looks beneath the rock and discovers an envelope with his name on it. The envelope contains a letter and twenty fifty-dollar bills. Frightened, he reads the letter later in his room:

Dear Red,

If you're reading this, then you're out. One way or another, you're out. And if you've followed along this far, you might be willing to come a little further. I think you remember the name of the town, don't you? I could use a good man to help me get my project on wheels.

Meanwhile, have a drink on me—and do think it over. I will be keeping an eye out for you. Remember that hope is a good thing, Red, maybe the best of things, and no good thing ever dies. I will be hoping that this letter finds you, and finds you well.

Your friend,
Peter Stevens

Now Red is faced with a decision, but there's really no question. As Red says in the story, there are just two choices: "Get busy living or get busy dying." This realization is triggered by his friend's gift of money and the offer of a new life. It's also triggered by Andy's faith in Red, which melts his resistance.

So Red, now fifty-eight, jailed since 1938, decides to get busy living and, after ordering two shots of Jack Daniels, boards a Greyhound bus heading south. His choice illustrates his transformation from fear to hope, from imprisoned by fear to freedom. In the final passages, the theme is underlined:

> I hope Andy is down there.
> I hope I can make it across the border.
> I hope to see my friend and shake his hand.
> I hope the Pacific is as blue as it has been in my dreams.
> I *hope*.

There are many uses for revelations and epiphanies in a novel, but perhaps the richest vein to mine is character arc. When a reader witnesses a character such as Red changing, he too feels hope, and this sort of vicarious involvement in a character's life is why we read fiction. When you're creating characters, pay special attention to their flaws, lacks, denials, and weaknesses. The story will determine how the character will overcome these traits, but if you can stage revelations that force him to reevaluate his understanding of himself and his world, and create epiphanies that create deep change, you'll be investing in characters that readers will remember.

MINING CHARACTER FLAWS

As Red proved in *Rita Hayworth and Shawshank Redemption*, a character's self-image can be inaccurate or outdated. Interestingly, in real life and in fiction, people always act in ways that defend and uphold their beliefs about themselves, even when those beliefs are at odds with reality. These beliefs are often where revelations and epiphanies come into play. A character's flaws will always be tied to her self-concept, which in turn is tied to her character arc. The events you design in the story will force your character to change in the direction she most needs to change.

A character's flaws, whether real or perceived, are deeply illuminating, create inner and outer conflict, and allow readers to know truths about a character that she sometimes doesn't know about herself. When you create a character's flaws, make sure they directly impact the direction of the plot. For example, if a character is cowardly, then she should face a situation that calls for courage. An epiphany or some key revelation might also occur that causes her to understand that she's not always cowardly, or why she's cowardly and how she can change.

Use other cast members to nudge your characters to overcome their flaws. Notice how Red needed Andy's help to understand his own strengths and lend him hope, which overcame the negative example of Brooks's suicide. Notice, too, how Red's flaws (lack of hope and belief in himself) were ingrained from his circumstances—a prison sentence.

Fiction writers are fortunate in having fictional characters to manipulate and orchestrate to illustrate what it means to be human in a complicated and difficult world. Epiphanies are terrific plot devices to alter the course of your story, but they also deepen characters and provide intimacy so the readers can know characters. Revelations in fiction always matter, and they drive the story. Readers read because they want to discover what is going to happen next, why characters act as they do, and the secrets or past events that shape their behaviors.

chapter 6
Flashbacks

> When it is a long damp November in my soul, and I think too much and perceive
> too little, I know it is high time to get back to that boy with the tennis shoes, the
> high fevers, the multitudinous joys, and the incredible nightmares. I'm not sure where
> he leaves off and I start. But I'm proud of the tandem team.
>
> —Ray Bradbury

Fiction writers wrestle with many structural decisions when crafting a novel, and flashbacks—that is, memories and scenes that depict events that take place before the time frame of the story—are among the trickiest of such decisions. Writers hear lots of rules about flashbacks—avoid using them in the opening chapter; avoid using them in the last few chapters; never use them unless they're absolutely necessary to the story. In truth, there are a number of editors who lament that flashbacks are overused. Why? Because the reader's interest lies in the unfolding events in the present, and often events that happened in the past are not as involving as those occurring in the now.

THE FUNCTIONS OF FLASHBACKS

Despite their bad rap, flashbacks are one of the most useful devices in a writer's arsenal of tricks. They add depth to motivations, character histories, and themes, and impart information that cannot be told during the linear sequence of a story. If a character is an adult when the novel begins, flashbacks can reveal how she evolved. When used correctly, flashbacks also answer questions raised as the story goes along, especially those relating to a character's childhood influences.

Flashbacks are inserted chiefly to supply context. If your character is a high-priced lawyer without scruples, a flashback reveals why and how he lost his moral compass. Or, if your lawyer is a person of utmost integrity, it could be interesting to know how his values were shaped. If your story features a family feud, a flashback scene can be used to depict the dramatic event that started it. Similarly, if your story is set in a small town that was changed by a murder ten years earlier, a trip back in time is just the ticket to recapture the horror and ramifications of the murder.

When possible, use flashbacks to accomplish more than a single task. For instance, here are four key ways flashbacks can be employed to enhance your fiction.

1. TO INFLUENCE PACING

Flashbacks are typically slower than front story, especially if those present-day events are portrayed in vivid action scenes. Flashbacks can also be used to delay the present or to distract the reader from it. If your story has a major secret, mystery, or revelation at its core, you can use flashbacks to prolong the outcome and milk the suspense.

You can also slip in a series of flashbacks to convey events from a character's past while she struggles with a decision or issue in the now. So, while the flashbacks reveal the character's core and illuminate her struggle, they also delay her choice and allow tension to build.

When mixed with flashbacks, intermediate crises and goals also work to prolong climactic scenes. The flashbacks and intermediate events create a series of doorways that take the reader deeper into the story and the protagonist's psyche, enriching the whole, but also delaying the story's crescendos until the last possible moment.

2. TO SET OR CHANGE MOOD

When the reader returns from the flashback, the mood of the story will be colored by the events or information the reader was just was privy to. If your character flashes back to a sorrowful event, such as the death of her mother, then this sorrow is likely to follow the character and the reader into the next scene. Conversely, if your character recalls a more cheering event, such as watching her toddler playing with a puppy on a spring day, the mood after the flashback will be upbeat.

The trick to creating mood in a flashback is in identifying the emotion of the memory and scene, and then choosing words and details that accurately depict it.

The more haunting the memory or flashback, the more intense the emotion. If you write flashbacks without attention to emotion and thus mood, they will fall short.

If you want to depict a character favorably, you might want to compare her eyes to a summer sky. A dog can be depicted as cuddly or vicious—but generally you won't use blatant announcements. Lighting can split the sky with garish drama to create unease, or a room can be filled with shadows to suggest gloom or secrets. A place might smell like lavender or mildew. Even the smallest detail can suggest an emotion and mood—a hollow laugh, a weak smile, slumped posture, or even a slight hesitation.

Make nuanced choices, and your reader will adjust her emotional thermostat to the moods you've created. And remember that these choices are as important in the unfolding story as they are in the past.

3. TO REVEAL BACKSTORY

Backstory consists of events that happened before the story and that are crucial to understanding some aspect of the story or characters. While backstory is discussed in chapter two, it's important to acknowledge it here as a natural associate of flashbacks. Why? Because characters without pasts lack substance.

If your character is grown, and especially if he is eccentric, criminal, or just plain difficult, showing snippets of his childhood through flashbacks explains how he became who he is. After all, readers are always intrigued by characters' pasts and how those long-ago influences continue to shape them.

Don't let the temptation to reveal all of your character's backstory through flashbacks overtake you. Instead, balance your character revelations, understanding that readers relate better to events happening in the present. After all, the shadows from the past affect our knowledge, but the dramatic events of the front story are generally most revealing.

4. TO EXPLORE CHILDHOOD MEMORIES

Childhood memories have a special potency and can infuse your characters with depth and reveal motivations. In the real world, the remembrance of smells, sounds, and sights of the past steals into our bodies, stirring our senses and passions, and so it is with fictional characters. The meaning of your character's life resides in these memories, connecting him to a younger

82

and generally more vulnerable self, along with the world as it existed in earlier decades. Childhood memories contain a laser-like focus, an intensity and clarity that can enhance a story line.

But memory is a slippery thing and comes calling when least expected. A distant scene will appear unbidden; a tragedy will refuse to leave our consciousness. Characters are sometimes haunted by their pasts and sometimes able to step back into a distant time to relish life again. When your character is mining the past, the reader wants to know what the memories mean. A reader knows that often we understand ourselves, our families, and our tragedies only long after events occurred. In real life we spend our lives puzzling over the meaning of things, and so can your characters.

When revealing childhood memories through flashbacks, try to use memories that are poignant or that reflect on a major event, such as a death in the family. In *The Mammoth Cheese*, Sheri Holman introduces a flashback from protagonist Margaret Prickett's childhood immediately after the character has spent a harrowing night delivering breech twin calves. It is late, and though she's ready to collapse, Margaret spots laundry that needs to be hung outdoors to dry and hauls the metal tub out into the yard. It is while pinning up laundry that a memory comes in, pricked by the night, the weather, and events from the past few days:

She remembered, almost as if it were a dream, a night just like this when she was a girl; the night of the comet. The same anticipation hung in the air, the same thrilled foreboding. The wind lifted her hair just as it was doing now, while she and her cousins raced like blinded bats across the field between her grandmother's house and the railroad tracks. There was supposed to be a comet that night and they were going to stay up to see the fiery red ball steak across the sky and set the world on fire.

They ran and shrieked and played until something moved in the air, and the moon went dark, and collectively, like animals huddling before a storm, they came together in a clump at the center of the field. A strange electricity tickled their skin and caught in their lungs and they knew as sure as they lived, the comet must be at hand. Far away, as far away as Richmond, thunder grumbled. The cousins held hands and waited with an anticipation and desire so great it seemed to lift them off the ground and leave them hovering over the mowed stalks of field corn. What would the comet look like when it came? Would they be instantly combusted and tossed as sparks through the black night sky? Would they ever be the same? Then suddenly, just as the anticipation threatened to explode them from within, there was a flash, and a streak of lightning, emerald green and thick as a girl's arm, hit down just in front of them. The cousins scattered. Margaret, cheated of her comet, opened her mouth to cry *What happened?* But all she tasted was metal on the railroad tracks.

The flashback ends when headlights swing into her driveway, and her farmhand steps out of his truck. This flashback works particularly well because the author wisely chose a childhood memory rich with magic, wonder, anticipation—an event that didn't go exactly as planned—that uniquely parallels and complements the birth of the calves.

When using memories, here are a few things to keep in mind. First, flashbacks work well after an emotionally draining event to provide a way to calm characters' and readers' emotions and provide the reflection that lends meaning to the previous scene. The aftermath of an intense scene, where characters react emotionally and take stock, is called the sequel. While not every scene in every novel requires a sequel, sequels are often an appropriate place for a flashback or recollection.

When working with a character's memories, keep in mind that you and the reader will never know everything about his past. You might want to list events or influences the reader needs to know to understand his motivations and how he sees the world. Not all the items on your list will be revealed in flashbacks, but it's helpful to refer to your list as you write.

Remember to create characters whose actions suggest their pasts and how they were shaped by childhood, instead of providing blow-by-blow accounts of every childhood memory, trauma, or glory.

TYPES OF FLASHBACKS

There are four types of flashbacks: recollections, frame stories, flashback scenes, and dreams. They vary greatly in length, with frame stories being the longest and recollections the shortest. Sometimes a writer will use more than one device; sometimes, as in the case of the frame story, only one is needed.

RECOLLECTIONS

A recollection is the simplest and least obtrusive flashback. It's a brief, single memory averaging a few sentences or several paragraphs. This fragment of memory doesn't disrupt the story for long. Unlike other types of flashback, a recollection doesn't necessarily take the character or the reader to a different time frame. Instead, it opens a brief window into the past, and this window grants only a glimpse, then slams shut. The potency of the memory and the shadow it casts dictate how long these recollections last and how they influence the character.

Your character's recollections should resemble the reminiscences we entertain during our real lives. Your mind constantly flits in and out of time, and sometimes you dwell on a memory for only a few seconds, sometimes a bit longer. Work to reproduce those fleeting moments as well as longer memories (flashback scenes).

Elinor Lipman's *Isabel's Bed* is written with a mostly forward-facing plot. It's the story of forty-one-year-old Harriet Mahoney, a struggling writer who is down on her luck after her live-in boyfriend of twelve years dumps her for a younger woman. Answering an ad, she moves to Cape Cod and into the home of Isabel Krug to ghostwrite Isabel's scandalous life story. The house is a magnificent dwelling with inspired architecture, separate wings, rounded walls, and ocean views. Chapter four begins with Harriet's brief recollection of a childhood dream:

> I had a recurring dream in my childhood: I'd walk into my bedroom closet to the small attic door inside, open it—something I was afraid to do while awake—and find a hidden suite of rooms, sunny and beautiful, which made our small house something of a magical duplex.
>
> Isabel's kitchen had a similar effect on me. I had missed it on my trips between the car and my new room, had thought about it briefly when the wine appeared, and had assumed there must be an efficient, prize-winning galley around one of these bends.

Thus Lipman quickly zips to the past and back into the present, but the short recollection adds to the reader's impression of the house.

FRAME STORY

This book-ended type of flashback is a unique structure that creates a story within a story. It uses a prologue and epilogue in the present (although they are not always clearly named as such), and then the entire tale is told as one long flashback that takes place after the action is over. (Frame stories are also discussed in chapter eleven.)

Two of the most famous frame stories are Joseph Conrad's *Heart of Darkness* and Mary Shelley's *Frankenstein*. As in the case of these two novels, a character or narrator may recall events that happened years earlier. At other times—for example, in a mystery such as Sue Grafton's Kinsey Millhone series—the story is told soon after it ends. No matter how much time has elapsed since the story action, the frame story requires a reason for the distance. Perhaps, as in *Frankenstein*, the events were so disturbing that the narrator is still sorting out his feelings about them. Or, in the case of a detective following up on a case, perhaps the legal ramifications weren't sorted out immediately after the plot ended, and time was needed for arrests, trials, and an outcome.

William Styron's *Sophie's Choice* is another well-known frame story, and again, because the events of the story are horrific, the narrator needed time to reflect back and understand exactly what had happened. Set against the backdrop of the Holocaust and post-war New York, the main characters, Sophie and Nathan, are already dead when Stingo, the narrator, begins the story. In describing the events of the summer of 1947, he attempts to unravel the motives and tragic events leading to their double suicide.

Daphne Du Maurier's *Rebecca* is another example of a frame story. It begins with these famous first lines:

> Last night I dreamt I went to Manderley again. It seemed to me I stood by the iron gate leading to the drive and for a while I could not enter, for the way was barred to me.

In this opening, the narrator is pondering her dream about Manderley, a seaside estate in Cornwall. As the dream is recalled, we learn that Manderley now lies in ruin. The story switches to years earlier, beginning in Monte Carlo, where the young and unsophisticated narrator (who is never named) meets and marries Max de Winter. Afterward they move to Manderley, where the lingering presence of the dead but larger-than-life Rebecca de Winter not only haunts the lavish home, but also the narrator's new husband.

If most of your story is about a character's past, or if your story is mostly about the *why* of the story events, then a frame story structure is suited to your plot. A frame structure also works if some hidden puzzle piece is suddenly revealed and shows the mysteries of the past in a new light. While the frame structure provides distance because the action has already happened, the events must still unfold with a gripping immediacy and significance. The

events are never so far in the past that they've ceased to matter—they still cast
a long shadow over the characters' lives and emotions.

FLASHBACK SCENE

Perhaps the truest and most common flashback form is the flashback scene.
These flashbacks are comprised of a single scene, several scenes, or an entire
chapter and usually contain setting details and dialogue. The flashback scene
takes your reader from the present and creates the longest interruption of the
front story. If your story contains multiple flashback scenes, it isn't necessary to
present them chronologically. Allow the reader to slip in and out of time and meet
your characters at different stages.

Anna Quindlen's *Blessings* makes excellent use of flashback scenes to reveal
crucial past events. This novel has two story lines: In the first one, a young couple
abandon their newborn at a country estate called Blessings, and Skip Cuddy, the
estate groundskeeper, finds the baby and begins caring for her. The second story
line traces events that happened to the elderly estate owner, Lydia Blessing, years
earlier and how these events, recalled with poignancy, still trouble her.

Lydia's history and the riddles it contains are expertly woven into the present-day story through flashback scenes and recollection, and her long-ago
tragedies and secrets provide as much momentum as Skip's struggles with fa-
therhood in the front story.

Midway through the book, a scene depicts Lydia eating dinner with her
daughter, Meredith. Backstory, via a series of flashback scenes, is nimbly intertwined into the dinner conversation. The flashback reveals that Lydia became
pregnant at nineteen after sleeping with a married man. Desperate, she turned to
her brother's friend for help as they ate breakfast in a diner:

> Neither of them said much until Benny reached over and took her hand. "What's
> the matter, Lydie?" he said, and she started to cry. The only words that would come
> were "I need." "I need I need I need" between wet sobs and heaves and then an-
> other trip to the ladies.
>
> "What do you need, Lydie?" he said when she'd come back.
>
> "I need help," she said softly.
>
> "What kind of help?"
>
> "I need someone to marry me."

There was a silence. ...

Benny said, "I'd marry you. I'd be happy to marry you."

Now, Meredith said, "The landscaping is looking lovely, Mother."

Lydia's head came up slowly, like one of the water birds fishing around the pond that tried to pretend that they weren't there, that they were really a rock or a stick or a part of the dock. She hadn't been following the conversation.

Notice how Quindlen portrays Lydia emerging from the past using *now* to transition into the present, and how the ongoing dinner anchors the reader in the present while allowing explorations into the past.

If you're interested in how to connect several flashbacks scenes within a single present-day scene, *Blessings* is a good novel to examine. It also illustrates how to parse out and withhold flashback information to create a separate layer of intrigue in the story.

Beginning writers have a tendency to make flashbacks sketchy or indistinct, but since a flashback scene must evoke emotions in the characters involved (and thus the reader), a ghostly outline won't work. Imbue flashback scenes with sensory details and immediacy so that the past has a distinct reality.

DREAMS

Dreams, a less traditional form of flashback, are used in the front story to reflect current concerns, but can also reveal backstory and its influences. The advantage of using dreams is that you can inject emotionally charged information within a short segment and portray especially haunting events in a format that readers relate to. Since most readers have experienced disturbing or revealing dreams, they are inclined to key in to the emotional significance of a dream.

Because dreams are such a mysterious phenomena, embedded with metaphor and symbolism, they must be handled with the utmost delicacy. I'd like to impose a warning here: If a dream is the only means through which a character realizes important information about her past, it's best to find another method. To make a dream significant to the story, it needs a nudge from the front story to set it in motion. This nudge might be a new setting, the arrival of someone from the character's past, or even the result of a character undergoing therapy. Dreams introduce variety to a story and provide another glimpse into a character's psyche.

However, be careful not to overuse dreams, and make sure the ones you do use are up to the task. Dreams that aren't intriguing or powerful enough to telegraph their meaning will bore readers. It might be helpful, if you're writing a dream sequence, to watch several films such as Hitchcock's *Spellbound* or David Lynch's *Mulholland Drive*, noticing their use of spooky and visual elements.

Another reason for using dreams is to reveal that your character suffers from a trauma or a full-blown case of post-traumatic stress disorder, where dreams and nightmares are such a common occurrence that they're a hallmark of the condition. Post-traumatic stress disorder is an anxiety condition brought on by an extreme stressor, such as being directly involved in or witnessing a traumatic occurrence.

Animal Dreams, by Barbara Kingsolver, uses flashbacks scenes, dreams, and Native American myths to enhance the story line. Because much of the story line is focused on the protagonist's desire to understand the past, Kingsolver frequently moves back and forth in time, using various tactics. The story centers on Cosima (Codi) Noline, who returns to her hometown of Grace, Arizona, to teach biology, confront her past, and care for a father who has Alzheimer's. The past holds a lot of pain for Codi: the death of her mother when she was three, a difficult relationship with her distant and demanding father, and a traumatic secret. In this excerpt, from the opening of chapter six, Codi's secret is revealed to readers through her memory of dreams she used to have:

> I was fifteen years old, two years younger than my own child would be now. I didn't think of it in those terms: losing a baby. At first it was nothing like a baby I held inside me, only a small impossible secret. Slowly it grew to a force as strong and untouchable as thunder. I would be loved absolutely. But even in the last months I never quite pictured the whole infant I might have someday held in my arms; that picture came later. The human fact of it was gone before I knew it. But evidently the word "lost" was somewhere in my mind because I've had thousands of dreams of losing—of literally misplacing—a baby.
>
> In one of the dreams I run along the creek bank looking among the boulders. They are large and white, and the creek is flooded, just roaring, and I know I have left a baby out there. I thrash my way through mesquite thickets, stopping often to listen, hearing nothing but the roar of the water. I feel frantic until finally I see her in the middle of the water bobbing like a Cortland apple, little and red and bright. I

89

wade in and pull her out and she lies naked there on the bank without so much as a surname, her umbilicus tied with a man's black shoelace such as my father might wear. I see her and think, "It's a miracle she's survived."

Notice how visual and sensory the dream is—it contains surreal events that many of us have experienced in our own nighttime dramas. Because Kingsolver has created an intricate plot, the reader understands that Codi is dreaming about her miscarriage as well as another real incident from her childhood. Codi doesn't remember the event, but other characters do.

There are more dreams scattered throughout the story, but there are several things to learn and to emulate here. First, when a character dreams about the past or present, the dream needs to cause things to happen. Codi faces her past because her recurring nightmare leads to insomnia, which in turn leads to other happenings in the story. Generally, dreams are used for understanding some aspect of the dreamer's life, and if the character cannot understand the dream, it's hoped that the reader will.

PLACING FLASHBACKS

Pay attention to where you position flashbacks, because intrusions from the past must always be justified. Because fiction attempts to create a trancelike state in your reader's mind, you dare not disrupt the trance unless it's essential to the story.

While time is slippery in fiction, the linear progression of the events in your story is the basis of its structure. Fiction writers who craft a story without planning the order of its events risk creating a muddled mess. Zipping around in time without proper planning can leave a reader light-headed and bewildered. Plodding at turtle speed in simple chronological order won't provide moments of high drama or brilliant insight.

Generally, flashbacks are best introduced during lulls in the story or when a character is alone to enliven a static scene or to add intimacy and depth to a sequel. Avoid flashback scenes and recollections during intense action scenes, turning points, and in climactic scenes. During these moments, readers want to be glued to the unfolding drama, and will resent being distracted by the past. The exception might be a brief recollection during an action scene, but here too, the recollection must be meaningful and the trigger for the recollection must be apparent.

90

Readers need to sense the logical march of time in the unfolding events , even if time dips back and forth between past and present. If you move around in time with care, and do not insert flashbacks frivolously, you'll be fine.

FLASHBACKS IN THE BEGINNING

Your openings can start with a whisper or a bang, but they must hook the reader by introducing questions about what is going to happen next and what the impact of the first incident will be on the protagonist's fate. Since your opening must accomplish all this heavy lifting, there is no need to distract with digressions into the past.

Flashbacks that are placed near the opening work best when the story begins at a feverish pitch, such as with a murder, trauma, or accident. In these cases, flashbacks introduce the cast or explain how things became so intense. This sort of flashback controls pacing, allowing the reader to catch his breath and understand the context for what has just happened.

For example, a flashback placed soon after a car accident in the opening pages of Ron McLarty's *The Memory of Running* provides context and data about the story world. Within a few paragraphs we learn the make of the car, the date and place of the accident, and that the victims had been driving from a cabin set on a beautiful Maine lake.

The opening doorway also creates sympathy for the protagonist, Smithy Ide, because by the fourth paragraph of chapter one, we learn that Smithy is overweight, drinks too much, and has a dull and dead-end job, no girlfriend, and no future. Remember that, once the reader starts feeling pity for the protagonist, he will follow the character through the story and, over time, his pity will be transformed to empathy as the protagonist struggles to pursue his goals.

If you feel the need to place a flashback in your opening, remember this: No matter how intriguing or eloquent, flashbacks not only stop the story, they also leech its intensity. Justify their presence in your opening and use them sparingly throughout your story.

Also, make certain that the present-day story, especially the opening salvo, is more intriguing than or as equally intriguing as past events. In *The Memory of Running*, for instance, the inciting incident is sufficiently dramatic to overshadow the past. At times, the past might overshadow or share billing with the present, but the general guideline is that the front story should contain the most drama.

FLASHBACKS IN THE MIDDLE

The middle of a novel, that vast territory after the first plot point but before the climax, occupies most of the story. In these chapters, conflict and motivation intensify as problems worsen for the protagonist. This is one of the best places to insert flashbacks, because by the time the reader reaches the middle, he has come to know the main characters and understand the main conflict.

Elinor Lipman's *Isabel's Bed*, discussed earlier, uses an entire chapter to deliver a large amount of backstory in the form of a transcript from a murder trial, complete with testimonies from expert witnesses. This technique works well: The information appears realistic, contains lots of dialogue for immediacy, reveals another side of Isabel as she testifies, and introduces secondary players at an emotionally strained moment—always a good time to introduce characters. *Isabel's Bed* has thirty-five chapters, so this long flashback chapter comes at about the one-third mark, and plenty of intrigue and conflict have already been introduced.

Consider emulating Lipman's method of using a trial transcript or a similar device to deliver a lot of information in a single chapter. Since not every story involves a trial, think of other devices, such as a home movie, journal excerpts from the past, or a character arriving at a setting where significant events in the past occurred, opening a doorway to memories of long ago.

FLASHBACKS IN THE END

It's best to avoid flashbacks at the end of novels. Endings are the destination of your front story, and the reader wants to be riveted to the final moments as they press urgently toward a climax of action and emotion. If you digress to the past, or wait until the last possible moment to reveal an important flashback scene, it steals the limelight from the climax. So, it is generally advised that endings and the final scenes of the story remain in the present.

Dual Time Frames

There is an exception to the warning about inserting flashbacks in the ending: a story that has dual time frames. While chronological order is simpler to write, many story structures shift back and forth in time, because the past story is as important as the present-day story. *The Memory of Running* is an example of such a novel.

In *Fried Green Tomatoes at the Whistle Stop Café*, Fannie Flagg clarifies the back and forth structure by featuring each time zone as a single chapter, with each chapter headed by a dateline. She adheres to her pattern throughout the novel, proving the importance of backstory to front story, and using the past to change the present.

In *Fried Green Tomatoes at the Whistle-Stop Café*, Evelyn Couch meets Ninny Threadgoode in the visitor's lounge of a nursing home. Evelyn doesn't know the loquacious elderly woman, but she's drawn into her conversation. As the novel progresses, Ninny slips in backstory about Idgie Threadgoode, her sister-in-law and the protagonist of the past time frame:

> Idgie used to do all kinds of crazy harebrained things just to get you to laugh. She put poker chips in the collection plate at the Baptist church once. She was a character all right, but how anybody ever could have thought that she killed that man is beyond me.

Here Ninny introduces the story question, *Who murdered Frank Bennet and why?* When backstory is unraveled as a series of flashbacks that answer the story question, the events have a forward thrust like the front story, so the reader's mind will be traveling ahead on a dual track. In the case of *Fried Green Tomatoes at the Whistle Stop Café*, as the past unfolds, the present will never be quite the same again, because tales from the past are used as a catalyst for Evelyn Couch to make changes in her life. She finds courage in the stories of the daredevil Idgie Threadgoode and her friends in Whistle Stop.

WHEN *NOT* TO FLASH BACK

Flashbacks are not designed for the writer's amusement, but rather the reader's education. If your flashback is *not* going to elucidate, illuminate, or provide context, then you probably don't need it.

It is also advisable not to use a flashback in a novel-length manuscript when you only have one or two flashbacks to insert. You're better off setting up a pattern of at least half a dozen flashbacks at fairly regular intervals, rather than taking one or two lonely excursions into the past. If there are only one or two flashbacks, the reader will be jarred by the digressions and they will stand out as an abnormality.

If you still believe that you have invaluable information about the past to impart, you can use exposition or other devices, like newspaper clippings, letters, or diaries. Let's consider exposition. In the opening chapter of Alice Hoffman's *Turtle Moon*, she describes how in May in Verity, a small town in eastern Florida, everything goes haywire. She refers to specific past events, then moves into the present:

> People in Verity like to talk, but the one thing they neglect to mention to outsiders is that something is wrong with the month of May. It isn't the humidity, or even the heat, which is so fierce and sudden it can make grown men cry. Every May, when the sea turtles begin their migration across West Main Street, mistaking the glow of streetlight for the moon, people go a little bit crazy. At least one teenage boy comes close to slamming his car right into the gumbo-limbo tree that grows beside the Burger King. Girls run away from home, babies cry all night, ficus hedges explode into flame, and during one particularly awful May, half a dozen rattlesnakes set themselves up in the phone booth outside the 7-Eleven and refused to budge.
>
> At this difficult time of year people who grew up in Verity often slip two aspirins into their cans of Coke; they wear sunglasses and avoid making any major decisions. They try not to quit their jobs, or smack their children, or run off to North Carolina with the serviceman who just fixed the VCR. They make certain to stay out of the ocean, since the chemical plant on Seminole Point always leaks in the first week of May, so that the yellowfin float to the surface, bringing sharks closer to shore.

Hoffman uses about three paragraphs to describe the conditions in May, creating feelings of unease and curiosity. Her first sentence also refers to the past:

> The last major crime in the town of Verity was in 1958, when one of the Platts shot his brother in an argument over a Chevy Nomad they had bought together on time.

We can see that Hoffman's opening sentence and background information foreshadow the future events and tease the reader. Hoffman didn't need a flashback to set all this in motion, and you might try a similar strategy.

GRACEFUL ENTRANCES AND EXITS

Flashbacks need to be entered by graceful means, tipping off the reader to a change in time and place. Transition sentences, which link time and place and

94

create flow, don't need to be elaborate or obtrusive to be effective. They can be as simple as "It all began the day she met Regan." Consider this example from F. Scott Fitzgerald's *The Great Gatsby*, in which Nick, the narrator, suggests that Gatsby cannot repeat the past. Gatsby is determined to try to recapture his former relationship with Daisy, which leads into this flashback:

> He talked a lot about the past, and I gathered that he wanted to recover something, some idea of himself perhaps, that had gone into loving Daisy. His life had been confused and disordered since then, but if he could once return to a certain starting place and go over it all slowly, he could find out what that thing was. ...
>
> ... One autumn night, five years before, they had been walking down the street when the leaves were falling, and they came to a place where there were no trees and the sidewalk was white with moonlight. They stopped here and turned toward each other.

Fitzgerald uses ellipses and the simple phrase "one autumn night, five years before" as his signal of a time change. While ellipses are generally no longer used in this fashion, what is notable here is that a flashback beginning doesn't need to be an announcement, and works best when it appears natural.

When following your characters in and out of the past, try to avoid transitions that refer directly to your characters' brains at work, such as "Mary thought back to the day she first met Tom." Or, "My mind drifted back to that beautiful day in May." Sometimes referring to thoughts in this manner is your only option, but there's usually a better option. Pay attention to the methods best-selling authors use to transition into the past.

If you're writing in past tense, begin the flashback in the past perfect and use *had* a few times to clue the reader that you're entering another time zone. Then, once you're back in time, switch to the simple past tense. If you're writing in the present tense, use the past tense throughout the flashback. Sometimes you don't need to use the past perfect tense as a transition:

> As she looked deeply into the hypnotist's light, her memories came tumbling back. The night of Gerald's disappearance, she arrived home late; too tired to notice that he was not home before her. Weary from a long day at the hospital, she slipped into bed without giving much thought to her husband's absence.

When the flashback ends, it must be clear to the reader that you're shifting back to the present, picking up where the story left off:

> But that was twenty years ago and now Regan must be middle-aged. We all are, she sighed, and left the room.

To chart a story back to the now, you might want to repeat an earlier detail, action, or image. Or, use a simple means of returning with a brief transition word or phrase such as *now*. Alternatively, you can use a device such as an unusual word, event, sensory awareness, or object, or create a summary statement, such as:

> By Saturday, the office crisis that had so dominated her thoughts was now replaced by preparations for Angela's wedding.

Triggers help create a smooth transition into the past. These catalysts can be a song, place, person, object, sensory stimulation, or event that plunges the character into a memory. Your character can smell lilacs drifting in through an open window (scents are quite evocative), spot a character who reminds her of a former lover, overhear a song, or hear a familiar voice.

It helps if triggers are associated with strong or unresolved emotions. Your character can hear a song from her teenage years or spot the vintage car driven by a high school boyfriend, her first heartbreak. After the flashback ends, the reader needs to slip back into the present through a doorway, like Alice slipping in and out of the rabbit hole in *Alice in Wonderland*. Examine your favorite novels, noting the sentences just before and after flashbacks and how the author planted the trigger and handled moving around in time.

EDITING YOUR FLASHBACKS

When editing your completed draft, scrutinize your flashbacks, asking yourself if the flashbacks interfere with the story's trance. No matter which types of flashbacks you employ, they must pulse through your story with forward momentum. Check also that any flashbacks more than a few sentences long simmer with tension or conflict.

Evaluate your flashbacks with an eye toward consequences. Does the backstory revealed have consequences for the characters? Does it illuminate conflict in the front story? Is the past in the flashbacks linked to a character's turning points or crucial realizations?

Make sure your flashbacks do not tell more than they show, or you'll sap them of emotion and immediacy. Telling distances the reader. Avoid this hazard by infusing your flashbacks with emotion, tension, and conflict and writing them as scenes, not summaries.

Keep proportions in mind. Longer novels have more room for excursions into the past, and can also withstand longer, more detailed flashbacks. The shorter the novel, the fewer and shorter the flashbacks.

During revision, note how many entrances you use in your flashbacks. Circle every word that refers to some movement in time: *now, later, then, next, when, often*, etc. Make certain each segue is concise, clear, and necessary to clue the reader. You can also insert line breaks on both sides of a flashback to indicate movement in time.

If one character is asking another character about her past, craft dialogue that is eloquent and concise. Make certain the character who receives the information responds to it somehow; that the information is vital to the overall plot; and that the information has an emotional core—that is, it's somehow unforgettable, disturbing, or cathartic. Look to *Isabel's Bed* for a good example of using dialogue to discuss the past when the characters are strangers at the outset of the story.

Finally, review the action before and after the flashbacks. Avoid slipping a flashback in the midst of an exciting or emotional scene, an action scene, or important moment. This is like slamming on the brakes while you're driving at eighty miles per hour. If your scene depicts a heated argument, a physical fight, a collision, or an accident, don't slip back in time; stay focused on the conflict and peril.

{ * }

There are many reasons why flashbacks fail. They're often poorly designed, overly long, and awkwardly constructed (meaning the writer has not created graceful segues in and out of the past). That said, they're still one of the most useful tools in your repertoire. Just follow the guidelines set forth in this chapter and remember that each flashback must be handled with caution.

chapter 7

Foreshadowing

{

What I like in a good author isn't what he says, but what he whispers.

—Logan Pearsall Smith

oreshadowing suggests, whispers, or plants information, and deepens the reader's sense of anticipation by laying down traces of what will happen later in the story. Foreshadowing causes tension because events are hinted at, but not explained. It also lends future events authority and adds layers and depth that readers appreciate. When you insert foreshadowing, you're telling the reader, "Don't be surprised if this happens later in the story."

Foreshadowing has three main functions: to build unity in a story, to create credibility for future events, and to increase tension and suspense. One of the earliest suggestions for foreshadowing came from short story master Anton Chekhov, who explained that if you plant a gun in the first act, before the story ends, someone must shoot the gun. In other words, if you have imbued an element or object in the story with significance, then you must deliver the payoff.

Foreshadowing builds a foundation of plausibility and logic. This is necessary because, while readers enjoy surprises in a story, they like to be in on the surprise, and won't enjoy feeling mystified or blown off course when the surprise happens.

When and how much to foreshadow varies with the needs of the story—too much, and you kill suspense; not enough, and the story doesn't quite gel. The best foreshadowing raises a question or uneasiness in the reader's mind, but sometimes you don't want the reader to realize that the question has been planted. Good foreshadowing slips in like a slight wind change, not like thunder. It can be woven into small or quiet moments, or into dialogue, and is especially effective when ending a scene or chapter.

Foreshadowing requires planning and an understanding of exactly where you're headed in the story. Some writers etch in foreshadowing instinctively, but many are forced to intertwine it into a later draft after they've determined if they've missed opportunities. Foreshadowing can also tie unrelated events together, causing the reader to see an event in a new light. When used early in the story, foreshadowing suggests a wide range of possibilities; as the story progresses, the range of possibilities narrows. It's generally best to stop foreshadowing at about the three-quarters mark in the story, since the final scenes are reserved for immediacy and emotional payoffs. Spend the last chapters developing the climax, not hinting that it's forthcoming.

What Can be Foreshadowed

Foreshadowing is used to lay the groundwork for: (1) set pieces (the largest, most dramatic scenes), (2) character transformations, and (3) secrets. Let's take a closer look at each.

1. SET PIECES

Set pieces are the cinematic scenes in which you pull out the stops and the drama heats up, allowing the tension and opposition that have been boiling to explode. In a movie, a set piece is where the budget is blown, and can be anything from a huge song and dance number to a Civil War battle.

For set pieces to be effective, they require a buildup, and that's where foreshadowing comes into play. It's like when you're traveling along a lonely highway and see mountains looming ahead in the distance: The reader senses that the set piece lies ahead because tension is building, and actions become inevitable until the upcoming scene arrives and delivers a wallop of excitement.

There is no required number of set pieces, but there are usually six to ten in a novel, with at least one each for the beginning, middle, and ending sections. (Note that the climax is a set piece scene.) Set piece scenes often host fights, show-

99

downs, boardroom squabbles, or murders. They can also host weddings, funerals, parties, or family gatherings.

In a novel, the early set pieces will not be set up with a lot of foreshadowing, because you're still introducing characters, conflict, and the story world. Your later set pieces will be foreshadowed more because by then the reader will be familiar with the story and players, giving you more room to slip in foreshadowing.

2. CHARACTER TRANSFORMATIONS

Foreshadowing builds characters by introducing traits and values. When a character lies, especially with little provocation, the reader wonders if he'll lie again and questions his values. If a character faints at the sight of blood in an early scene, then when a high-stakes medical emergency happens later, the reader leans in wondering how he'll react. Readers enjoy speculating about how a character is going to act under pressure or threat, and these actions are often foreshadowed.

A character's motives are always foreshadowed. If a character acts in ways that are especially generous or stingy, fearful or bold, readers want to know why. If your private investigator breaks into an office to steal documents, the reader should know that she's risking her license because she cares about her falsely accused client, and that she also gets a secret thrill from her illegal acts. If your sorcerer casts a spell on the princess, then the reader needs to know that he plans on taking over the kingdom or wants the princess to fall in love with him. If your army captain leads his squadron into a jungle riddled with booby traps and dangers, we need to know that he's trying to impress his father, a retired major who thinks he's not man enough for the job.

Foreshadowing is also necessary when a character is undergoing a major change in beliefs, actions, or direction. The bigger the character's transformation, the more foreshadowing is required. In the movie *Thelma and Louise*, what started out as an escape/adventure turns into a suicide pact as the women launch their convertible into nothingness in the final moment.

For such a dramatic ending to be believable, the viewer needed to experience the characters changing along the way, and witness their friendship bond. It was also important for the viewer to see them in the context of their status quo: fed up with their lives, abused or mistreated by their men, with little hope for the future. To make the ending work it had to be foreshadowed with scenes proving their anger and desperation, and to add poignancy the viewer had to witness their exhilaration in their short-lived freedom.

Foreshadowing is important to reveal the motivations of an antagonist or villain. Bad guys can be particularly tricky to fashion because they have a big job to accomplish—they must exude a certain amount of star power, threaten the protagonist's well-being, exhibit comprehensible motives, and act in a way that's perfectly in sync with their personalities and goals.

For example, when a mystery opens and the reader is told that the victim died by a particularly gruesome method, this information foreshadows what the villain is capable of. It also creates anticipation for when we finally meet him, and suspense over whether he's going to kill again. One of the questions looming over a story featuring a bad guy is how far he will go to achieve his goals. The reader is always afraid to find out, but keeps reading to allay his fears.

3. SECRETS

When a secret has a central role in a novel or story it must be foreshadowed. Secrets can be almost anything, but when they're shameful or desperately concealed they are more powerful. In *Bee Season,* a novel about the disintegration of a family, author Myla Goldberg both hides and foreshadows a devastating secret involving Miriam Naumann, the mother of the family. As the story progresses, Goldberg provides the reader with clues that become meaningful once the secret is exposed.

Here, Goldberg provides the reader with a glimpse of Miriam, capturing the sense of restlessness that surrounds her and foreshadowing what's to come:

> Miriam Naumann is a hummingbird in human form, her wings too fast to be seen without a stop-motion camera. The silver in her hair makes her seem electric, her head a nest of metal wires extending through her body. Eliza can only imagine the supercharged brain that resides inside, generally equates the inside of her mother's head with the grand finale of a July Fourth fireworks display.

Because the reader isn't immediately aware of the fact that Miriam is mentally ill, and because the full implications of her illness aren't made clear until much later in the story, these remarks craftily hint about her brilliant but damaged mind.

FORESHADOWING DEVICES

A variety of devices can be used to foreshadow, so plan on using more than one method to create a whisper campaign. The devices are many: dreams, actions, mannerisms, gestures, news events, emotions, overheard conversations, or characters overreacting or underreacting to certain news or events. Let's examine some of these methods more closely.

CHARACTER TRAITS

Foreshadowing is crucial to fully depict a character and reveal personality traits or fatal flaws, such as in Alfred Hitchcock's *Vertigo*, based on a novel written by Pierre Boileau and Thomas Narcejac. A complicated, multi-layered story, *Vertigo* is rich in symbolism, but much of it is held together with foreshadowing. The main character suffers from a severe fear of heights, resulting in a crippling case of vertigo. As the story progresses and the protagonist loses more and more to his fear, it becomes clear that he must face his phobia once and for all. But can he beat it? If you're unclear about where foreshadowing lies in novels you're reading, watching *Vertigo* might clarify how it is used.

In all fiction, a protagonist's character traits (and flaws) are linked to every aspect of the plot. They predict if she will achieve or fail to achieve her goals, how she reacts to the story problem and setbacks, how she deals with confrontations and crises, and how she behaves in intimate moments. A story is a huge canvas upon which a character's traits are revealed. When a character succeeds, fails, or changes in the final moments of a story, the reader believes in the ending because earlier actions have foreshadowed this result.

MOOD

Just as every party, holiday, or bustling office on payday are infused with mood, so are scenes in fiction. Mood infects and reinforces the reader's emotions, aids in understanding key moments, and enhances his enjoyment of the story events. *Turtle Moon*, by Alice Hoffman, depends heavily on mood to reinforce the story. The first chapter begins by talking about how May is a time of danger, and danger arrives when a woman running from her past is murdered. The following illustrates how Hoffman uses moods to foreshadow:

Even people who are afraid of the dark know that the worst nightmares usually happen at noon. It may be because of the gravitational pull of the sun in the center of the sky, or simply because this is the hour when everyone's defenses are down, and they expect nothing more than bread and fruit.

This segment suggests something is about to go wrong, and violence is forthcoming. If you create scene cards or an outline, you might want to briefly note the mood that permeates each scene. In a novel, moods might range from boisterous to tragic, with many permutations in between. Once you've named the moods for your scenes, examine your descriptions and word choice to determine if they deliver.

SYMBOLS

Symbolism creates meaning, but it can also foreshadow future events and moods. When an image or object is used repeatedly in a story, it becomes a symbol. A symbol can come from the natural world, such as a flock of birds, a desert, fire, or ocean. In *Bee Season*, the younger child, Eliza, displays a startling ability to win spelling bees. Her father is a quiet man, a cantor and intellectual whose study is symbolic in the story and foreshadows the family's relationships and changing roles:

When Saul closes the study door behind him, he closes the book of the everyday world as well, placing it upon a distant shelf until familial duty or emergency calls him back.

The study is described as a small room, made smaller by piles of papers, notebooks, and walls lined with bookshelves:

The average paper density increases toward Saul's desk, which emerges from the tumult like a piece of flotsam tossed by the paper tide. Saul's desk spares no room for distracting doohickey or clever calendar, covered as it is by books and notes, loose and bound. ...

In this room governed by disorder the shelves are the exception to the entropic rule. Saul's library is arranged alphabetically, recent paperbacks brushing spines with age-seasoned leather-bound volumes. English texts adjoin Hebrew and Yiddish. ... While the library's overall organization might cause many a self-respecting academic to blush, to Saul the study is a paper-lined nursery in which his scholarly interests may grow and blossom by the light of two 80-watt soft white bulbs.

This detailed description provides the reader with a sense of Saul's main traits and magnifies the significance of the study. Before the spelling bees begin, Eliza is shut out of her father's study, but Eliza's new prowess excites her father's interest and she starts spending time with him there. There is also a huge secret within this family, and the study—with its door closed, shutting out other family members—symbolizes how little they know about each other. In your own work, look for objects, places, and aspects of nature that can whisper about what is to come and lay down traces for the most dramatic moments. Readers have an intuitive understanding of symbolism, so don't be afraid to use it.

DIALOGUE

A reader's eye is naturally drawn to dialogue because it is staged, action-intensive, and auditory. But although fiction dialogue mimics real conversation, it is a highly stylized version of it. It is more succinct, leaves out unimportant information, is often embedded with conflict, and is often suggestive. And, like other techniques, dialogue can hint at the truth of something or suggest things to come. In Ernest Hemingway's *The Sun Also Rises*, after Mike meets the unattainable Brett, his infatuation is foreshadowed in a quick dialogue exchange between his friends:

> We said good night. "I'm sorry I can't go," Mike said. Brett laughed. I looked back from the door. Mike had one hand on the bar and was leaning toward Brett, talking. Brett was looking at him quite coolly, but the corners of her eyes were smiling.
>
> Outside on the pavement I said: "Do you want to go to the fight?"
>
> "Sure," said Bill. "If we don't have to walk."
>
> "Mike was pretty excited about his girl friend," I said in the taxi.
>
> "Well," said Bill. "You can't blame him such a hell of a lot."

Because Brett is also the object of the narrator's desire, the reader starts speculating along with the characters about how Brett feels about the men, if a rivalry will develop, and how things will end. The best dialogue hints to foreshadow, but isn't an obscene wink and can be as simple as a character expressing doubts or misgivings.

OBJECTS

Character's belongings and physical objects make a story tangible and solid. When you place objects in a story, especially personal objects, always know what they mean to the owners and the story. For example, Amy Bloom's short story, "A Blind Man Can See How Much I Love You," is about Jane, who undergoes a sex change operation, and the effects of this operation on everyone involved, especially Jane's mother. The story opens with foreshadowing using objects, in this case, photographs:

> Jane Spencer collects pictures of slim young men. In the bottom drawer of her desk … she has two photographs of James Dean, one of a deeply wistful Jeremy Irons in *Brideshead,* arm in arm with the boy holding the teddy bear, a sepia print of Rudolph Valentino in 1923, without burnoose or eyeliner, B.D. Wong's glossies in Song Liling and as his own lithe, androgynous self, and Robert Mapplethorpe slipping sweetly out of his jeans in 1972. She has a pictorial history of Kevin Bacon, master of the transition from elfin boy to good-looking man without adding bulk or facial hair.

Thus the reader is introduced to Jane's desires and the story conflict. Objects used for foreshadowing can be sentimental, such as a character's souvenirs from childhood, or grisly, such as a villain's collection of souvenirs from his victims.

ACTIONS

Fiction is made up of large actions, such as fight scenes, and small actions, such as a character getting ready for an important meeting. Large and small actions can foreshadow the climax, reveal themes and truths in the story, and hint at the depths of a character. In *The Dogs of Babel*, author Carolyn Parkhurst cleverly inserts foreshadowing into the opening paragraphs of the fourth chapter. The story follows Paul Iverson as he struggles to understand his wife's death from a fall. In this foreshadowing segment, he describes how he once visited a college friend who lived in New York on the nineteenth floor of a building. A couple lived next door, and one night the man climbed onto the balcony and jumped. Iverson recalls:

> My friend was in bed when it happened—it was about one A.M. and he heard a short piercing scream and then nothing more.

Iverson and his friend spend time looking down from the balcony and speculating about the trajectory of the man's body. After his wife dies, Iverson looks back at the months before her death and ultimately concludes it was suicide, like the

105

death of the man who jumped from the New York balcony. Since Iverson has been loathe to admit that his wife killed herself, this earlier memory (and foreshadowing device) helps set the stage for his eventually accepting the truth.

SECONDARY CHARACTERS

Secondary characters are the unsung heroes of fiction. Because many writers use them more as props, rather than using them to make things happen or orchestrate the protagonist's transformation, they are often not effectively utilized. Secondary characters can also foreshadow actions and motives of main characters, as well as tip off readers about upcoming events. Author Liza Cody's protagonist Anna Lee is a former cop turned operative for a small detective agency in London. In *Under Contract*, Anna is hired as the bodyguard for a rock star, Shona Una, who has been receiving threatening letters. When Anna arrives to meet Shona, she rings the bell of a large house with shuttered windows that looks deserted (foreshadowing), and is greeted by a secondary character who serves to foreshadow both the strained relationship Ann will have with Shona and entourage, and Shona's secrets:

> At last the door opened. The chain was on and a suspicious face looked through the crack. Anna held up her security badge and said, "Anna Lee. Mr. Horowitz sent me."
> "No one told me," the face complained. A pale hand emerged from the gap allowed by the chain, fingers snapping impatiently. Anna put the badge into it. The hand withdrew and the door shut. Ann waited, still shivering.

Since you should always look for ways to slip tension into scenes, small moments like this hostile greeting instead of a welcome work well.

SETTING

Setting is perhaps the most often-used tool for foreshadowing, since readers are accustomed to its ability to create mood. After all, we begin reading about haunted castles, spooky islands, and magical kingdoms in childhood. Readers instinctively understand that a place suggests (and thus foreshadows) danger or delight, death or rebirth. In *Under Contract*, Liza Cody continually uses setting to foreshadow and create tension. Chapter nine begins after Anna wakes from a nightmare, restless and unable to sleep. She leaves her flat and returns to the house where Shona lives:

The night in London is never quite dark, never quite still. There are always a few with somewhere to go or work to do. And there are always a few who can't sleep. The city at night is like a big animal, groaning and twitching when it should be unconscious—the restless fleas on its back giving it no peace even at the smallest hours. ...

In Addison Road topaz raindrops fell from the bare branches of trees and dropped on the shining paving stones. Anna slowed the car to a crawl as she approached Shona Una's house. It looked as dead and empty as it had earlier.

Cody's setting details are quite deliberate here, especially words such as *dead*, which weave unease into the moment.

Another example of foreshadowing using setting is found in Tobias Wolff's novel *Old School*, where the reader learns early in the story that the private boys' school is a place where literature and poetry are revered and emulated. This emulation will lead to the protagonist's downfall. The first lines signal this:

Robert Frost made his visit in November of 1960, just a week after the general election. It tells you something about our school that the prospect of his arrival cooked up more interest than the contest between Nixon and Kennedy, which for most of us was no contest at all.

Explaining that the momentous Kennedy victory paled in comparison to Frost's visit implies much about the atmosphere of the school, suggesting that the story takes place in a setting where a boy will do anything to succeed as a writer.

DESCRIPTION

You can imbue simple moments with tension or creepiness with a single descriptive word. In *Under Contract*, Cody's carefully drawn descriptions of a rock concert foreshadow future events, and reflect the unease and violence seething around Shona. Anna Lee is in the balcony of a concert hall when she hears Shona perform for the first time:

The impact of the sound came not so much through the ears—it started with the feet from the huge roaring vibrations in the floor, and spread upwards until the whole body was immersed. It was loud enough to shake muscle from bone. And all the while strobing white light pierced the eye and flickered straight into the brain like the onset of epilepsy. The great structure of girders, now ablaze with thousands of flashing bulbs, descended gradually from the rafters and spun slowly above the audience like a ferris wheel.

With its violent connotations (shaking muscle from bone), this description leads to escalating suspense and danger immediately following the performance.

PREMONITIONS

A character's premonitions, along with clichéd settings such as "a dark and stormy night," are probably the two most overused foreshadowing devices, but they are also powerful means to create a sense of unease that whispers in your story. After all, most people experience premonitions from time to time, and in many situations this sort of intuition is invaluable.

In Liza Cody's *Under Contract*, detective Anna Lee has a premonition that something is wrong as she is watching Shona's final number, where the singer wears a black and red costume with stark white makeup that makes it look like her eyes and mouth are cut from a sheet. After this ghost-like description of Shona's costume (more foreshadowing), Cody writes:

Ann shivered suddenly and turned away. … She started to run and arrived back-stage just as the band came off.

Keep in mind that writers often overuse premonitions. This means that each premonition must be handled deftly and must keep with the character's personality and possibly her occupation. Anna Lee is the perfect character for experiencing a premonition, because her job demands finely honed instincts.

Another tip about premonitions: They work best when you use newly minted images, interpretations, and sensory language. In Alice Hoffman's *Turtle Moon*, a character's premonition is delineated with a fresh eye, and suggests the kind of danger most of us try to avoid, as in the example below:

Lucy is at the mall when she knows something is wrong. She can feel a sharp edge at the back of her throat, as if she's forced to swallow a knife.

The words *knife* and *throat*, so closely juxtaposed, add another shiver to this fore-shadowing and prove that a single sentence can be highly suggestive.

ADDITIONAL WAYS TO FORESHADOW

You can use almost anything in a story to foreshadow future events. Light glistening on a new engagement ring might foreshadow the character's future happiness, just as the stone cracking might suggest troubles to come. Here are a few more devices to add to your repertoire.

1. PLANTS AND RED HERRINGS

Plants are a cross between foreshadowing and clues. These are used often in mysteries and thrillers—the dog that didn't bark the night of the murder, the person from the past who suddenly appears just as things start going wrong for the protagonist, or the character in mismatched clothes whose color blindness will be a major clue.

Plants generally aren't sitting out in the open. You need to disguise them a bit. For example, the character from the past might have legitimate business in the story: Perhaps his mother just died and he's in town for the funeral and to settle her estate. You can disguise plants by placing them within ordinary moments (such as a character running an errand), or next to dramatic moments, so the reader is diverted by the larger action. The point is that a plant doesn't call attention to itself.

Sometimes writers use red herrings, or false clues, to lead the reader astray. Red herrings are a time-honored device in writing mysteries and suspense, but again, a little goes a long way. It might be helpful to think about where the term *red herring* comes from. In England, anti-fox hunting activists would trail fish, such as smoked herring, along the ground in the area where the hunt was to take place to throw off the hounds.

The purpose of a red herring is to fool the reader, but the problem is that readers don't always like being fooled. They like options to choose from, being teased with possibilities, and misdirection and reversals, but they don't like being played with. Red herrings, when not handled deftly, can have that effect. For example, if you're writing a murder mystery and the reader follows Tom, the chief suspect, all through the story, and then you spring the real killer, Ethan, at the last moment, the reader will feel cheated.

2. TRAGEDY

Sometimes tragedy seems like a common occurrence in our society, but it's actually uncommon by definition—for example, an untimely death or an accident or a serious illness that strikes an otherwise healthy person. In fiction, as in life, a tragedy can break a person, change him forever, or strengthen him. Tragedy that happens in the backstory or early in the novel can also foreshadow future events. It's important that you don't insert tragedy into backstory or inflict it on a character just because you can, but rather to toss in complications, change motivations and outcomes, and cause character transformation.

3. BLATANCY

At times, a character or narrator speaks directly to the reader about what has already happened or is about to happen. "But this was a decision I would come to regret" is this sort of foreshadowing. This trumpet effect is best used to foreshadow an event that will happen much later, not immediately after the announcement. Examples of this type of blatancy are everywhere in Lemony Snicket's A Series of Unfortunate Events books, and are used to increase anticipation and underline the dangerous plight of the Baudelaire youngsters. In fact, the series' first book, *The Bad Beginning*, opens with this sort of device:

> If you're interested in stories with happy endings, you would be better off reading some other book. In this book, not only is there no happy ending, there is no happy beginning and very few happy things in the middle. This is because not very many happy things happened in the lives of the three Baudelaire youngsters.

The opening continues in this manner, and the story is interspersed with a series of asides such as:

> There are many, many types of books in the world, which makes good sense, because there are many, many types of people, and everybody wants to read something different. For instance, people who hate stories in which terrible things happen to small children should put this book down immediately.

Naturally, a young reader is going to wonder what terrible things lie ahead. You need a good reason to use this sort of device. In Snicket's case, he is designing a series with orphans who suffer from bad luck and the incompetence and evil intents of adults. The voice is an odd mix—outraged, judgmental, and confiding. If you've incorporated an intrusive or omniscient narrator, if you're telling an old-fashioned tale, if you've given away the ending in the beginning as in a frame story, or if you want the reader in on the game as in the Lemony Snicket stories, blatant foreshadowing can be fun.

However, if you're writing a serious suspense story or psychological thriller, blatancy won't work. When unraveling a mystery, the reader wants to play detective along with the character. In mysteries and thrillers, for example, the murderer's identity or the chief secret in the story must be craftily suggested, yet hidden, so sleight of hand is especially crucial. Also, in many genres where suspense is a large element of the story, the reader likes to pit himself against the author and guess at the story's outcome.

If you're questioning whether your foreshadowing devices might be too blatant, as opposed to a whisper about future events, agent and author Noah Lukeman suggests the following in his book, *The First Five Pages*:

> Look back over your foreshadowing (if any) and consider if, in the context of your book as a whole, it might be too overt. If so, there are three basic ways you can tone it down: (1) cut back the sheer space devoted to it; (2) make it more cryptic; and (3) move it further from the event it foreshadows.

This is good advice for foreshadowing you worry is intrusive, as well as for all other types.

4. WEATHER AND SEASONS

There's a good reason why a character's sense of danger escalates during severe weather and storms and why a character is more optimistic when the sun shines. Weather is a powerful backdrop for creating moods and action. Since it is unpredictable and volatile, weather can foreshadow random violence, danger, or passion. Seasons, on the other hand, are predictable, symbolic, and suggestive, and can suggest a whole range of things in your novel.

When something is amiss with a season, as in the opening paragraphs of Ernest Hemingway's *A Farewell to Arms*, trouble and heartache are foreshadowed.

> In the late summer of that year we lived in a house in a village that looked across the river and the plain to the mountains. In the bed of the river there were pebbles and boulders, dry and white in the sun, and the water was clear and swiftly moving, and blue in the channels. Troops went by the house and down the road and the dust they raised powdered the leaves of the trees. The trunks of the trees

too were dusty and the leaves fell early that year and we saw the troops marching along the road and the dust rising and leaves, stirred by the breeze, falling and the soldiers marching and afterward the road bare and white except for the leaves.

The plain was rich with crops; there were many orchards of fruit trees and beyond the plain the mountains were brown and bare. There was fighting in the mountains and at night we could see the flashes from the artillery. In the dark it was like summer lightning, but the nights were cool and there was not the feeling of a storm coming.

This opening is laced with foreshadowing, but one of the most disturbing lines for the reader is "the leaves fell early that year." The reader worries when nature acts queerly, just as when nature explodes with storms and earthquakes. Nature acting strangely opens the door for stranger happenings in the world of humans. This opening, where Hemingway uses *bare* twice, also foreshadows how war is abnormal and extraordinarily tragic. Mountains and leaves are normal; troops marching past until their dust powders the leaves is not. If the troops can affect the countryside with their sounds and dust, what else are they capable of?

5. SMALL GOALS

The conflict in novels is created when a protagonist pursues goals that are not easy to achieve. Along the way to his major goal of the story—to find the murderer, find true love, climb a mountain, or overcome his past—the protagonist also pursues smaller goals. These wins and losses can foreshadow the final goal. For example, if your character is trying to solve a murder, he might obtain DNA evidence, trick a witness into admitting an important truth, and discover a previously overlooked clue. Of course, there will also be setbacks and dead ends in the case, but the series of small failures and successes sets the stage for his ultimate victory or loss.

CAREFULLY PLACED WORDS

In foreshadowing, words are used with the utmost skill, often doubling the intensity of a moment or hint. It can be helpful to collect words with unpleasant, sinister, or dangerous implications, such as *shroud, ghostlike, shadowy, cheerless, murk, carnage, bloodletting, shiver, pall, conceal, impale,* etc.

112

The first line of Peter Robinson's *The Hanging Valley* is:

It was the most exhilarating feeling in the world.

In this case, Robinson's setup actually foreshadows exactly the opposite of an exhilarating or pleasant experience. After this tease, sixteen paragraphs describe how Neil Fellowes, a "humble wage clerk," was enjoying "fell-walking" in the Yorkshire Dales:

He had been climbing for well over an hour: nothing too *dangerous*—no sheer heights, nothing that required special equipment. Fell-walking was a democratic recreation: just plain hard work. And it was an ideal day for walking. The sun danced in and out between plumb white clouds, and a cool breeze kept the temperature down. Perfect late May weather.

Neil savors his feelings of elation and takes in the panorama of hills and a wooded valley with unusual foliage so magical that he feels like the valley is out of Tolkien's Lord of the Rings series. Everything about the hike seems too good to be true, too lush and beautiful.

But Neil's elation doesn't last long. As the reader knows, danger lurks even in the sweetest valleys in Tolkien's epic. Neil spots what he thinks is a wildflower and, nearing it, notices a cloying unpleasant smell. Then he finds the body. He notices two things: that it has no face and that the flesh is crawling with insects. The discovery is doubly horrific because of the preceding word play describing the valley.

SUBPLOTS AND FORESHADOWING

When subplots are carefully conceived, they foreshadow or suggest important events in the main plot or the climax. Subplots are woven or braided into the main plot, subsidiaries of the main conflict. In the best stories, the subplots always keep looping back to the main actions, but also reinforce what the writer wants to prove about the story world and the people in it. Because subplots are linked, they can also foreshadow elements in a novel.

We talked earlier about a detective achieving small goals that foreshadow his solving the case. If a subplot has a positive outcome, such as a reunion with an estranged family member, it can foreshadow a positive outcome. On the other hand, if the detective loses something or someone important to him, that might also reflect on the main story. Perhaps the subplot involving loss reflects the story premise that law enforcement comes at too high a price for those involved when an innocent bystander is killed.

{ * }

The operative word in this chapter is *whisper*. Foreshadowing is subtle, often a barely visible element, tugging at the reader's nerves. You might want to think about how good you feel after a hard workout at the gym or a long walk or run. Yet for all its subtlety, foreshadowing serves a powerful purpose: It makes the important moments in fiction more potent because of the anticipation that came before.

chapter 8
Imagery & Other Charms

{

The most ordinary word, when put into place, suddenly acquires brilliance. That is the brilliance with which your images must shine.

—Robert Bresson

*I*magery and figurative language are used by poets, preachers, politicians, copywriters, and songwriters, as well as by fiction writers. Both use language to shape the reader's experience and understanding. These techniques are not merely decorative, but necessary. They can be a means of expressing something that is not the literal meaning, can convey abstract ideas, and can add complexity and implications.

Because so many fiction techniques lie between the lines and stem from an oral tradition, imagery, like many other techniques, is deliciously suggestive and often subtle. Used artfully, imagery acts almost like a sixth sense, whispering to the reader's subconscious.

There is an old saying that every picture tells a story. As a fiction writer, you're always painting pictures that tell stories in your reader's imagination. Or, if you prefer, you're directing movies that play out and tell stories. In Salman Rushdie's *Midnight's Children*, this brief scene illustrates how imagery is used to paint a picture:

One Kashmiri morning in the early Spring of 1915, my Grandfather Adam Aziz hit his nose against a frost-hardened tussock of earth while attempting to pray. Three drops of blood plopped out of his left nostril, hardened instantly in the brittle air and lay before his eyes on the prayer-mat, transformed into rubies. Lurching back until he knelt with head once more upright he found that the tears which had sprung to his eyes had solidified, too; and at that moment, as he brushed diamonds contemptuously from his lashes, he resolved never again to kiss earth for any god or man. This decision, however, made a hole in him, a vacancy in a vital inner chamber, leaving him vulnerable to women and history.

There are so many tools that a writer uses to bring stories to life, to stamp a lasting impression. Let's explore why imagery and other techniques are important ingredients in your writing repertoire.

THE IMPORTANCE OF USING IMAGERY

Images, as we just saw in Rushdie's excerpt, are word pictures that grant power and richness by involving the reader's senses. Imagery has been used since ancient storytellers and poets first starting putting their work onto the page. For example, in Homer's *The Iliad* you'll find:

> Grey-eyed Athena sent them a favorable breeze, a fresh west wind, singing o'er the wine-dark sea.

Homer could have easily written "then the west wind picked up," but notice how, without the imagery, the idea doesn't connect as firmly or beautifully in the reader's mind. We use imagery to appeal to the reader's associative powers, allowing an image to appear as a whole in the reader's imagination, complete yet connecting with all the sensations surrounding it. Images usually have a strong visual impact, but they also evoke the feeling or sound or smell or taste of things. They intensify the unspoken, often creating patterns that resonate with meaning and help to explain or stand in for difficult-to-describe concepts and emotions. Imagery also works to create a mood; suggest connections between things to make their meaning more powerful; slow the pace, as with a lush description; add a layer of meaning; and emphasize, exaggerate, or make a point.

Every word and phrase on every page represents potential. Each has implications and nuance. When choosing words, meaning must be considered, but also tone. Language and style involve a series of choices you make to ensure that your language connects in the reader's mind, and, by extension, with the reader's emotions. If you do not create images in the reader's mind, along with refrains that enhance the images, you will lose his attention.

Of course, there are times when it's necessary to describe a person, object, or event directly, such as "The sun blazed directly overhead," "Mary winced at his words," or "The clown pranced into the ring."

Yet there are many times when you don't want to express things directly—when ideas or scenes need to play out more subtly. Instead of instructing the reader, use imagery to engage his imagination, allowing him to bring his own understanding into a scene.

THE CONNECTION BETWEEN IMAGERY AND MOOD

Mood is the soundtrack of fiction and, as with movies, without a soundtrack fiction is not complete and captivating. Mood makes readers worry about heroines stranded in lonely castles amid fog-bound moors. It feeds suspense and tension, and in fact is inseparable from them. It is essential to genres like horror, thrillers, and action, but is necessary to every moment in every story where you want your reader to feel a certain way. You can stage your characters in dramatic events, but without setting up the proper mood, the characters' actions will fall short.

Let's think for a moment about the kind of moods you want to induce in readers: tense, dreamy, gloomy, nostalgic, panicked, terrified, sexually tense, worried, rapturous, sad, etc. Here is an example of mood found in D.H. Lawrence's *Sons and Lovers*:

> She went to the fence and sat there, watching the gold clouds fall to pieces, and go in immense, rose-colored ruin towards the darkness. Gold flamed to scarlet, like pain in its intense brightness. Then the scarlet ran to rose, and rose to crimson, and quickly the passion went out of the sky. All the world was dark grey.

Sensory descriptions are the perfect means to create moods (in this case, one of gloom), but are also a chance to add imagery to scenes, as Lawrence does in this description of a sunset. He's also using a timeless technique that you can emulate—equating some aspect of nature with a mood, emotion, or idea.

THE POTENCY OF COMPARING AND CONTRASTING

Comparing and contrasting are basic to all communications. When you use figurative language, your descriptions soar, meaning is reinforced, and lushness is added to your pages. Figurative language is the comparison of two unlike things to lend meaning to the compared object, person, or place. It takes the reader beyond ordinary description and creates energy and excitement. Figurative language comes in several forms: simile, metaphor, personification, and symbols. No matter what device you use, your purpose is always clarity.

Fiction relies on figurative language for depth. In *The Great Gatsby*, F. Scott Fitzgerald describes Daisy Buchanan's voice as "being full of money," a comparison that jangles with energy, but also clarifies. Daisy is old money, and since the novel explores the differences between old and new money, this distinction is important. A comparison can startle, cause the reader to understand powerful connections between two unlike objects, and awaken the reader's curiosity.

Often when writers use comparison, they link a known object with something that is less well known. Comparison is a terrific tool for characterization because it creates a solidity, a compass point in the reader's mind. From Michel Faber's *The Crimson Petal and the White*, here are two brief character descriptions containing comparisons:

Colonel Leek is the landlady's uncle, a pot-bellied stove of a man.

And:

Not that Henry Calder Rackham is working as hard now as in earlier years, his involvement in the company being more deskbound now. He's still fit as a horse, mind you.

Faber could have written that Leek is stout or Rackham is physically fit, but the comparisons bring these men to life. Comparison is also helpful to describe a character's feelings or states of being. Again, Faber writes:

Caroline's guts make a noise like a piglet.

In other words, Caroline was hungry. Notice too how this comparison makes her hunger desperate and primitive.

Comparisons also make places understandable and intriguing. Here is part of a longer description from *O Jerusalem* by Laurie R. King. It is the early 1900s and Sherlock Holmes and Mary Russell are seeing the ancient city for the first time:

> Walking toward the setting sun, we came to the Mount of Olives, a great sprawl of tombs and gravestones, and there at our feet lay Jerusalem. She is a jewel, that city, small and brilliant and hard, and as dangerous as any valuable thing can be.

Notice how this comparison foreshadows the dangers that await Holmes and Russell.

The question that you should ask yourself constantly as you write is, "What does this remind me of?" If you're writing about a character who is exceptionally fat, write "Marilyn is a round as X," and then start brainstorming, "an apple," "a teakettle," "a walrus," "a mattress left out in the rain." Just keep jotting down connections until the right one shows up on the page.

Comparison in fiction can also be indirect. Since snakes are commonly connected to evil or stealing, you imply volumes when you give a character a snakelike smile. Names like Faith, Prudence, or Goodwin can suggest that the character has positive qualities.

FIGURATIVE LANGUAGE DEVICES

Now that you understand the value of figurative language, let's examine some of its forms.

SIMILE AND METAPHOR

A simile is an explicit comparison stated by using *like, as, than,* or *resembles.* This is the simplest form of figurative language. Some examples of simile are "heart like a stone," "thin as a rail," "run like the wind," "swift as a gazelle," and "shy as a schoolboy."

Metaphor, another device that tells us that something is like something else, is an *implied* comparison between two unlike things, for example, "Her heart, that blood-fueled engine." The word *metaphor* stems from the Greek and means "to borrow or transport," thus metaphor borrows meaning from one place and carries it to another. A metaphor is a bit more difficult to construct than a simile, but it's worth the effort. The best metaphors create a dual reality and add resonance and those layers of meaning I keep referring to. Metaphoric language inspires wonder in your reader and also induces tension and excitement. When you work with metaphoric language, you're in good company.

119

Aristotle once said that "The greatest thing in style is to have a command of metaphor," and the poet Wallace Stevens said "Reality is a cliché we escape from by using metaphor."

If using metaphoric language doesn't come naturally to you or you find it daunting, it's important to remember that metaphor is part of everyday language, found in such common phrases as *fish out of water* and *hard hearted*. Pay attention to metaphoric language when you hear it, or possibly jot it down in your writer's notebook.

In Amy Bloom's short story "Silver Water," about a family coping with a daughter's schizophrenia, she uses figurative language throughout to add impact. The use of figurative language is especially effective because Bloom chooses fresh and original comparisons that help the reader see with new insight. The reader first meets Rose via this description by her sister, Violet:

> My sister's voice was like mountain water in a silver pitcher; the clear, blue beauty of it cools you and lifts you up beyond your heat, beyond your body.

Bloom could have told the reader that Rose had a powerful voice or a pure voice, but this description, stirred through the senses, has more potency, especially since it was also chosen for the story title.

PERSONIFICATION

Personification is giving human characteristics to an inanimate object, animal, abstract concept, idea, or something from nature, as in the phrase *Mother Nature*. It's a comparison you use to show something in an entirely new light, to communicate a certain feeling or attitude toward it, and to control the way a reader perceives it. For example, if you want the reader to feel uneasy or fearful, you might write "The fog crept in like a corpse crawling up from the grave."

Personification is used widely by fiction authors, but it might have slipped past you unnoticed. Here is an example from Toni Morrison's *Tar Baby* that depicts nature as sentient:

> When laborers imported from Haiti came to clear the land, clouds and fish were convinced that the world was over. ... Only the daisy trees were serene. ... It took the river to persuade them that indeed the world was altered. That never again would the rain be equal, and by the time they realized it and had run their roots

deeper, clutching the earth like lost boys found, it was too late. The men had already folded the earth where there had been no fold and hollowed her where there had been no hollow, which explains what happened to the river. It crested, then lost its course, and finally its head. Evicted from the place where it lived, and forced into unknown turf, it could not form its pools or waterfalls and ran every which way.

This sort of description is found often in magical realism and adds to the sense of enchantment, whimsy, and poetic flow. But personification works in all types of fiction because humans see the world through their own experiences and can accept human qualities in all sorts of nonhuman entities.

SYMBOLS

The word *symbol* is Greek for "to throw together." Symbols unite people and ideas, make concepts visible, and whisper reminders to the reader. Sometimes symbols are used to suggest something unknown, but often they are a shorthand for a known commodity or idea. Symbols can be objects, characters, colors, or aspects of nature used to represent abstract concepts or ideas. Used extensively by advertisers, symbols are things that stand for something else. In *Man and His Symbols*, Carl Jung defines a symbol as:

> [a] term, a name, or even a picture that may be familiar in daily life, yet that possesses specific connotations in addition to its conventional and obvious meaning. It implies something vague, unknown, or hidden from us.

Symbols can convey specialized meaning, such as in flags, crosses, or religious icons, but you can also think of the yellow Labradors that often appear in television commercials as symbols of family, safety, and perhaps the American dream. The swastika, the symbol of the Nazi government, is perhaps the most negative symbol in our culture, along with a burning cross.

Symbols are found in everyday life in social gestures, such as shaking hands. Storytellers have been using symbols for centuries: In Shakespeare's *Hamlet*, Yorick's skull is used as a potent symbol of death.

Dave King's novel, *The Ha-Ha*, has a central symbol, the ha-ha, a sunken fence used to divide land without altering the landscape. The brain-damaged protagonist, Howard, is a groundskeeper and maintenance man at a convent. His favorite times are while steering the John Deere mower, often driving perilously close to the ha-ha.

As the story progresses, we see Howard flirt with the dangerous ha-ha, but the ha-ha has deeper implications in the story and actually symbolizes the complicated protagonist. At times sensitive and hopeful, at times filled with rage and regret, Howard's brain injury, like the ha-ha, is barely concealed, and creates a rift within him that he must confront.

The symbol of the ha-ha is central to the story. In your own story, you might use smaller symbols scattered throughout instead of an overriding one such as King uses. You might want to use universal symbols like spring water for purity, dawn or springtime for a fresh start, the Statue of Liberty for freedom, or a cemetery for grief. Fiction writers often work with a culture's associations with a place or object. It is helpful to keep in mind that if you use an image (such as the ha-ha) repeatedly, it will attain the status of a symbol.

COMPARING, MADE EASY

Comparing and contrasting in fiction clarifies and electrifies. The best comparisons wed two unexpected images or objects. Here's a cheat sheet of sorts to illustrate the means of comparison.

Simple Comparison: Compare X to Z
   The sun is a furnace today.

Simile: X is like Z, or X is as Z
   The sun is like a dragon breathing fire from the sky.

Metaphor: X is implied to be like Z
   In her couture ensemble, she was dressed in money.

Irony: X is not Z
   With a friend like Miles, who needs enemies?

Personification: X has human characteristics
   The cat smiled as it delicately licked its paws.

MORE CHARMS

There are many charms that appeal to a reader's senses and add emphasis. The following are several techniques to use in your own writing.

ALLITERATION

Sound communicates meaning and mood and must always be part of your writing repertoire. Alliteration is similar, repeated sounds that occur at the beginning of words or within words. It's used to create melody, establish mood, call attention to important words, and point out similarities and contrasts. For example, "wide-eyed and wondering while we wait for others to waken."

ASSONANCE AND CONSONANCE

Assonance is the repetition of vowel sounds, and consonance is repetition of consonant sounds. Here is an excerpt from Ntozake Shange's novel *Sassafrass, Cypress & Indigo*. As an exercise, underline each *s*, *l*, and *o*, and then look for other repeated sounds and alliterative pairs.

> The South in her, the land and salt-winds, moved her through Charleston's streets as if she were a mobile sapling, with the gait of a well-loved colored woman whose lover was the horizon in any direction. Indigo imagined tough winding branches growing from her braids, deep green leaves rustling by her ears, doves and macaws flirting above the nests they'd fashioned in the secret, protected niches way high up in her headdress. When she wore this Carolinian costume, she knew the cobblestone streets were really polished oyster shells, covered with pine needles and cotton flowers.

ALLUSION

An allusion is a reference to another work of art or a cultural icon. For example, "the road ahead loomed like the Grand Canyon before me." Or, "Mary entered the room wearing a Mona Lisa smile."

ANALOGY

Analogies explain relationships, comparing two things because they have something in common. The two things compared can be alike or opposites.

Analogies work well to convey complicated or technical facts or information, and abstract thoughts and concepts. For example, "The federal debt is so high, if the United States was a family it would be homeless; if it was a corporation, it would be bankrupt."

ANTITHESIS

Antithesis is when one thing or idea is the exact opposite of a second thing or idea as in "good is the antithesis of evil" or "hope is the antithesis of despair." These contrasting ideas can be joined or juxtaposed in parallel grammatical patterns as "cold hands, warm heart" or Alexander Pope's statement, "To err is human, to forgive divine."

HYPERBOLE

Hyperbole is an exaggeration that often contains humor and can be used to help a reader see something in a fresh light, highlight a moment, deliberately mislead the reader, or illustrate how a character thinks. It's most effective in dialogue and introspection, and is common in the language of children and teens. For example, "I've told you a bazillion times that I hate broccoli." Or, "My husband is the most considerate and handsome man alive. I've told him so ten thousand times."

IRONY

Irony can be used to say something other than what you really mean. If a character walks into a room where a couple is fighting, he might remark, "Sounds like you two are having a jolly old time." Or, if the temperature is a sweltering 106 degrees in the shade, he can remark about what a lovely day it is.

ONOMATOPOEIA

This device involves using words, usually verbs, to mimic the sound of a thing or an action. In the hands of a sly writer, onomatopoeia slips into the brain and ignites the senses. It can be used to paint scenes of a gaudy bazaar in Morocco, or a dank and noisy nineteenth-century shirt factory. It forces your readers to hear the tourists' chatter and merchants' whine, or the clatter and din of sewing machines. Some examples include *glisten, simmer, blast, careen, stammer, squawk, zoom, gallop, claw, creak, sizzle, dazzle, whoosh, plunge, pluck, prune, slather, bludgeon, wiggle, roam, wobble, sidle, tweak, growl, yap, tiptoe.*

Beware of Bloated Language

Good writing glitters but is not gaudy. It is picturesque, not bloated. The main thing when using imagery and figurative language is to not try too hard. Beware of piling on figurative language without a distinct purpose in mind. Figurative language must be handled carefully, with utmost precision. If sloppy, it confuses and muddles meanings. If overdone, it feels false and forced. The best imagery and figurative language is natural and engaging. Choose thoughtful images and comparisons, not gimmicks. Because a little goes a long way, think of metaphoric language as the seasoning in a complex dish, not the main ingredients.

Also, don't take the lazy way out. If you've heard a simile many times before, so has your reader. You need to invent your own—the fresher the better.

When writing similes, don't make trite comparisons, such as "the meadow was as flat as a roadway." Comparisons, especially similes, should jolt the reader just a little. He should feel pleasure and recognition upon reading.

Also, be sure to make your comparisons match in scale. You can compare a large dog to a pony or even a horse, but if you use an elephant it just comes off as exaggeration. Along these lines, don't trivialize tragedies, disasters, intimacy, or important moments or events with trite comparisons. Often the more painful emotions and moments are best communicated with understatement.

Writers have a tendency to tack metaphoric language onto endings. If the story has very little figurative language until the final sentences, the ending will come off sounding false, as if the writer was grasping for flourishes. Metaphors don't always work in endings, especially in short stories. While they don't need to be avoided altogether, often a better or more graceful device is understatement, a quote or dialogue, or a poignant image.

{ * }

Fiction is intricate, and imagery and figurative language are enormously powerful in creating this intricacy. They are especially helpful in conveying the unusual or difficult to explain, and are a means to create nonliteral distortions and constructions that provoke interest and make readers see things in a new way.

chapter 9
Pacing

> *Fiction is like a spider's web, attached ever so lightly perhaps, but still attached to life at all four corners. Often the attachment is scarcely perceptible.*
>
> —Virginia Woolf

 acing is a tool that controls the speed and rhythm at which a story is told and the readers are pulled through the story events. It refers to how fast or slow events in a story unfold and also to how much time has elapsed in a scene or story. Pacing can also be used to show time passing, characters aging, and the effects of time on story events.

Pacing differs with the specific needs of a novel, story, or segment of fiction. A far-reaching epic will often be told at a leisurely pace, although it will speed up from time to time during the most intense events. A short story or adventure novel might quickly jump into action and deliver drama. Pacing is part structural choices and part word choices, and uses a variety of devices, like flashbacks and sequels, to control how fast the story unfolds. When driving a manual transmission car, you choose the most effective gear needed for driving uphill, maneuvering city streets, or cruising down a freeway. When pacing your story, you choose the devices that move the scene along at the right speed.

Writers hear many warnings about moving too slowly through events, causing the story to sputter or bog down. But fiction can also rattle along at a breakneck speed, leaving readers unsettled. The delivery and pace of fiction requires variety and a thoughtful approach. Not every novel can move at the same tempo, and not every scene can unfold at the same clip. Sometimes fiction needs to slow so that the impact of what is happening or has just happened can be appreciated by the reader, and sometimes it needs to race along like a runaway steed.

William Noble, in *Conflict, Action & Suspense*, provides this insight about pacing:

> Story pace essentially means two things: smooth, event writing without anti-climaxes, without lengthy static prose; and carefully constructed scenes that blend with one another and build to a satisfying climax. Pacing our story means controlling it, and that, in turn, means taking the long view and measuring each scene against the entire story line.

Keeping Noble's definition in mind, let's look closer at how fast or slow a story should unfold and why.

The Speed of Things

Not all delivery modes in fiction are created equal, and understanding the speed of each mode is important. Here's a quick glance at the speed of various elements:

Action: fast

Exposition: slowest—sometimes so slow it's deadly

Description: slow

Dialogue: fast/super fast

Summary: super fast

Transition: medium

SPEEDING THINGS UP

You need speed in the opening, middle, and climax of your story. Sure, you'll slow down from time to time, especially to pause for significance and to express characters' emotions, but those times will usually appear just before or after a joyride of skin-tightening speed.

A quick pace comes from a number of devices, but also from an understanding of structure and from seeing the manuscript as an interconnected entity. A quick pace is comfortable—never rushed, careless, or contrived. You want the reader to be on edge and involved, not exasperated because things are happening so fast he can't quite take it all in.

One fairly easy method of speeding up your fiction is to remember that stories need to be front loaded—your first chapters, as well as scene and chapter openings, should introduce change, conflict, and intrigue so that the reader plunges ahead with curiosity.

DEVICES FOR SPEEDING THINGS UP

There are lots of tools at your disposal to hasten your story. Some are better suited for micro pacing—that is, line by line—and some are better suited for macro pacing—pacing the story as a whole. Let's take a closer look at each device.

• **Action.** Action scenes are where you "show" what happens in a story, and, when written in short- and medium-length sentences, they move the story along. Action scenes contain few distractions, little description, and limited transitions. Omit or limit character thoughts, especially in the midst of danger or crisis, since during a crisis people merely focus on survival. To create poignancy, forego long descriptive passages and choose a few details that serve as emotionally charged props instead.

• **Change.** When your plot dashes off in a new, unexpected direction, this too hurries the pace and increases the reader's interest. Changes happen in small moments and actions, in a character's failures and setbacks, and in things not going as expected. Each scene requires at least one change, and each chapter requires a series of changes. If you cannot grasp this concept, dissect a few chapters written by your favorite author and underline wherever a change occurs. Change also includes emotional reversals, new characters entering a scene, interruptions, and a character (and the reader) receiving new information. Change pushes a story forward; few changes slow it down.

• **Cliffhangers.** When the outcome of a scene or chapter is left hanging, the pace naturally picks up because the reader will turn the page to find out what happens

128

next. Readers both love and hate uncertainty, and your job is to deliver plenty of unfinished actions, unfilled needs, and interruptions. Remember, cliffhangers don't necessarily mean that you're literally dangling your character from a rooftop as the scene ends. If your characters are in the midst of a conversation, end the scene with a revelation, threat, or challenge.

- **Dialogue.** Rapid-fire dialogue with little or no extraneous information is swift and captivating, and will invigorate any scene. The best dialogue for velocity is pared down, an abbreviated copy of real-life conversation that snaps and crackles with tension. It is more like the volleying of ping-pong or tennis than a long-winded discussion. Reactions, descriptions, and attributions are minimal. Don't create dialogue exchanges where your characters discuss or ponder. Instead, allow them to argue, confront, or engage in a power struggle.

- *In medias res.* This Latin term is long-standing advice for starting scenes in the middle of events rather than starting every scene from the beginning. In nineteenth- and twenty-century fiction, many stories began with slow opening sequences, a leisurely stroll into the story world. Contemporary fiction, with few exceptions, has reversed this trend, and stories and scenes often dive into the midst of action—and often into the midst of conflict—at the last possible moment.

- **Prolonging outcomes.** Suspense and, by extension, forward movement are created when you prolong outcomes. While it may seem that prolonging an event or moment would slow down a story, this technique actually increases the speed, because the reader wants to know if your character is rescued from the mountainside, if the vaccine will arrive before the outbreak decimates the village, or if the detective will solve the case before the killer strikes again.

- **Scene cuts.** Also called a jump cut, a scene cut moves the story to a new location and assumes that the reader can follow without an explanation of the location change. The purpose is to accelerate the story, and the characters in the new scene don't necessarily need to be the same characters as in the previous scene.

- **A series of incidents in rapid succession.** Another means of speeding up your story is to create events that happen immediately one after another. Such events are presented with minimal or no transitions, leaping via scene cuts from scene to scene and place to place.

- **Short chapters and scenes.** Short segments are easily digested and end quickly. Since they portray a complete action, the reader passes through them quickly, as opposed to being bogged down by long, complex actions and descriptions.

- **Summary.** Instead of a play-by-play approach, tell readers what has already happened. Since scenes are immediate and sensory, they require many words to depict. Summary is a way of trimming your word count and using scenes for only the major events. You can also summarize whole eras, descriptions, and backstory. Summaries work well when time passes but there is little to report, when an action is repeated, or when a significant amount of time has passed.

- **Word choice and sentence structure.** Language is the subtlest means of pacing. Think concrete language (like *prodigy* and *iceberg*), active voice (with potent verbs like *zigzag* and *plunder*), and sensory information that's artfully embedded. If you write long, involved paragraphs, you should break them up.

Fragments, spare sentences, and short paragraphs quicken the pace. Crisp, punchy verbs, especially those with onomatopoeia (*crash, lunge, sweep, scatter, ram, scavenge*) also add to a quick pace. Invest in verbs that are suggestive to enliven descriptions, build action scenes, and milk suspense.

Harsh consonant sounds such as those in words like *claws, crash, kill, quake, quarrel,* and *nag* also push ahead. Words with unpleasant associations also ratchet up the speed: *hiss, grunt, slither, smarmy, venomous, slobber, slaver,* and *wince.* Energetic, active language is especially appropriate for building action scenes and suspense, and setting up drama and conflict.

A fast pace means trimming every sentence of unnecessary words. Eliminate prepositional phrases where you don't need them: For example, "the walls of the cathedral" can be written as "the cathedral's walls." Also, examine your passive linking verbs and trade them in for active verbs.

Scrutinize sentences for repetition in dialogue and other redundancies, such as "past history," "little kittens," and "doleful mourners." It's also considered repetition when the same words appear too often in a story or too close to one another.

SLOWING THINGS DOWN

If your story zips ahead at full speed all the time, it might fizzle under this excess. There are plenty of times and reasons for slowing down, especially to emphasize a moment so readers can experience its emotional impact. There are also times when a sedate or dignified pace is called for, or you want to slowly build a scene to maximize the payoff. Readers want to relish love-making or wedding scenes, especially if they come after hundreds of pages of the characters being too afraid of their feelings to venture into the bedroom or walk down the aisle. Readers also want to spend time at celebrations, funerals, and births, and with characters who are gossiping or struggling with difficult decisions.

DEVICES FOR SLOWING THINGS DOWN

Your job is to vary moods, tension, and pace. Readers don't want to feel intense emotions all throughout the story. Too much intensity (and violence) creates a kind of shell shock—readers shut down their emotions as a self-protective measure. Provide readers with slower moments where emotional highs and lows can be savored. Here are the perfect tools for just that:

• **Description.** Readers enter your story and reside there for the days and nights that it takes to complete the story events. Description is an important tool for causing a reader to linger amid the story world. But there is a fine line between just the right amount of description and overkill. When possible, put description in motion, as when a character is walking or driving through a place.

• **Distractions.** There are times when you want to distract the reader with small actions, such as a character cooking or gardening, or with weather or setting details. Distractions can be used to engage your reader's emotions. In the middle of an emotionally charged or pivotal scene, give your character another task, such as handling an object, applying makeup, looking out the window, or recalling or connecting the moment to a memory or realization.

• **Exposition.** Exposition stops the story or breaks away from action to dispense data and facts. It is most needed when fiction involves technology, science, or historical explanations. It can provide context and perspective, such as biographical or geographical information, characters descriptions, and time references.

Because straightforward exposition is so slow, trim it down to the essentials and remember that storytelling comes first and facts need to be blended in. Delivering exposition via dialogue can accelerate the pace while still providing readers with essential information.

- **Flashbacks.** Flashbacks halt the momentum of the front story. They can be risky because they can slow the story too much or too often. If flashbacks go on for pages or are not clearly linked to front-story events, they can be especially troublesome. Deliberately place flashbacks to pause and add insights.

- **Introspection.** A viewpoint character's thoughts or musings are another device for slowing a scene. Avoid, however, enclosing a character's thoughts in quotation marks or making references to mental processes, such as "Marty thought long and hard about what do next." Instead, slip the thoughts in without announcing their presence, so they mimic the character's dialogue and reflect his mood.

- **One step forward, one step back.** Protagonists need to stumble, make mistakes, experience reversals, and hit dead ends. If your protagonist succeeds again and again, the story becomes both predictable and too fast paced. Troubles and setbacks slow the pace, increase suspense, and keep readers interested.

- **Sequels.** A sequel is the aftermath of an action scene, especially one that is intense. Sequels are staged so your character can sort through her feelings, assess the changing situation, and then make decisions about what to do next. Not every scene requires a sequel, but if characters never react to events or devise plans for the future, the story will feel episodic and lack depth. A sequel allows a reader to catch her breath along with the character and take in what has happened. Sequels often involve introspection, musing, or talking things over with another character.

- **Word choice and sentence structure.** You can also slow down a story on a word-by-word and sentence-by-sentence basis. Think of the texture of sentences and call on all the senses for your purposes. Soft-sounding words, especially verbs (*soothe, simper, prolong, stroke*), soft *s* (*the silent snow sifted downward*), and vowels all slow the pace. Repetition, lengthy sentences (especially run-ons), and long paragraphs also slacken the pace.

NOVELS WITH GREAT PACING

Secret Sanction and *The Kingmaker*, Brian Haig

Alex Cross series, James Patterson

Dating Dead Men, Harley Jane Kozak

No Witnesses, Ridley Pearson

Outlander, Diana Gabaldon

Isabel's Bed, Elinor Lipman

Good Faith, Jane Smiley

The Bone Collector, Jeffery Deaver

Stephanie Plum series, Janet Evanovich

Blood Work, Michael Connelly

Absolute Power, David Baldacci

Get Shorty, Elmore Leonard

Skinny Dip, Carl Hiaasen

PACING YOUR SCENES

You cannot talk about pacing without applying it to individual scenes. There is no right or wrong pace to begin a story—you can start with a tragedy, an earthquake, or a languid description—but you must maintain the pace that your story opening promises. You must justify the opening action, and it must prompt the reader to keep reading.

While an electrifying beginning allows you to slow down afterward and introduce elements at a more leisurely pace, you don't want to open with melodrama, like a hurricane washing through without warning. Since the reader doesn't know the characters yet, it's dangerous to stage them screaming, fighting, or fainting. And if the characters are operating at a full tilt in the opening, where are they going to go from there? How will their character arcs play out?

A slower beginning, however, has its own set of problems, as it still requires a payoff at some point within the first few chapters. Slower beginnings are also in danger of being bogged down with large clumps of information or backstory.

Not all scenes have the same purpose in the story and thus don't have the same pacing requirements. Some scenes are created to build tension and complications for set pieces and upcoming scenes. Some are designed to deliver information or to create a sense of place. For example, perhaps your protagonist is a cop and you're at the three-quarters mark in your novel. The story events have him ragged and embattled, so to slow the pace you stage a quiet scene where he cooks lasagna for his girlfriend. Your character catches his breath and talks over the case before you steam ahead into more conflict and danger.

We've been talking mostly about the speed at which a story unfolds, but let's bring in another element—the emotional pace in scenes. Not every scene can be fraught with angst, sorrow, or agony, just as they cannot all be breezy, silly, or madcap. At times you'll be writing emotionally charged scenes, and at times you'll be writing less passionate scenes.

The scenes where you want the reader to pause and feel deeply are similar to the times in real life when you feel deeply, the moments when you know you've blown it at love, acted in some way that is unforgivable or regrettable, or lost someone or something dear to you. They are the moments when you're frightened, worried, or realizing the enormity of some event that you cannot control. Of course, not all scenes with emotional impact are negative—they can also depict the birth of a longed-for baby, a blissful wedding, a handicapped person overcoming a physical obstacle, or a troubled kid winning a spelling bee. Scenes that deliver poignancy cause readers to savor what it is to be human and feel deeply.

PACING DIFFERENCES IN COMMERCIAL AND LITERARY FICTION

Commercial (or genre) fiction and literary fiction have differing needs for story and emotional pacing. Mystery readers expect murder, detection, and solutions, just as readers of thrillers expect a hearty dose of suspense, violence, or a threat of violence. Genre fiction also includes Westerns, action-adventure, fantasy, science fiction, horror, and erotica.

Fiction that doesn't fall into these categories is called literary or mainstream. In mainstream fiction there is a focus on language, character development, and inner conflict. Theme is often important, and endings can be more ambiguous than in genre fiction. In a sense, readers of mainstream are tolerant—they don't expect a fast pace and are tuned in to moods and nuance. Mainstream can support more exposition, flashbacks, and emotion than genre novels.

Commercial fiction tends to have a stimulating, brisk pace, while literary fiction has more of a relaxed pace. The exception to the fast pace in thrillers and action-adventure is the necessary exposition that provides context and technical information. Exposition might explain a nuclear submarine, a mutant virus, or cannons built on seventeenth-century frigates. If you're writing in a genre, examine the proportion of exposition that a published author uses—it is likely to be 80 percent action to 20 percent exposition.

Fantasies and science fiction often require the writer to build a world that is different from ordinary reality, and therefore contain more exposition than other genres. However, you shouldn't spend a considerable portion of your story describing elaborate empires or gadgets simply because you can. If you write science fiction or fantasy, post this note next to your computer: "Story comes first." If you focus on hardware, tribal alliances, and epic histories, your reader will lose sight of what your protagonist wants and why obtaining it will be difficult.

Similarly, mysteries can bog down with one witness interview after another, railroad schedules, an array of suspects' alibis, forensic evidence so complicated it takes an advanced degree to decipher, and tedious logistics. Mysteries need to be crafted with a huge dose of suspense. To do this the writer must endanger the protagonist and other characters, adding twists and surprises to keep the pace boiling away.

The lesson here is that you can deliver the pace the readers of your genre have come to expect and appreciate by adjusting the details and conflicts of your story.

PACING AND THE PASSAGE OF TIME

Pacing also proves that time is passing in your story. Beginning writers sometimes fail to create devices that offer proof of time rolling along. The Victorian novelist

Anthony Trollope once commented that each character in a story should age a month if a month of time has passed.

With this in mind, shadows, sunlight or the moon can show how time has passed in a single day. Or, a character can age, become progressively more ill, gain or lose weight, or otherwise transform her looks to prove that a longer segment of time has elapsed. The methods for depicting time's passage in your story are inexhaustible. (For more transitional methods, see chapter eighteen.)

EDITING FOR PACE

Pace is often corrected during your editing process, when you have a finished draft to work with. One of your first editing tasks is to make certain that your story contains all the scenes and information necessary to tell the tale, and that the pacing is varied and fast enough to hold the reader's interest. If it works for your story's chronology, alternate slow and fast scenes during editing. Here are more tools for editing for pace:

- Evaluate the length of your flashbacks. As with scenes, you want to enter a flashback at the last possible moment, then leave as quickly as possible.

- Analyze individual scenes that drag. Try tightening the dialogue and adjusting the tension by adding surprises and tweaking details.

- Examine the plot for places where you are withholding or delaying information readers need to know. Delay outcomes until the last possible moment, squeezing suspense and increasing pacing by doing so.

- Scrutinize your final scenes, making certain that they are trimmed of extraneous information and don't introduce new characters.

- Make certain that you have not used too many short sentences, because when overused they slow a story like a series of speed bumps.

- Heighten the emotional impact of scenes by using imagery, symbols, and metaphor (for more on this, see chapter eight).

$\mathscr{P}$ACING $\mathscr{C}$HECKLIST

Here is a checklist to use during your editing process.

☐ Does the opening capture the reader's interest and imagination?

☐ Does the story contain a mix of sentence lengths and types?

☐ Have you revealed time passing?

☐ Are there a variety of emotions on display in your scenes?

☐ Have you foreshadowed major events?

☐ Do the scenes contain emotional reversals and other changes?

☐ Have you included sequels after emotionally charged scenes?

☐ Do scenes and chapters end with thrusters and cliffhangers that push the story ahead?

☐ Do you use scene cuts and have you trimmed unnecessary transitions?

{ * }

Pacing cannot be separated from other elements of fiction, such as tension, suspense, style, and viewpoint. It is a structural device that can be mastered over time, just as you can perfect your harmony part when you sing in a choir. Pacing is learned by critically reading published works, then applying this knowledge to your own story. It is also helpful to read your story out loud, stage a reading where readers interpret it aloud, or ask for feedback from readers. Pacing is an element that can most easily be noticed when it's not working.

Movement in fiction happens when characters are acting, interacting, talking, fighting, and going places. Interlace these movements with description, and then increase action as the climax looms, and you'll have conquered the first step in writing with a firmly controlled pace.

chapter 10

Prologues

The novel is an organic event that requires prepared ground to do its work.
—Philip Gerard

A prologue is introductory material set apart in time, space, or viewpoint (or in all three) from the main story that creates intrigue for upcoming events. To qualify as a prologue, the information or events must exist outside of the framework of the main story. This stand-alone device must be absorbing, distinct, and beguiling in its own right. Often, an effective prologue will contain drama and dialogue so that it is immediate rather than reportorial. Prologues are always loaded with specific and sensory details.

A prologue's job is to provide a potent insight into the world of the story that cannot be provided through the unfolding of events. It can also be information that cannot be discovered by the protagonist, but is still necessary to the story.

Prologues can take place five years or five centuries before the drama begins, but somehow the gap of time between the prologue time and story time must be bridged. But not all prologues are written strictly from the past. Sometimes they stem from the future or are told from a viewpoint that will not be heard from again.

Although the prologue exists outside the flow of the narrative, it is always linked to the story events, characters, and themes. There are no hard and fast rules for length, but most prologues are at least several paragraphs and can run to twenty or more pages. However, try to keep prologues brief and vital, no longer than a chapter.

The Benefits of Using a Prologue

A prologue requires a strong reason for being, so it must be inherently dramatic and entertaining while casting an illuminating light on events, characters, or theme. The reasons for and benefits of using a prologue are many. Here are eleven of the most essential functions prologues can accomplish for your story. They can:

1. Sweep the reader into some crucial aspect of the story and ignite her imagination. One of the great benefits of including a prologue is that by doing so you can introduce information at a place where it can carry a lot of weight—the beginning. For example, a prologue can be based on an act of violence, such as a particularly grisly murder that lies at the heart of your story. By placing the murder in the prologue, you alert the reader to the extreme dangers of the story world, cast light on the villain's nature, and raise questions about the murder's aftermath. Such a prologue is found in Dan Brown's *The Da Vinci Code*, which begins at night in the Louvre Museum, where a renowned curator has been attacked and is being confronted by his attacker as a far-off alarm begins to shrill.

2. Introduce essential facts about the protagonist's past or future. In Rebecca Wells's prologue to *Divine Secrets of the Ya-Ya Sisterhood*, she introduces the protagonist, Sidda, at age six:

> Sidda is a girl again in the hot heart of Louisiana, the bayou world of Catholic saints and voodoo queens. It is Labor Day, 1959, at Pecan Grove Plantation, on the day of her daddy's annual dove hunt. While the men sweat and shoot, Sidda's gorgeous mother, Vivi, and her gang of girlfriends, the Ya-Yas, play *bourree*, a cut-throat Louisiana poker, inside the air-conditioned house. On the kitchen blackboard is scrawled: SMOKE, DRINK, NEVER THINK—borrowed from Billy Holiday. ...
>
> That night, after dove gumbo (tiny bird bones floating in Haviland china bowls), Sidda goes to bed. Hours later, she wakes with a gasp from a mean dream. She tiptoes to the side of her mother's bed, but she cannot awaken Vivi from her bourbon-soaked sleep.
>
> She walks barefoot into the humid night, moonlight on her freckled shoulders. Near a huge, live oak tree on the edge of her father's cotton fields, Sidda looks up into the sky. In the crook of the crescent moon sits the Holy Lady, with strong muscles and a merciful heart. She kicks her splendid legs like the moon is her swing

and the sky, her front porch. She waves down at Sidda like she has just spotted an old buddy.

Sidda stands in the moonlight and lets the blessed mother love every hair on her six-year-old head. Tenderness flows down from the moon and up from the earth. For one fleeting, luminous moment, Sidda Walker knows there has never been a time when she has not been loved.

This moment provides powerful insights into Sidda's past and is a dramatic departure from the abrupt events in chapter one, where a newspaper headline describes Vivi as a "tap-dancing child abuser." After this opening gambit, the story tracks Sidda's attempts to make peace with her mother and her past.

3. Introduce out-of-sequence information or events. The prologue to Stephanie Kallos's *Broken for You* is set in the future and written in a dreamy, surreal voice:

While the woman sleeps and dreams of all that breaks, come into this house of many rooms. Once your eyes adjust to the darkness, beginning to take in what is visible, you may notice a silence that is not quite silent. There is another language being spoken here, a tongue that emanates from white clay, fire, the oils of many skins, the fusion of rent spirits and matter. The woman hears this language always, even in her sleep, because those who speak to her are never silent. But for you, the innocent, there may only be a humming, a distant drone.

The prologue continues for two more paragraphs, then concludes with an admonition to the reader:

Leave now. Come back later, when the house is not bereft and its inhabitants are not desperate. There will be employment for you then. You'll feel more at home. Your hands will have a purpose, your relationship to these objects and their guardian will be clear and comfortable. Come back when you're ready. You'll find what you've been looking for.

This prologue not only introduces future events, but demonstrates how the best prologues multitask (which we'll discuss in greater detail on page 148). Besides whisking the reader to the future, the prologue hints at conflict, trouble, and mystery. It also hints at one of the story's themes, guilt, and creates a mystical, odd mood that carries over into future chapters.

4. Establish a distinct mood and atmosphere as you reveal vital information.
Maxine Hong Kingston's novel *China Men* is about Chinese men immigrating
to America, building railroads, raising families, and assimilating or not assimilating into American culture. It begins with two short prologues, the first a grisly
little myth about how a man looking for Gold Mountain (America) arrives at the
Land of Women, where he is transformed into a woman, including having his feet
bound. The second prologue is from the narrator's viewpoint and describes how
the narrator and her siblings waited at the gate for their father to arrive home from
work, and once ran up to a stranger they mistook for him. Both of these stories
are infused with a strong dose of Chinese sensibility and are disquieting, setting
the mood for events to come, many of them tragic.

**5. Provide information or backstory that cannot be told in the main body of the
story.** Prologues are often used to describe events and influences that occurred years,
even eons earlier or that are set far apart from the main story line. These events or influences are crucial to understanding the story and provide context. For example, the
prologue of Penina Keen Spinka's *Picture Maker* spins a creation myth explaining
how the world was formed and how Indian clans were established in the Northeast
and Great Lakes regions. It also summarizes European history during this era and
explains that the tale begins when a girl named Picture Maker is born.

6. Create a hook or question that begs to be answered. A hook in a prologue
creates buzz about the upcoming story, and is especially helpful in creating a
sense of foreboding and mystery, and anticipation of revelations to come.

Lisa Shea's disturbing little novel *Hula* begins with a prologue entitled "A
Good Enough Place to Hide," which depicts children at play—if you can call it
that—torturing their dolls and hiding:

> When our father finds us, we have to march around the yard and then lie
> down on our bellies with our arms up over our heads. Sometimes he pretend-
> shoots us with his gun.
>
> "You're dead, soldier," he says. I pretend I don't have any arms or legs or a head.

After this portrayal, which is especially effective since it's told in the matter-of-fact
voice of a child, the reader is naturally gripped with fear, wondering what might
happen to these children and whether their father is mentally stable.

7. Play with the reader's emotions before getting down to the nitty-gritty of telling the story. "A Good Enough Place to Hide" is a great example of a prologue that plays with a reader's emotions. Another prologue that accomplishes this appears in Rebecca Wells's *Little Altars Everywhere*. It is based on a sensuous dream that Sidda Walker is having about being five and raucously dancing to a Little Richard song with the encouragement of her mother:

> Arms and legs have new lives of their own. Every single part of me dances. And that 45-rpm record plays over and over and over, and we're singing with Little Richard now, we're blowing saxophones! … [S]omething secret, something sweet, something strong is shooting up from the earth straight into my body, making my limbs quiver, making me crazy-dance all over the place right there in my orange and white sunsuit.

With this provocative recollection, the reader is drawn into the story and the complex emotions of mother and daughter.

8. Introduce the rules of the story world, especially if history or complicated events will affect the story. A prologue can explain the workings of the story world, which is especially helpful for fantasy, science fiction, or historical fiction. It can also comment on a world or events not strictly involved with the protagonist.

Barbara Kingsolver's *The Poisonwood Bible* is about the Prices, a missionary family, and their disastrous attempts to convert natives of the Congo. It has multiple viewpoints, which allows the same story to be told from different angles, enhancing tension and adding dimension. The prologue is told from the mysterious viewpoint of Orleanna Price. It begins:

> Imagine a ruin so strange it must never have happened.
>
> First, picture the forest. I want you to be its conscience, the eyes in the trees. The trees are columns of slick, brindled bark like muscular animals overgrown, beyond all reason. Every space is filled with life: delicate, poisonous frogs war-painted like skeletons, clutched in copulation, secreting their precious eggs onto dripping leaves. Vines strangling their own kin in the everlasting wrestle for sunlight. The breathing of monkeys. A glide of snake belly on branch. A single-file army biting a mammoth tree into uniform grains and hauling it down to the dark for their raven-

ous queen. And, in reply, a choir of seedlings arching their necks out of rotted tree stumps, sucking life out of death. This forest eats itself and lives forever.

These first sentences transport a reader far from his ordinary world into the depths of a jungle, a place of teeming life and danger, with rules all its own. A prologue such as this one can be especially effective to introduce a time and place unlike our ordinary world.

9. Pass on information from another viewpoint. Most often, a prologue is written in the same viewpoint and style as the story. But sometimes, for good reason, the prologue comes from another vantage. While a prologue can be written from a different viewpoint, it still must be woven from a similar fiber so it does not sound like it comes directly from the author.

If you've written your prologue through an alternate viewpoint, such as that of a minor character, then the reader must meet that character somewhere later in the story. The exception to this might be a character who is set many years or centuries apart from the story. Generally, when reporting on happenings widely separated by time, the viewpoint is omniscient.

10. Establish who is telling the story and why. Helen Fielding's *Bridget Jones's Diary* is an intimate, breezy novel that follows the thirty-something protagonist through a year of challenges, setbacks, and triumphs. The prologue consists of New Year's resolutions, written as two lists beginning with "I WILL Not" and "I WILL."

These resolutions introduce Bridget and her heart's desires, but also foreshadow upcoming events and announce the tone, adventures, and concerns of the novel.

11. Introduce a cast of characters. This is especially helpful if there is a large cast, the story lacks a single protagonist, or the story is particularly complex. The prologue to Karen Joy Fowler's *The Jane Austen Book Club* begins with a captivating first sentence: "Each of has a private Austen." It then goes on to introduce the six members of the Central Valley/River City Jane Austen book club. Each character is awarded a brief sketch that includes physical descriptions and backstory. The sketches are cleverly drawn to demonstrate the characters' differences and to make readers wonder how this disparate group came together and how its members will remain intertwined.

143

Prologue Pitfalls

Some experts claim that a prologue should be written only as a last resort, when there is no other way of revealing the information. The warnings about using prologues stem mostly from the fact that a prologue is often composed of backstory. Because the reader wants to plunge into the drama, this excursion into backstory must be hugely significant.

Resist the urge to tell a reader everything you know about the story world and your characters. This urge is often overwhelming, but remember that you aren't a librarian or researcher—you're a storyteller. Don't let your prologues dump information that muddles the beginning with too much data.

Another hazard in using a prologue is that you can dilute suspense by exposing too much too soon. If you're giving away some important aspect of the future, such as the identity of the villain or murderer, or some other key moment, the story that unfolds must be especially engrossing and tense.

Since a prologue can stand apart from the rest of the story, writers are often tempted to go overboard with their concoctions. For example, they write stand-alone scenes that are so removed from the story in time and place that they're confusing or misleading. Although a prologue doesn't need to introduce your protagonist, it must be firmly connected to the story. A tenuous thread will not do. In other words, you shouldn't create an elaborate backstory for a minor character, or a tedious recitation of how harnesses were made in thirteenth-century England.

If you've written a prologue merely to create a mood or atmosphere, and no vital information is revealed, you can usually dump it. A prologue should evoke a mood or atmosphere (all writing should), but it cannot exist solely for this purpose. As you craft individual scenes, ask yourself how you want your reader to feel or what effect you're trying to create. Mood is created on a word-by-word basis, by choosing details that stir emotions and orchestrating pacing to slow down for important moments.

Three final warnings: (1) prologues should never be vague or confusing, (2) they should never be written in the passive voice, and (3) they should never be excerpts of a cliffhanger moment that appears later in the story (this is a technique from earlier centuries and will not appeal to contemporary readers).

Prologues as Setups

Like the first words of a novel, a prologue is written to send the first tingles of fear, doubt, or suspicion down the reader's spine. You want your reader to feel disturbed by the prologue, because disturbing events are tantalizing.

Donna Tartt opens both her novels, *The Secret History* and *The Little Friend*, with a prologue. In *The Little Friend*, the prologue is set twelve years before the events in chapter one. Often a prologue describes long-ago, unforgettable events that have influenced the characters so much that they are forever changed, and this is the case in *The Little Friend*. The prologue depicts the unthinkable: Robin, a nine-year-old boy, is murdered in his own back yard. The first line of the prologue speaks of a mother's guilt thereafter:

> For the rest of her life, Charlotte Cleve would blame herself for her son's death because she had decided to have the Mother's Day dinner at six in the evening instead of noon, after church, which is when the Cleves usually had it.

Thus the reader is informed of this murder's far-reaching effects. As the prologue continues and reader is informed that Robin's family doesn't talk about the day he was murdered. The prologue piques the reader's curiosity and at the same time fills in the blanks about that day for readers. While it might be argued that Tartt uses Robin's death as a shock factor, the prologue plays a key role in setting the story in motion by detailing an event that defines and fractures the family.

Portraying Tragedy in Prologues

A defining moment in a prologue carries more heft than one found in a flashback because it looms over the story and the characters. When you have such an event, particularly a traumatic accident or an untimely or violent death in the protagonist's inner circle, consider setting it in the prologue so that its front row placement is arresting and illuminating.

For example, in the prologue from Ann Packer's *The Dive From Clausen's Pier*, the protagonist and her boyfriend have reached a strained point in their relationship when tragedy strikes. It is Memorial Day, and they are at reservoir with a group of friends. The prologue's last paragraph sets up the events of the novel:

Then somewhere on the reservoir a motorboat started up, and we were still for a moment as we looked across the water to see if we could see it. I remember the sound so clearly, the sound of the boat and also the feel of the icy-cold beer can in my hand. I wish I'd done something to stop him then—jumped up and said I'd marry him that day, or burst into tears, or held on tight to his leg. Anything. But of course I didn't. I was already looking away, when from across the water there came the sound of the outboard revving higher. And then Mike dove.

Naturally, since the title refers to this dive, the reader wants to know about its ramifications. They aren't good. Mike is permanently crippled from the spinal injury that occurs, but then questions arise: How will his injuries motivate the protagonist? Will guilt rule her emotions? Will she find a way to love him despite his physical limitations?

So that murders and tragic accidents don't veer into melodrama, depict their long-ranging effects. Tragedy should ripple into every corner of a story, causing characters to be forever changed. Don't kill or hurt sympathetic characters simply because, as a fiction writer, you can, but rather to show that humankind is always burdened by tragedy. Then use these events to reveal a character under duress, forced to adapt, and motivated to act.

FORECASTING THE FUTURE

Prologues can function as reverse time shifts, allowing a protagonist or narrator to reflect and comment from the future on events that will happen, because he's already lived through them. Typically written in the same viewpoint and style as the rest of the novel, this type of prologue portrays the aftermath of key events.

The effects of the plot on the characters are either suggested or directly revealed, and the protagonist is somehow changed, damaged, haunted, or grieving. To bridge the time gap between the prologue and novel, you may portray a character writing a diary entry, report, letter, or memoir reflecting on what has already happened.

Often the character is much older when he thinks back to the occurrences of the past, as in Umberto Eco's *The Name of the Rose*, where the protagonist, Adso, looks back on his younger years. The prologue features the now elderly monk recalling and writing about an eventful week, when he and his mentor, William of

Baskerville, solved a mystery at a northern Italian abbey. Adso's musings whisk the reader to the fourteenth century, but do not give away how the mystery was solved. The second paragraph of the prologue introduces Adso:

> Having reached the end of my poor sinner's life, my hair now white, I grow old as the world does, waiting to be lost in the bottomless pit of silent and deserted divinity, sharing in the light of angelic intelligences; confined now with my heavy, ailing body in this cell in the dear monastery of Melk, I prepare to leave on this parchment my testimony as to the wondrous and terrible events that I happened to observe in my youth, now repeating verbatim all I saw and heard, without venturing to seek a design, as if to leave to those who will come after (if the Antichrist has not come first) signs of signs, so that the prayer of deciphering may be exercised on them.

After the prologue ends and chapter one begins, the reader slips into the past and discovers that Brother William of Baskerville is a sleuth Sherlock Holmes would approve of, as he and the young novice, Adso, arrive at the abbey where a monk's murder must be solved.

A prologue of this sort works best if the character relating it has somehow changed and has a different, more thoughtful, or more comprehensive understanding of what has happened. This gives the reader the benefit of watching the action unravel as the plot moves along, while also being privy to insider information.

THEMES IN PROLOGUES

Themes in fiction are the central idea or concern reflected in the story. Theme is used to connect elements in fiction, and novels can contain more than one theme. A theme greatly enhances a novel's depth to the point that, without a theme, the story is merely a series of actions or events. When introducing your theme(s) in a prologue, a careful balance is needed, so that the reader is not overwhelmed.

In Dennis Lehane's *Mystic River*, the prologue is titled "The Boys Who Escaped From Wolves," and is set in 1975, twenty-five years before the story action. Through the portrayal of a traumatic and haunting event, the prologue works to create a powerful backstory that ultimately affects the front story and its tragic climax. The prologue also introduces the novel's secondary theme, which is innocence lost.

In the thirty-three-page prologue, the reader is introduced to the Irish-Catholic world of South Boston and to three boys: Sean, Jimmy, and Dave. One day, when the boys are playing in the street, they're approached by two men, who claim that they're plainclothes policemen. However, they aren't cops, they're child molesters, and Dave, the least self-assured of the three, drives away with them and is imprisoned for four days in a dark basement before he escapes.

Keep in mind that if your prologue opens with a shocking incident, then it's crucial that the prologue ends on a powerful note. It must conclude with a cliffhanger or some thruster that demands that the reader keep reading.

THE MULTITASKING PROLOGUE

If you come away with only one insight from this chapter, it should be that the best prologues multitask, and do so gracefully. For example, the seven-page prologue in Sarah Dunant's *The Birth of Venus* begins with a scintillating hook; introduces the reader to a long-ago time and its mores and customs; provides backstory on the protagonist; reveals the protagonist's future; introduces several mysteries that demand a solution; reads like a captivating short story; stands apart from the main story in time, place, and viewpoint; suggests themes about women's roles in the sixteenth century; and accomplishes its main job of titillating the reader.

Earlier in the chapter, we looked at eleven prologue functions. Think about those functions now and compare them to the needs of your story. Which ones can fit with what you're trying to accomplish? Read Dunant's prologue for yourself, and notice how she weaves the different elements together, accomplishing so much so seamlessly.

PROLOGUES, FANTASY, AND SCIENCE FICTION

Fantasy, science fiction, and historical fiction often use prologues to establish a story world that is unlike the one the reader resides in. Why? Because sometimes the reader needs to enter the world first before the events in chapter one can be fully appreciated and believed. All fiction requires that the reader suspend disbelief, and the more extraordinary the story world, the more proofs required for it to seem plausible.

But herein lies the catch. Not every fantastical world requires a prologue. J.R.R. Tolkien doesn't use one in his Lord of the Rings series, and his Middle Earth was deeply complicated and teeming with strange creatures. Tolkien instead uses his protagonist as a guide to the world, making the epic a journey of discovery for both the character and readers.

Your litmus test for the decision to include or not include a prologue has several components. Ask yourself the following:

- Is the story world extraordinarily unusual and complex, so that many elements are not recognizable?
- Does the story world have technology that needs to be explained in increments?
- Does the story world have a particular set of ground rules not found in contemporary society?
- Is the story world directly affected by some aspect of its history?

Let's imagine that five hundred years ago in your fictional world a group of people were captured and enslaved. We must know this fact in order to understand the rebellious protagonist, who wants to lead his people to freedom. In an unconventional story world, the prologue can create proofs of the world and lay down the basic rules of the place.

To see some interesting and well-written fantasy and science fiction prologues, look at *Jurassic Park* by Michael Crichton, *A Sorcerer's Treason* by Sarah Zettel, *Crossfire* by Nancy Kress, *The Mists of Avalon* by Marion Zimmer Bradley, *Wolves of the Calla* and *The Drawing of the Three* by Stephen King, and *Jonathan Strange & Mr. Norrell* by Susanna Clarke.

THE CASE OF THE FRAME

As discussed earlier, a frame story structure is one where the timeline is not chronological, but instead begins with the present or immediate past (in a prologue), then travels back in time to a more distant past (in the body of the novel), before returning to the time of the opening (in an epilogue). There are two kinds of frame stories: The first, which was discussed in chapter six, is a story that is told as recollection or a long flashback after the action of the story is over. This is essentially a story within a story, as found in Umberto Eco's *The Name of the*

Rose and Mary Shelley's *Frankenstein*. In a frame story, we often find a character, usually in the role of narrator, trying to make sense of events or tragedies that have already happened.

The second type of frame is found in novels or films such as *The Red Violin*, where an object or subject serves as the frame that holds together a collection of smaller stories or vignettes that relate to it. Other examples in which smaller stories are woven into the whole are *Tales from the Arabian Nights* or Chaucer's *The Canterbury Tales*. The prologue in *The Canterbury Tales* establishes the time (April) and setting (medieval England, on the road to Canterbury) from which the story collection will unfold. It also sets its ground rules: A group of pilgrims on the road to a saint's shrine are telling stories to amuse each other, pass the time, and ultimately win a prize. The prologue also establishes that the narrator is one of the pilgrims, lending credibility to his observations about his fellow pilgrims.

{ * }

If you're still contemplating whether your prologue is necessary to your story, try leaving it out entirely and giving the manuscript to several readers. If they do not need the information provided by the prologue, you can likely get by without it. If they are confused by its absence, put it back in. Or, if it provides a hook and creates a forward flow, you can try using the prologue as your first chapter.

One last tip: A prologue must always be fascinating and dramatic. If your novel is published and you're called on to read it at a book signing, you will mostly likely be reading your prologue to an audience. It needs to have a compelling voice and a stand-alone quality, and drive the reader into the rest of the story.

chapter 11
Sense of Place

> {
> Place is one of the lesser angels that watch over the racing hand of fiction, perhaps
> the one that gazes benignly enough from off to one side, while others, like character,
> plot, symbolic meaning, and so on, are doing a good deal of wing-beating about her
> chair, and feeling, who in my eyes carries the crown, soars highest of them all and
> rightly relegates place into the shade.
>
> —Eudora Welty

*F*iction has three main elements: plotting, character, and place or setting. While writers spend countless hours plotting and creating characters and then imagining their character's arcs and dilemmas, often too little attention is paid to place. This is a fatal mistake, since the place fiction is staged provides the backdrop against which your dramas ultimately play out.

But setting is more than a mere backdrop for action; it is an interactive aspect of your fictional world that saturates the story with mood, meaning, and thematic connotations. Broadly defined, setting is the location of the plot, including the region, geography, climate, neighborhood, buildings, and interiors. Setting, along with pacing, also suggests passage of time. Place is layered into every scene and flashback, built of elements such as weather, lighting, the season, and the hour.

Here is a list of the specific elements that setting encompasses:

1. Locale. This relates to broad categories such as a country, state, region, city, and town, as well as to more specific locales, such as a neighborhood, street, house, or school. Other locales can include shorelines, islands, farms, rural areas, etc.

2. Time of year. The time of year is richly evocative and influential in fiction. Time of year includes the seasons, but also encompasses holidays, such as Hanukkah,

Christmas, New Year's Eve, and Halloween. Significant dates can also be used, such as the anniversary of a death of a character or real person, or the anniversary of a battle, such as the attack on Pearl Harbor.

3. Time of day. Scenes need to play out during various times or periods during a day or night, such as dawn, dusk, during the dinner hour, late afternoon, or, more specifically, at 8 P.M., 8 A.M., noon, or midnight. Readers have clear associations with different periods of the day, making an easy way to create a visual orientation in a scene.

4. Elapsed time. The minutes, hours, days, weeks, and months a story encompasses must be somehow accounted for or the reader will feel confused and the story will suffer from a lack of authenticity. While scenes unfold moment by moment, there is also time to account for between scenes, when a flashback is inserted, and when a character travels a long distance. (Various methods for showing the passage of time are discussed in chapter nine.)

5. Mood and atmosphere. Characters and events are influenced by weather, temperature, lighting, and other tangible factors, which in turn influence the emotional timbre, mood, and atmosphere of a scene. A fourteenth-century castle depicted in a Gothic romance, with its cavernous, chilly, and poorly lit rooms, can seem spooky and shadowy. On the other hand, a scene set in a charming seaside villa on the French Riviera with the sparkling turquoise of the Mediterranean in the distance might seem upbeat, opulent, or romantic.

Human influences also infect scenes with mood. For example, the atmosphere of a carnival midway, with its primary colors, balloons, and cacophony of sounds from the rides and barkers, might depict a frantic, gay, or gaudy atmosphere. Human influences also can come from architecture, artwork, and furnishings, such as in the hushed and ornate atmosphere found in an ancient European cathedral when it is empty of worshipers.

6. Climate. Climate is linked to the geography and topography of a place, and, as in our real world, can influence events and people. Ocean currents, prevailing winds and air masses, latitude, altitude, mountains, land masses, and large bodies of water all influence climate. It's especially important when you write about a real setting to understand climatic influences, as E. Annie Proulx did

152

when setting *The Shipping News* in Newfoundland. She used climate along with geography to influence every aspect of the story from the way the natives think and eat, to what they wear and how they make a living. Harsh climates can make for grim lives, while tropical climates can create more carefree lifestyles. Shrieking winds from a blizzard can prevent a character from sleeping well, which in turn makes it difficult for him to cope with his problems. Fog or a heavy snowstorm can make it difficult for a character to find his way home. An early frost can ruin a vegetable garden a family depends on. Climate and weather can also propel major events in a story, as in *The Shipping News*, when early impassable roads force Quoyle, the protagonist, to buy a boat, even though he doesn't know how to swim.

7. Geography. This refers to specific aspects of water, landforms, ecosystems, and topography in your setting. Geography also includes climate, soil, plants, trees, rocks and minerals, and soils. Ecosystems have hundreds of variations and include the Andes and Himalayas, the Nile and Amazon rivers, the Sahara desert, and the Everglades. Geography can create obvious influences in a story like a mountain a character must climb, a swift-running river he must cross, or a boreal forest he must traverse to reach safety. No matter where a story is set, whether it's a mountain village in the Swiss Alps or an opulent resort on the Florida coast, the natural world with all its geographic variations and influences must permeate the story.

8. Man-made geography. There are few corners of the planet that have not been influenced by the hand of humankind. It is in our man-made influences that our creativity and the destructiveness of civilization can be seen. Readers want visual evidence in a story world, and man-made geography is easily included to provide it. With this in mind, make certain that your stories contain proof of the many footprints that people have left in its setting.

Use the influences of humankind on geography to lend authenticity to stories set in a real or famous locale. These landmarks include dams, bridges, ports, towns and cities, monuments, burial grounds, cemeteries, and famous buildings (the Empire State building, the Eiffel Tower, the Taj Mahal, the Vatican, Buckingham Palace), as well as the Great Pyramids, Mayan ruins, the Great Wall of China, the Hoover and Aswan dams, the Panama and Suez canals. Consider too the influences of mankind using the land, and the effects of mines, deforestation, agriculture, irrigation, vineyards, cattle grazing, and coffee plantations.

9. Eras of historical importance. Important events, wars, or historical periods linked to the plot and theme might include the Civil War, World War II, the Vietnam War, medieval times, the barbarian invasion of Rome, the pirate wars that raged from the 1600s through the 1800s, the Bubonic Plague, the Great Depression, the gold rush in the 1800s, or the era of slavery in the South.

10. Social/political/cultural environment. Cultural, political, and social influences can range widely and affect characters in many ways. The political and social unrest of the United States in the 1960s, the mores and conventions of Victorian England, or the lawlessness of the Old West are examples. The social era of a story often influences characters' values, social and family roles, and sensibilities. An example of this use of setting is in John Updike's Harry "Rabbit" Angstrom books, where Updike takes his character from youth to death against the backdrop of societal and political changes, upheavals in sexual mores, and a changing economy.

11. Population. Some places are densely populated, such as Hong Kong, while others, such as the steppes of Outer Mongolia, are lonely places with only a few hardy souls. Your stories need a specific, yet varied population that accurately reflects the place. If the story takes place in a farming community, you need not only tractors and corn fields but farmers, mill owners, seed salesmen, veterinarians, the Ladies Auxiliary of the local Lutheran church, a pastor, and other characters likely to be found in this kind of community.

12. Ancestral influences. In many regions of the United States, the ancestral influences of European countries such as Germany, Ireland, Italy, and Poland are prominent. The cities and bayous of Louisiana are populated with distinctive groups influenced by their Native American, French-Canadian, and African American forebears. Ancestral influences can be depicted in cuisine, dialogue, values, attitudes, and general outlook. Garrison Keillor's mythical Lake Wobegon, a small town in the upper Midwest, is featured in his novels. Keillor populates his stories with people who possess Midwestern qualities, such as self-deprecating humor, modesty, good manners, a strong work ethic, and respect of their elders.

SETTING AND THEMATIC CONNECTIONS

Besides acting as the location for the plot, setting conveys historical or cultural influences and proves that the characters live in a world as vivid as our own. Setting, therefore, must be woven into the tapestry of characters' lives and hint at the deeper themes revealed in their actions.

Weave thematic connections into your setting, as in this opening from James Crumley's short story "Hostages":

> Between the hammer of the Midwestern sun and relentless sweep of the bone-dry wind, the small town of Wheatshocker seemed crushed flat and just about to blow across the plains. Long billows of dust filled the empty streets like strings of fog. ... Shadows as black as tar huddled protectively in the shallow dunes that lined the few buildings left on the main street. Most the windowfronts were are empty as a fool's laugh, while those with glass were etched in formless shapes by the sharp, ghostly wind.

It's easy to believe that in a place under the hammer of the sun, with dust like strings of fog and a bone-dry wind, something horrific might happen. The careful layering of setting details also suggests a theme, a certain and terrible ugliness found in human nature (especially when Crumley employs metaphors such as "empty as a fool's laugh").

Crumley's use of the 1930s as the backdrop for "Hostages" suggests the hopelessness and criminality of the Prohibition era. Whatever your themes—abandonment, loneliness, lawlessness, justice, the dangers of seduction—the setting can enhance these concepts.

MULTITASKING WITH SETTING

Whenever possible, work at using elements in your story to accomplish more than one task at a time. For example, you can use your setting, a castle in Scotland in the seventeenth century in November, to reflect an era, to indicate the season with constantly drumming rain, to create a dismal mood—since the sky is overcast and the rooms are lit by torches and candlelight—and to make life difficult for the protagonist, since there are few comforts in the chilly rooms.

Cold Mountain, by Charles Frazier, is a novel that uses setting to multitask. The main story line revolves around William Inman, who wakes in a Civil War

155

hospital, where he's being treated for gunshot wounds, and decides to go AWOL and head home to his beloved Cold Mountain, North Carolina. Inman's need to escape the hospital and the brutality of the war sets the story in motion. Echoing Homer's *The Odyssey*, the story chronicles his perilous journey home and is interwoven with a report from the home front from Ada Monroe, his sweetheart. Frazier uses setting to report on the journey, move the story forward, show time passing, reflect on themes, and depict a colorful and motley cast of characters, all while grounding the reader in the realities of day and night, heat and cold, and survival.

The setting is featured as Inman follows rivers, roads, and deer trails, sometimes relying on the Milky Way to find his way home. At times near starvation, and gravely ill from his wounds, Inman often journeys at night to escape detection. The South is depicted as a ruined, desolate land, which reflects the theme of the cost of war. Here is an excerpt that depicts one segment of the journey:

> The road soon climbed and crossed a little ridge and left the river behind. It wound through low hills. The moon had risen and Inman could see that the land lay open in great patches where the forest had been burned away to make place for fields. But nothing more toilsome than lighting a fire had been done with it, and so it was a country of black stumps set in runnel-cut clay stretching away bare to a far horizon. The charcoal of the stumps caught the moonlight and glittered. Inman looked about and thought, I could well be on a whole other planet from the place I'm aiming for.

Meanwhile, Ada's story is intertwined with Inman's journey. Her father dies of tuberculosis and leaves her alone on their farm, which soon falls into ruin as described here:

> She looked off across the yard to the kitchen garden where the beans and squash and tomatoes bore vegetables hardly bigger than her thumb despite the fullness of the growing season. Many of the leaves were eaten away to their veins by bugs and worms. Standing thick in the rows and towering over the vegetables were weeds that Ada could not name and had neither the energy nor the heart to fight. Beyond the failed garden stretched the old cornfield, now grown up shoulder high in poke and sumac. Above the fields and pastures, the mountains were just becoming visible as the morning fog burned away. Their pale outlines stood at the horizon, more like the ghosts of mountains than the actual things.

This use of setting reveals Ada's lack of farming skills, her surroundings, the time of day, and her state of mind. It also furthers the theme by illustrating the toll war has on the land when the men are called away to fight. Whenever possible, scrutinize your setting descriptions to determine if they can accomplish more than one task.

Creating a setting that multitasks, especially one that suggests themes, doesn't always happen in your first draft. As you rewrite, keep asking yourself what emotions you're trying to evoke. Then choose words with potency, and deepen each description by asking yourself "What does this remind me of?" Analogies, similes, metaphors, and comparisons of all types can enrich the work, sending ripples of added meaning into the reader's imagination.

ATMOSPHERE AND MOOD

Atmosphere and mood are used to immerse the reader in your story world and then needle him, creating emotions and layering the story with depth and subtext. Capturing the mood of a place is especially important when an author wants to evoke terror, anxiety, or horror, but also works for less intense emotions.

Horror writers are especially known for using setting to create apprehension in their readers. But no matter the genre, powerful drama penetrates the reader, slips into his veins and makes him feel jazzed or scared or languorous, depending on the needs of the scene. Carefully constructed setting details instruct the reader how to feel.

Edgar Allan Poe, the godfather of suspense writing, populates his stories with creaky old houses and gloomy, secluded castles. He doesn't simply depict interiors, he haunts them with shadows, odd noises, and the spooky darkness of endless halls lit dimly by candlelight. In addition to interior details, there are exterior details such as bogs, graveyards, overgrown weeds, and trees that loom and twist.

One of his most famous stories, "The Fall of the House of Usher," opens with this somber depiction:

During the whole of a dull, dark, and soundless day in the autumn of the year, when the clouds hung oppressively low in the heavens, I had been passing alone, on horseback, through a singularly dreary tract of country; and at length found myself, as the shades of the evening drew on, within view of the melancholy House

157

of Usher. I know not how it was—but, with the first glimpse of the building, a sense of insufferable gloom pervaded my spirit. I say insufferable; for the feeling was unrelieved by any of that half-pleasurable, because poetic, sentiment, with which the mind usually receives even the sternest natural images of the desolate or terrible. I looked upon the scene before me—upon the mere house, and the simple landscape features of the domain—upon the bleak walls—upon the vacant eye-like windows—upon a few rank sedges—and upon a few white trunks of decayed trees—with an utter depression of soul which I can compare to no earthly sensation more properly than to the after-dream of the reveller upon opium—the bitter lapse into every-day life—the hideous dropping off of the veil.

This opening makes it clear that this is not going to be a pleasant holiday in the country, and thus the reader is immediately put on notice that a distressing experience will unfold. The dismal setting also whispers secrets suggested by the vacant, eye-like windows, and raises questions about why the house is so gloomy and strange, and why it hasn't been maintained. Because the secrets are horrific, it's necessary to create a remote and dismal place where they can be acted out.

THE SUGGESTIVE NATURE OF SETTING

Setting whispers, hints, and sets the stage for events to unfold. Settings can suggest misery or happiness, triumph or betrayal, or other emotional connotations. Using setting to suggest adds the layers and nuance that we've discussed in previous chapters. In "The Fall of the House of Usher," for example, the Ushers' ancestral home suggests the story's end, as well as the home's dark and decaying mood.

Spooky events need atmospheric staging: There's a good reason that storms, so typical of horror novels, work for crucial scenes. When the sky is exploding and lightning is chasing across the sky, the setting telegraphs to readers that anything can happen, that nature is out of control, and that murderers or madmen can run loose, wreaking havoc. Darkness is effective because many people fear the dark and because humans operate at a disadvantage in the dark.

While weather is great for creating atmospheric influences, interiors can work equally well. Interiors characterize the people who live in them. In the Ushers' rooms, even the draperies suggest something creepy:

I endeavored to believe that much, if not all of what I felt, was due to the bewildering influence of the gloomy furniture of the room—of the dark and tattered draperies, which, tortured into motion by the breath of a rising tempest, swayed fitfully to and fro upon the walls, and rustled uneasily about the decorations of the bed.

Let's take this technique a step further. People have memories, associations, and preconceived notions about certain places. For example, many of us have warm memories of and associations with our grandparents' homes. But associations can have larger connections. Take the deep South for example. Most of us connect the South to all sorts of images, from plantations and lovely gardens to antebellum charm and gracious cities like Charleston and Savannah. The South can also conjure up images of lynchings and the Ku Klux Klan. Associations depend on the individual.

Thus, at times you will play on a reader's preconceived notions of a place. Mountains are majestic, but can also be dangerous, lonely, and isolated. Deserts bring to mind unbearable, relentless heat, rattlesnakes, and a bleak, unbroken landscape. Anne Rice plays on readers' preconceived notions of graveyards when she sets her vampire stories in the above-ground tombs of New Orleans.

HORROR, MYSTERIES, AND SETTING: PLAYING ON THE UNEXPECTED

Horror fiction, like its predecessor, Gothic fiction, is meant to frighten and unsettle. Gothic stories often feature mystery and the supernatural, the clash of good and evil, and a sense of doom and decay woven together with ghosts, family curses, madness, and desire. Gothic fiction is the first tradition where setting acted like a character in the story and was tied to every element of the plot. This genre often used remote settings, rambling mansions, and crumbling convents and monasteries.

Contemporary horror stories also use castles, haunted houses, graveyards, deserted buildings, and lonely places because they create an emotional response and dread *before* the ghosts and ghouls show up. J.K. Rowling uses her Hogwarts castle for all sorts of happy circumstances, but its labyrinth of dimly lit halls, wings, and echoing rooms is also a convenient prowling ground for ghosts and evildoers. Once you understand how Gothic and horror settings amp up fear, you can apply this knowledge to all types of stories and all types of emotions.

However, sometimes setting is most effective when it's used to go against a reader's expectations, as in P. D. James's *A Taste for Death*, where two corpses are found in the quiet vestry of St. Matthew's Church. The double murders are discovered by an elderly volunteer and a boy there to arrange flowers. This type of unexpected discovery in the most unlikely of settings strikes a memorable note with readers and helps writers avoid using a setting that is formulaic. Similarly, the reader doesn't expect a gang of murderous bank robbers to be playing poker in a farm kitchen in James Crumley's "Hostages," making that scene all the more powerful.

Ray Bradbury uses a carnival setting, usually a place for fun and cotton candy, for terror in *Something Wicked This Way Comes*. Stephen King and Dean Koontz place evil where the reader doesn't expect it, so when it starts roaming a school or playground or rustic countryside, the heebie-jeebies are worse than if the malevolent force were lurking in a ruined castle. Because the reader doesn't have scary emotional connections with and expectations of innocent places, the setting details need to work harder because they're going against type.

Horror stories play on the reader's private fears, exploiting the frightened child within, who is holding his breath, hoping the bogeyman is not lurking in his closet. The bogeyman is so frightening because he's in the closet close enough to pounce, not in a remote castle. In King's novella *The Mist*, people are trapped in a supermarket when a fog filled with nightmare creatures surrounds the store. Since we all need to visit supermarkets, this cranks up the fright factor, the left-over-from-childhood dread that no place is safe.

Using setting to go against type also links neatly to themes. There is nothing so shocking as innocence defiled or order destroyed, two themes often explored in mysteries and suspense. So think of where innocence reigns, such as in a toddler's bedroom, with its faint smells of baby powder and washed cotton. If a villain breaks into this sanctuary, where the walls are decorated with ducks and bunnies and the crib is piled with stuffed animals, the violation would be doubly horrific and underline the theme that the world is a dangerous place.

Similarly, when places of justice and order (courtrooms or government buildings) or places of beauty (art museums or majestic shorelines) are defiled by a criminal element or violent acts, there should be a clear link back to themes that suggest that everyone and every place is corruptible. Small towns are often used as settings because they suggest an innocuous, simple way of life, but can also swarm with secrets, scandals, and crime, contrary to their innocent appearance.

THE EFFECTS OF WEATHER AND CLIMATE

More than a prop, setting creates a living, breathing place. A wild storm ravaging the landscape not only enhances mood, but plays an active role in the story. As a writer, you should always look for ways to make settings interact with the events of the story. Weather is only one aspect of setting that works as a catalyst, meaning it causes things to happen. You can create a scene where an attack comes in the dark, when a character is most vulnerable and fuzzy from sleep. Rain can wipe out footsteps and clues at a crime scene, fog can hide the murderer's identity, and ice can cause car accidents.

Weather and setting can cause reactions in your characters: a heat spell causes tempers to flare, a prolonged cold spell isolates characters indoors and make them cranky and restless, or overcast skies cause depression.

In *Snow Falling on Cedars*, David Guterson uses a fierce snowstorm that hits San Piedro, a fictional Pacific Northwest island, to isolate the players in his drama, causing an emotional reversal in newspaperman Ishmael Chambers. The storm also provides an extended metaphor as the snow covers the landscape, and the islanders cover up the past and their roles in it.

The racially mixed islanders of San Piedro live in close proximity and know each family's history and often its secrets, and the island locale serves to insulate the islanders from the rest of the world. Miyamoto, an accused murderer, is put on trial in early December during the anniversary of the attack on Pearl Harbor, which in turn heightens tensions and lends added meaning to the trial. This anniversary and the wrongs committed against the Japanese islanders also places history on trial.

CHARACTERIZATION WITHIN SETTING

Characters' homes disclose more than their decorating style and ocean view; they illustrate characters' tastes, personality, income, class, and mood. A kitchen with dirty dishes piled everywhere or stacks of unopened mail is revealing. Setting can demonstrate a lot about a character's personality, as when a bachelor has an

161

obsessively neat apartment or when a widow keeps her dead husband's clothes in the closet. Or, the reader might wonder about the coping skills of a young mother when there's a smelly, brimming diaper pail, fingerprint smudges on every surface, and toys and dirty laundry scattered throughout the house.

Creating a Constant Milieu

In fiction, everything needs to contribute to a living, breathing story world. For instance, if your story is set during the winter, think about how the sunlight will refract off the snow and how your character's breath will be seen in the air as the cold pierces her lungs and stings her face. When she steps indoors, her cheeks will be chapped and her fingers numb. After each new snowfall, she will be forced to shovel the driveway, and, when another storm sweeps in, coupled with freezing rain, it means that school will be closed.

Smart writers frame setting so that it is omnipresent, woven into every scene and employing every sense—a splash of light coming in through the window, an antique grandfather clock ticking and melodically chiming in the hallway, the homey smells of bacon and coffee drifting throughout the house.

Isolating Your Characters

Writers, especially horror writers, often use setting to isolate their characters, stage elaborate showdowns where the cavalry will *not* arrive to help, and eliminate escape routes. Stephen King opted for a prison setting in his novella *Rita Hayworth and Shawshank Redemption*, and Daniel Defoe used an island in *Robinson Crusoe*.

Geography and weather are used most often as devices for isolation. In Michael Crichton's *Jurassic Park*, the author maximizes the sense of isolation by having the characters face off against prehistoric creatures on an island from which there is no escape—and all during a major storm. King uses a combination of weather and location to create isolation in two of his most famous stories, *The Shining* and *Misery*. In *The Shining*, the Overlook Hotel oozes malevolence, and isolates Jack Torrance, a frustrated writer who is becoming increasingly unstable; his wife, Wendy; and son, Danny. The story is conveniently set during a long winter when snow piles high after a blizzard, isolating and endangering the family as Jack loses his hold on reality.

When you isolate a character, you're usually ruling out rescue, so the protagonist must struggle alone (or with a small group) for survival. In *Misery*, author Paul Sheldon's car accident on a mountain road delivers him into the hands of Annie Wilkes in her snow-bound cabin. King doubles Sheldon's isolation by giving him injuries that prevent him from escaping.

However, isolation doesn't always mean danger. The stories of Jane Austen and George Eliot play out in the English countryside, with only a few excursions to the city or shore. The story world is circumscribed by geography, status, and technology. Women without means spent most of their time at home, with brief walks outdoors or in the garden and occasional social engagements. They didn't own elaborate carriages or employ many servants, so they were forced to amuse themselves, and in a sense, wait for the world—and gentlemen callers—to come to them.

FISH-OUT-OF-WATER SETTINGS

This old setup plunks a character into an alien landscape, where he doesn't know the rules, doesn't possess the skills or knowledge to successfully navigate the new place, and must learn quickly to survive. William Golding's *Lord of the Flies*, in which a group of posh boarding school boys becomes stranded on an island, might be the ultimate fish-out-of-water story. Other noteworthy contenders include James Dickey's *Deliverance*, where four businessmen take on the rapids of an Appalachian River; *One Flew Over the Cuckoo's Nest*, where Randle Patrick McMurphy, the healthy protagonist, finds himself in a mental hospital; and Charlotte Brontë's *Jane Eyre*, where Jane's position as a governess at Thornfield finds her trying to cope with strange goings-on and a moody employer.

Most war stories follow a fish-out-of-water scenario, with the men and women involved struggling for survival and learning profound lessons. In *Cold Mountain*, Ada finds herself the mistress of a small farm after her father dies. After chopping firewood until she's soaked with sweat, she pauses and writes a letter to her cousin in Charleston:

> I cannot begin to recount all such rough work that I have done in the time since father died. It has changed me. It is amazing the physical alterations that can transpire in but a few months of labor. I am brown as a penny from being outdoors all day, and I am growing somewhat ropy through the wrists and forearms.

Ada's letter illustrates that often the purpose for pitting a character against setting in a fish-out-of-water story is transformation.

In most fish-out-of-water stories, the main conflict is between the protagonist and the setting. The story usually evolves around identity, self-discovery, and the challenges of survival, and often provides social commentary. Because the character is often inept and out of his depth, his situation causes reader empathy, forces the character to confront his fears, and plumbs the depths of his character. The character's missteps and mistakes can also provide comedy, but mostly reveal the character's core values and personality.

The fish-out-of-water model doesn't necessarily need to be the central conflict in the story. For example, in Louisa May Alcott's *Little Women*, Jo March has a personality unsuited to the genteel standards set for women in the mid-1800s, revealed in scenes such as when she serves as the companion to her wealthy, proper aunt, or attends a formal dance and ruins her gown and gloves with her unladylike antics.

THE ORDINARY PAVES THE WAY FOR THE EXTRAORDINARY

If you've created an environment that a reader can see, hear, and experience, he'll believe in the actions that happen in a story. For example, when a world has window shades, soda cans, dust, books, a baseball mitt tossed near the front door, pillows scattered on the sofa, and other ordinary objects, the reader will be anchored in a place he can believe in. If these ordinary items create a real place, then when the *extraordinary* events happen in the story—the murder is committed, the infidelity is discovered, the disease takes its toll, the criminal is caught, the child is kidnapped—these events are believable because the reader is anchored in the story world.

Also, when tragedy strikes or a huge drama explodes, the ordinary details of a character's life, such as a broken vase, a lover's toothbrush left behind, or an empty chair, can lend poignancy. There is an old line that says, "Don't tell me about the tragedies of war; show me the child's shoe discarded by the side of the road." In the same sense, you can use objects or small moments and discoveries to speak volumes.

CREATING YOUR OWN CAULDRON

Every novel needs what is called a crucible or cauldron, a predicament coupled with a place where the main characters are forced together, where the drama simmers, sometimes sputters, and often boils over. The cauldron is the vessel that holds the story—part bonding principle, part pressure cooker. A cauldron can be a place of no escape, but it is also a situation, circumstance, or ordeal. Include it under setting because it can be seen and understood and has a powerful influence on plot.

In Harper Lee's *To Kill a Mockingbird*, the fictional Maycomb County, Alabama, and the South, with its segregation laws, provide the cauldron. A fishing village on the north coast of Cuba, as well as Santiago's boat and the sea itself, provide the cauldron for *The Old Man and the Sea*. In *Snow Falling on Cedars*, the island serves as microcosm for the drama to play out. Just remember that without a cauldron, your characters have no reason to become entangled.

FAMILY CAULDRONS

A family unit can also function as a cauldron because it creates an irreversible bond that forces interactions and enhances or creates conflict. When a family is the cauldron in a story, the emotions and reactions to events are heightened, the dynamics are intricate, and the stakes are high.

Examples of family cauldrons appear in Joyce Carol Oates's *We Were the Mulvaneys*, which looks at how a family copes with a daughter's rape; *The Brothers Karamazov* by Fyodor Dostoyevsky, which is about patricide; and John Galsworthy's *The Forsyte Saga*, which tracks an upper-class English family through several generations. Other examples can be found in *The House of the Seven Gables*, by Nathaniel Hawthorne; *Jane Eyre*, by Charlotte Brontë; *Sons and Lovers*, by D.H. Lawrence; and *The Beautiful and the Damned*, by F. Scott Fitzgerald.

SOCIETAL CAULDRONS

A cauldron can be forged by the mores, standards, or rules set by a society, such as in Hawthorne's *The Scarlet Letter*, which is set in a Puritan New England community that exacts punishment for a woman's adultery. John Fowles's *The French Lieutenant's Woman* is set in Victorian London and portrays Sarah Woodruff, who is jilted by her lover, a French officer, and becomes an outcast because of her affair.

The social norms of times such as the Victorian era are rich territory for exploring themes, as in Kate Chopin's *The Awakening*, which chronicles a woman wakening to her own desires in a society with stifling conventions. *The House of Mirth*, by Edith Wharton, portrays the downfall of Lily Bart, who is torn between desire and the constraints placed on women of high society. Wharton was known for chronicling the Old New York society she was born into, as in *The Age of Innocence*, where the mores of the wealthy precipitate the conflict. Her friend Henry James often portrayed American expatriates in Europe and the differences between the Old and New World, as in *The Wings of the Dove*.

COMMON CAULDRONS

Cauldrons are part setting, part circumstance, because you need a hold over your characters—physical, familial, social, or emotional barriers to prevent their escape. Here is a brief list of settings that provide cauldrons for unfolding stories. These examples come from movies, television shows, and novels.

- Famous Cities: *The Maltese Falcon, Pulp Fiction, L.A. Confidential*
- Castle/Dungeon: *Dracula*, Harry Potter series
- Corporation: *Wall Street, Disclosure, Prey*
- Courtroom: *To Kill a Mockingbird, Kramer vs. Kramer, Bleak House*
- Desert/Oasis: *Lawrence of Arabia*
- Crime Family: *The Sopranos, The Godfather*
- English Countryside: *Emma, Far From the Madding Crowd, Middlemarch*
- English/French/Dutch Colonialism: *A Passage to India, Things Fall Apart, Heart of Darkness*
- Farm/Rural Area: *Witness, Of Mice and Men, A Thousand Acres*
- Island: *Lord of the Flies, Jurassic Park, The Shipping News*
- Jungle: *The Island of Dr. Moreau, Romancing the Stone, The Poisonwood Bible*
- Mental Institution: *One Flew Over the Cuckoo's Nest; Girl, Interrupted*
- Mining: *Deadwood, The Treasure of the Sierra Madre*
- Manor House: *Rebecca, Jane Eyre, Wuthering Heights*
- Monastery/Convent: *The Name of the Rose*
- Moor: *The Hounds of the Baskervilles, The Moor*
- Mountains: *The Shining, Misery*
- Nazi Germany: *Sophie's Choice, Stones From the River, Schindler's List*

- Ocean Liner/Sea: *Titanic, The Old Man and the Sea, Frankenstein*
- Old West/West/Texas: *Deadwood, Stagecoach, Lonesome Dove*
- Orphanage: *Oliver Twist, The Cider House Rules, Little Men*
- Planet: *The Left Hand of Darkness, The Little Prince*
- Plantation: *Gone With the Wind, Out of Africa*
- Prison: *The Fixer, Little Dorrit, The Count of Monte Cristo*
- River: *The African Queen, The Adventures of Huckleberry Finn*
- Schools/Institutions: *The World According to Garp, The Cider House Rules, Old School*
- Small Town: *To Kill a Mockingbird, Fried Green Tomatoes at the Whistle Stop Café, Salem's Lot*
- South: *Divine Secrets of the Ya-Ya Sisterhood, Fried Green Tomatoes at the Whistle Stop Café, To Kill a Mockingbird*
- Space: Star Wars series, *Alien, Dune*
- Sports Fields: *The Natural, Field of Dreams, Bull Durham*
- Submarine: *20,000 Leagues Under the Sea*
- Train: *Murder on the Orient Express*
- Traveling Carnival: *Something Wicked This Way Comes*
- Utopian/Anti-Utopian/Futuristic Society: *Atlas Shrugged, The Handmaid's Tale, Brave New World*
- War/Revolution: *Platoon, The Winds of War, Catch-22*

CRAFTING YOUR OWN SETTING

The level of setting detail necessary in your story depends on its complexity. A science fiction, fantasy, or historical novel will require a fair amount of setting information and world building. A contemporary novel set in a real place will require smaller amounts, while a story in a mythical place such as Faulkner's Yoknapatawpha County, Mississippi, will need more.

Generally, try not to explain the obvious (the ocean was vast), the trite (Bali looked like paradise), or the normal (the sand was beige). Instead, concentrate on unusual and fresh descriptions.

If you're creating a fairly simple transition where your purpose is to transport your character down a hallway, a street, or a beach, the reader doesn't need a description of every car that passes or the color of the walls. Hone in on a few details that paint a larger picture.

Be sparing with modifiers, saving them for extraordinary elements or creating a mood. Thus, don't describe "green grass," "tall trees," or "blue skies." However, if the grass is brown or burned, that might tell us that there has been a heat wave, or if the trees are stunted or looming, these descriptions might describe a mood.

Accentuate the positive. Don't write "The room lacked sunshine coming through the blinds." Instead, write "The room was dim, the lowered blinds blocking out the afternoon sun."

Be wary of writing a travelogue, a catalogue, or an overlong block of setting description, because these can be static and slow the pace. Choose the most distinctive details, breaking up description and interspersing it with dialogue or action, instead of clumping it together on the page.

Never make assumptions about historical details, but research for accuracy. Allow the facts to provide the perimeters for the story. With accuracy in mind, you'll remember that a six shooter needs to be reloaded, a horse cannot gallop nonstop for twelve hours, and a hero cannot make it across a desert without water.

Use weather, but be wary of constant weather reports that stand in for more direct ways of depicting setting. Also be wary of beginning every scene with a weather update. Further, don't always paint with the obvious: It does not need to rain every time your character is depressed or whenever a painful event is happening in the story.

If you're creating a fantasy or science fiction society, you might want to first list everything you know about another author's fantasy world. For example, if you're writing a trilogy and you're a huge Tolkien fan, make a list of everything you know about Middle Earth and use it as road map for the depth of detail you will need to create for your world. You need to know its laws and judicial and political systems, history, taxation, religions, class structures, agriculture, typical crops and natural resources, modes of travel, birds, animals, and dangerous predators. Are there forests, mountains, bodies of water, landmarks, and stars? What about class structure? Are there rich and poor, slaves, serfs, servants, guilds, artisans, or armies? What is the level of technology? If you've created a pre-industrial place, then you need to account for how people travel, how goods are brought to market, and how objects are made. You'll need convincing weapons and clothing made by hand. Also plan for the more arcane details—diseases, national holidays and festivals, highways and roads, architecture, foods, and alcoholic beverages.

One last bit of advice about using setting: Contemporary readers are sophisticated and don't need every nook and cranny explored, unless the writer has a specific purpose in doing so. When using a setting detail, ask yourself if it can multitask.

NOVELS WITH MEMORABLE SETTINGS

Like fictional characters, the best settings linger in the reader's memory and imagination. Here is a list of particularly memorable settings and cauldrons.

The Winds of War, Herman Wouk

Moll Flanders, Daniel Defoe

The Bridge of San Luis Rey, Thornton Wilder

To Build a Fire, Jack London

Ulysses, James Joyce

Breakfast at Tiffany's, Truman Capote

Native Son, Richard Wright

For Whom the Bell Tolls, Ernest Hemingway

Heart of Darkness, Joseph Conrad

Midnight's Children, Salman Rushdie

The Natural, Bernard Malamud

The Prince of Tides, Pat Conroy

East of Eden, John Steinbeck

The Mambo Kings Play Songs of Love, Oscar Hijuelos

The Murders in the Rue Morgue, Edgar Allan Poe

The Naked and the Dead, Norman Mailer

The Name of the Rose, Umberto Eco

TIPS FOR CREATING THE POWER OF PLACE

While we've covered many of the aspects of your story's turf, here are additional reminders to help you shape your story's place with depth and richness. If your setting details are flat or simple, you might be missing an opportunity to deepen the conflict, reveal characters, and tease or torment your reader.

1. Realize that some aspects of setting contain natural connotations. Dawn suggests a new beginning, a full moon suggests werewolves prowling, and so on. Seasons reflect the cycles in life, and spring suggests possibility and renewal.

2. Try to use details that can change over the course of the story, such as a garden that hibernates, blossoms, and then fades. Gentrification, industrialization, or decay can alter an urban neighborhood. Use political and social change to depict broader influences.

3. Use smells to describe pleasant and unpleasant elements. Smells are hardwired into a reader's brain and are easily accessed, so are especially effective to describe the grotesque or sensual, or to evoke memories.

4. Use lighting and differentiate between the quality of light that filters into your scenes during various seasons and times of day. The noon sky in December has a distinctly different quality than in July, just as morning light filtering through antique lace curtains will be different than light seeping in through closed wooden blinds.

5. When possible, reveal description through a character's viewpoint and set it in motion.

6. The first sentences or paragraph are often the most compelling for immersing your reader in a specific setting, but don't overload the openings of every scene with setting details. Use the beginning as a foundation, and add more bricks as the story progresses.

7. Physical detail is not the only way to introduce setting. Data, lists, or statistics are also effective if the voice is handled carefully, such as in the opening to Jane Smiley's *A Thousand Acres*.

8. If a town or community is the cauldron for a novel or story, use setting to reflect the makeup of the population, including attitudes, mores, ethnic and cultural backgrounds, class, and education level. How are outsiders and strangers treated? Are they welcomed? Distrusted? Are there only a few churches in the community, or do Catholic parishes dot every few blocks? What denominations populate the town? What do the religious affiliations suggest about the people who live there? What types of cars are parked in the driveways? Are the streets clean? Are yards tidy?

9. Take special care with details if your setting is famous or infamous, such as the prison on Alcatraz. Using a well-known locale (Paris, New Orleans, New York) requires strict attention to accuracy and a flair for capturing the essence of the place.

10. Lend authority to your settings by learning the specific names of plants, bodies of water, climate influences, animals, and architectural styles.

11. Describe all aspects of architecture, including interiors, designs, and furnishings, with complete accuracy, using a sprinkling of technical terms.

12. Scrutinize every setting description as you edit your final drafts. Is it necessary to the reader's understanding of the scene? Does it multitask? Does it create mood or emotion? Is it too long?

13. Create scene cards or a list of the scenes, including their time and locale, in order to track time elapsing in story.

{ * }

Writers create intricate settings because readers rely on visual and sensory references, but also because setting shapes characters and influences the events and moods in a story. The possibilities in using place, as in creating characters, are endless. Depicting place in your story is an opportunity for creative choices, a chance to delineate a place (either real or make-believe) that fascinates or disturbs you. Setting also provides possibilities for showing conflict with nature, depicting causality, and building a substantive world.

chapter 12
Sensory Surround

{

The beginning of human knowledge is through the senses, and the fiction writer begins where human perception begins. He appeals through the senses, and you cannot appeal through the senses with abstractions.

—Flannery O'Connor

*G*ood writing haunts us. The best stories linger in our minds the way the final notes of a symphony linger in the air. When a story slips within a reader, it does so because of vivid character development, action that creates worry, and the connections that lie beneath the words. Sensory details are part of that layer and create a deep reservoir of meaning.

You breathe life into fiction by translating the senses onto the page, producing stories rooted in the physical world. Action and dialogue arrest the reader's attention, but sensory details support them, giving them a feeling of reality.

However, sensory information can't be dumped into a story in gaudy heaps or offered bit by bit like a gift you're obligated to buy but don't really want to spend money on. Writing requires a sensory surround effect that creates a tapestry, a galaxy of interwoven sensory ingredients.

SENSORY FUNDAMENTALS: UNLOCKING THE STORY

Sensory details penetrate the reader's nervous system, memory, and imagination, serving to catapult the reader into the world of the story as well as into his remembrances and emotions. But this cannot happen without highly specific details that can be imagined wholly and viscerally, such as a ragged hemline, purple pansies, crooked teeth, rap music blaring from a low-rider, or a rusty swing set.

Such details reveal specialness and importance—the places in the story where the reader should take note. Not every scene or action is unfolded with the same weight or importance. Some scenes are transitions, some are building blocks for larger, more dramatic moments, and some occur in places the reader has already visited. You won't lavish as many details on these scenes; you'll get down to business and march through the scene. In more important scenes, spend more time and use more words and details, and your readers will linger there because the level of drama warrants it. Because sensory details engage and grab readers, use them whenever possible to begin novels and stories as well as scenes and chapters. In fact, sensory surround coupled with drama tugs the reader into your story and forces him to keep reading.

SHOW, DON'T TELL

This advice, so often heard, means involving the reader by concrete examples and dramatizing whenever possible. Instead of giving the reader the directions or outlines of an experience, place her in the midst of the experience with unfolding action. When the reader is given concrete information, she can draw her own conclusions and become involved. Showing requires that the writing be solid, not abstract, and this means that at least one of the senses must be involved to show a specific reality.

Here are the opening sentences from John Peyton Cooke's short story "After You've Gone," which not only convince the reader of a specific reality, but, because of the sensory details, pull her into the story, perhaps against her will:

> I loved it so much, I was cradling it in my hands, fondling its stock, bracing its chamber between my thumbs, staring into its barrel like you'd look into a lover's eyes, in search of some kind of truth. It stared back at me deeply and gave me the ultimate truth: *Yeah, you got it right, Grant. I'm your trusty Glock. You can count on me. I'm going to kill you.*
>
> I kissed its muzzle. My tongue tasted oil. ... It was all I could do to keep from turning my Glock on myself right then and there.

The lesson here is that by the time reader witnesses this character kissing a gun muzzle and tasting the oil, she needs to find out what is going on. Curiosity isn't aroused if you tell the reader something like "Harry was a troubled soul who was contemplating suicide." The word *suicide* always grabs anyone's attention, but a character kissing a gun captures the imagination. It makes the experience immediate and removes the distance between reader and character. Let's keep the *show, don't tell* dictum in mind as we look closer at how we can employ sensory surround.

INSTILL SENSORY SURROUND WITH THE FIVE SENSES

When you settle into a seat in a darkened movie theater, you feel the seat against your back and bottom, you smell popcorn and the flowery perfume of the woman seated in front of you, and your feet stick to spilled soda on the floor. Because we watch movies in the dark and because the movie screen is gigantic, our senses are heightened, and the setting alerts us that we're about to watch a drama unfold. When the movie begins, the sound piped in from the surround sound system, the enormous and captivating screen images, and the rustle and reactions of fellow movie goers all create a sensory surround that makes the drama riveting and enfolds you into the experience. When creating fiction, you want to mimic this experience, causing the reader to feel as if he is in the middle of the action, his senses activated, witnessing events and characters that are bigger than life.

Many writers scatter a sensory detail here or there when, instead, they need to use them throughout the story, especially during important scenes. Without sensory details and powerful description, a reader cannot settle into a story, because it is too spare. A lack of adequate sensory detail also creates confusion. Your story line is like a map that takes readers from beginning to end, but sensory information fills in the map so readers can follow the story's trajectory without getting lost at new roads or breathtaking vistas.

Now let's now examine each of the senses and how each can be used to engage your reader.

TOUCH

There is the touch of velvet, like the feel of a newborn's skin. A silk scarf draped around a neck. There is a lover's caress, light or insistent. The harsh bark of certain trees. Lemon juice in a fresh cut. Soft, thick grass under bare feet. Dried, parched grass during a drought. Oysters slipping down the throat. Touch is delicate, touch can scald. There is no world without touch, no life at all.

In *Word Painting*, author Rebecca McClanahan offers this explanation of its importance in our writing:

> Touch, by definition, is an intimate sense. It requires a body's immediate presence. The eye can see across long distances, the ear hear faraway noises, the nose detect aromas far removed from it. But in order to feel something or someone, we must be close. A well-written description that employs the sense of touch bridges physical and emotional distance.

Her explanation about touch's intimate appeal is extremely helpful to keep in mind. In real life, when someone wants to get your attention or create intimacy, touch works best—a pat on the back, a kiss, a hug, brushing hair out of another person's eye or tucking stray hair behind an ear, stroking, or tickling. Similarly, have weather, people, and things touch your characters, because when the character is touched, the reader feels it too.

In *Light on Snow,* author Anita Shreve weaves in an array of sensory details to capture the last weeks of December in New England. For example:

> My father brings a wave of cold air with him as he stomps the snow off his boots.

Shreve could have easily written "My father comes into the house and takes off his boots." Instead, she has him bring in the cold with him. Anyone who has ever lived in a cold climate knows how cold air clings to a person who has just been out in it. Just as cold penetrates, so does the sense of touch. Use it often in your stories.

TASTE

Many fiction writers avoid adding mundane details to their stories. Characters never sleep, walk their dogs, clean, or eat meals. Naturally, stories cannot be overwhelmed with ordinary activities, so they mostly depict extraordinary moments. However, mundane activities from our daily lives must also exist in fiction as lesser notes in the grand score of dramatic scenes. They are sprinkled throughout to lend credibility and, at times, to slow pacing or allow the reader to catch his breath after a harrowing event.

Mundane activities like eating and preparing food also create veracity. You've probably read stories where the characters never eat or care about food. The writer wasted an opportunity, because a character's eating habits are intimate and revealing. There's a huge difference in a character who is a vegan and one who eats a Big Mac and a double order of fries.

In the Harry Potter series, J.K. Rowling has cleverly turned the notions of an English boarding school upside down by inventing Hogwarts School of Witchcraft and Wizardry. The dorm rooms have four-poster beds, there are cozy fires, and the food is amazing—especially to Harry, who previously survived on scant portions. In *Harry Potter and the Sorcerer's Stone*, the menu for Harry's first dinner at Hogwarts is listed for impact:

> Harry's mouth fell open. The dishes in front of him were now piled with food. He had never seen so many things he liked to eat on one table: roast beef, roast chicken, pork chops and lamb chops, sausages, bacon and steak, boiled potatoes, roast potatoes, fries, Yorkshire pudding, peas, carrots, gravy, ketchup, and, for some strange reason, peppermint humbugs.

The menu reveals a lot about Hogwarts, and food can reveal a lot about your characters. And, as when our mouths pucker when we simply imagine a lemon, when a character eats, the reader participates in the meal also.

SOUND

In the real world, we're bombarded with sounds from the moment we awake (traffic noises, bird calls, or demands from children), until we settle into bed (shifting the blankets, thumping the pillow, and echoing the last sighs of the day). Sounds provide readers with satisfying proofs of a fictional reality.

Sounds can jangle or soothe. Sounds yank the reader into the now and focus the brain's attention, which is why dialogue is so compelling and necessary in a story. There are subtle sounds that can be used, such as birds twittering in the background, and potent sounds, like a gunshot ringing out.

Onomatopoeia—using words that sound like their meaning—is a potent device, although it's easy to overdo. But when onomatopoeic words explode onto the page, their swoosh and dazzle enter the reader's senses via a direct route.

When including sounds, mix ordinary and subtle sounds with those that are more unusual. This description from Tracy Chevalier's *Girl With a Pearl Earring* demonstrates how a voice can identify a person's class:

> I was chopping vegetables in the kitchen when I heard voices outside our front door—a woman's, bright as polished brass, and a man's low and dark like the wood of the table I was working on. They were the kind of voices we heard rarely in our house. I could hear rich carpets in their voices, books and pearls and fur.

Stephen King's novella *The Body* begins on the Friday preceding Labor Day weekend in the driest summer since 1907. But then the heat wave is broken by a storm that hits just as the boys find the body of Ray Brower. Listen to the sound of the storm in this passage, noting how it highlights the proofs of Ray Brower's death:

> Then the storm came back, viciously, all at once. Only this time it was hail instead of rain. Instead of whispering or talking, the woods now seemed alive with hokey B-movie jungle drums—it was the sound of big icy hailstones honking off treetrunks. Stinging pebbles began to hit my shoulders—it felt as if some sentient, malevolent force were throwing them. Worse than that, they began to strike Ray Brower's upturned face with an awful splatting sound that reminded us of him again, of his terrible and unending patience.

Fiction supplies readers with experiences that they will never have while living their ordinary lives. There is little likelihood that most of us will discover a boy's body, lying on the ground unprotected from the elements. Therefore, for readers to experience vicarious chills and thrills, embed all the senses into your writing.

SMELLS

Scents are vital to fiction, because our olfactory senses are wired directly to our memory and emotions. Often there is nothing so heady as a woman's perfume, so dreadful as the coppery smell of blood, so fresh as the sheets that have dried in the sun, or so expressive as the homey smells of a Thanksgiving feast. Just as every human has a distinct smell, so, too, should fictional characters. Writers should endeavor to use smells to describe characters as Sally Savic does in "God's Door":

177

I lean in for a better look. Harry smells of vermouth and damp earth.

Savic's example is particularly effective because the combined scents are unexpected and explode in the reader's imagination.

In *The Body,* King spends a lot of time describing Ray Brower's corpse, including the smells associated with it:

> Lightning forked blue across the sky, making the boy's single eye light up. You could almost believe he was glad to be found, and found by boys his own age. His torso had swelled up and there was a faint grassy odor about him, like the smell of old farts.

Smells are especially helpful when you report frightening or erotic events or specific emotions. As you go through life, collect smells from places, things, and people and file them away for use in your stories.

In your final editing process, notice how often you insert scents into the scenes. If you don't find them at regular intervals, slip them in before sending your manuscript to an editor. Smells are especially linked to emotions, so wield them regularly, but use great care so that a reader isn't bludgeoned by them.

SIGHT

Sight is the sense most commonly employed in fiction writing and while we go about our lives. There is so much to see, even when a person sits in the kitchen eating breakfast, that most people don't register the many visual details of the kitchen. We take sight for granted, or only notice the world closely when we're traveling.

Sight can transport a reader to a party, a funeral, a preschool, or an English moor in the 1800s. In every scene you write, you unfold a visual map of the place that explains if it is night or day, indoors or outdoors, filled with light or dim shadows.

In the opening of the third chapter of F. Scott Fitzgerald's *The Great Gatsby,* the reader is transported to the summer parties of the mysterious Gatsby. Although you can read these paragraphs to note Fitzgerald's use of color and visual details, he's also employing every sense:

> There was music from my neighbor's house through the summer nights. In his blue gardens men and girls came and went like moths among the whisperings and the champagne and the stars. At high tide in the afternoon I watched his guests diving from the tower of his raft, or taking the sun on the hot sand of his beach while his

two motor-boats slit the waters of the Sound, drawing aquaplanes over cataracts of foam. On weekends his Rolls-Royce became an omnibus, bearing parties to and from the city between nine in the morning and long past midnight, while his station wagon scampered like a brisk yellow bug to meet all trains. And on Mondays eight servants, including an extra gardener, toiled all day with mops and scrubbing-brushes and hammers and garden shears, repairing the ravages of the night before.

Every Friday five crates of oranges and lemons arrived from a fruiterer in New York—every Monday these same oranges and lemons left his back door in a pyramid of pulpless halves. There was a machine in the kitchen which could extract the juice of two hundred oranges in half an hour if a little button was pressed two hundred times by a butler's thumb.

At least once a fortnight a corps of caterers came down with several hundred feet of canvas and enough colored lights to make a Christmas tree of Gatsby's enormous garden. On buffet tables, garnished with glistening hors d'oeuvre, spiced baked hams crowded against salads of harlequin designs and pastry pigs and turkeys bewitched to a dark gold.

It's helpful when reading authors like Fitzgerald to notice how he makes simple sights extraordinary by using fresh and unusual word combinations, as when he pairs *salad* with *harlequin* and *pastry pigs* and *turkey* with *bewitched*. In your own writing, find places where you can elevate an ordinary description, but make certain the words used contain the proper connotation. This description heightens the mystery of Gatsby's character, introduces the opulence of these parties, and leads the reader by the hand through a typical evening on his bejeweled lawns. Thus *harlequin* and *bewitched* are appropriate when conveying wealth and exoticness, but would not work for a somber event.

Notice also how Fitzgerald and other masters use color. Color lends credibility to people, places, and objects in fiction, and also strikes a chord, connecting to the theme. A woman can be described as wearing a yellow dress, but if the color is called burnished gold, it can suggest wealth. An object can be crimson or blood red, the latter suggesting something frightening.

Details anchor the reader in a place, a moment, or a scene, and specificity deepens the reader's understanding of a scene. When specific senses are employed, the reader infers meaning, imagining that the character's grimace means that she hates her son-in-law or dislikes the taste of bourbon.

Specificity is also linked to purpose: Do you need the reader to linger? Will the detail push the story forward, or will it make the reader stop for some reason? The best details will underscore the emotions in a scene or paragraph.

Sensory information must appear as seamless and natural parts of the whole, but that is not easy. Create a natural effect with everyday details like ice in a glass or sweat on a person's upper lip. Look at the qualities of the object you're trying to describe.

If you believe that your own scenes and descriptions lack sensory information, use a highlighter pen and highlight each sense with a separate color—yellow for sight, pink for smells, green for sounds, etc. Try this on a few chapters where you suspect that the level of detail is too skimpy. What you should see on your pages is a rainbow of colors. If only one or two senses are represented, go back and start filling more in. You might also want to highlight the senses in a short story or a single chapter from one of your favorite authors, then compare your work.

CONVEYING MOOD AND TONE

Words should stir certain feelings in the reader, making him feel nostalgic, pensive, or terrified. Carefully chosen sensory information adds texture and heightens the impact of the scene. In a movie, the eerie strains of a cello signal a spooky moment; a crashing crescendo occurs when the killer appears with his gleaming, satanic grin; and low, lulling notes add to the sweetness of a love scene. As a writer, you must also create atmosphere and mood depending on the needs of the scene.

Elizabeth Berg's *True to Form* features Katie Nash during the summer of her thirteenth year. It is a summer filled with conflicts, family power struggles, and the intense emotions of adolescence. About midway in the novel, a brief chapter uses sensory surround as Katie wanders amid the season, which mirrors her emotions:

> It feels to me like summer has its feet planted far apart and its hands on its hips: I am here. Gardens are full of primary colors, grass sprouts from cracks in the sidewalk, bees fly heavy and low, like you could just reach down and grab one. You can smell the heat trapped in the concrete, that ironed pillowcase smell. Windows are open, and people seem open too—there is no hunching over from the cold, keeping your eyes on the sidewalk, concentrating on getting to where you're going so you can be warm and not freeze to death. When you pass by someone, you take

the time to nod a greeting or even stand and have a little conversation, the sun making a disc of warmth on the top of your head.

Curtains move in S-shaped dances from the breeze, or puff out dramatically, then fall straight and still, like they're denying they did anything. Kids with Kool-Aid mustaches run in and out of the house, banging the screen door and yelling to the mothers, and you can hear the faint voice of their mothers yelling back *not to bang the door,* how many times does she have to *tell* them to not *bang the door.* There is a different weight to the air. People sit on their porches after dinner, reading the paper or sitting idle, their hands behind their heads and their ankles crossed, waiting to see who passes by. There is a low happiness to them that they can't explain.

This scene also creates a setup for the scene that follows. During her walk, Katie stops in a field to write a poem.

I want to try a poem about a summer day. I want yellow and green in it; I want heat and drops of water and the slow flap of a new butterfly's wings.

Returning home and showing this poem to her stepmother marks a turning point in their relationship, but this moment would not have been possible without the intoxicating mood of summer woven into it.

Sensory surround prepares the reader for this moment, creates a mood, and makes the change in the character credible. Without techniques that magnify the story's theme, conflict, and mood, the story would feel flat.

REFLECTING AN ERA

When a novel or story begins, the reader needs to know if it is morning or evening, spring or fall, if the scene is happening indoors or outdoors. But she also wants to know if the story is set in 1860, 1990, or in the future. The era should permeate every aspect of a story, particularly influencing characters' values.

The Center of Everything by Laura Moriarty is a coming-of-age novel set during the 1980s in a small apartment outside of Kerrville, Kansas. The story explores unrequited love and the difficulty of finding compassion for the people we are closest to.

The story is peppered with clever proofs of the era. The novel begins when the protagonist, Evelyn, is ten:

> Ronald Reagan is on television, giving a speech because he wants to be president. He has the voice of a nice person, and something in his hair that makes it shiny under the lights. I change the channel, but it's still him, just from a different angle.

Thus the reader is plunked down into the Reagan era in America. If your story is set in an era different from our present one, keep a running list of all the ways that you are providing proofs of a distinct time, delivered through all the senses.

SENSORY DETAILS AND CHARACTERS

Let's discuss how sensory details shape characters, especially your main characters. There are so many problems in creating fiction that can bedevil a beginning writer, but one of the worst is failure to create realistic and fascinating characters. Sensory information creates characters who readers want to meet or possibly avoid, as in the case of your antagonist.

SHAPING MEMORABLE CHARACTERS

When a character shows up on a page, the reader needs to know what he looks like and his stance in the world, wither he's confident, mousy, bawdy, overwhelmed by grief, a practical joker, or a con artist. The list of character types is endless, but when your reader meets your characters, unless you're deliberately misleading your reader, she needs to understand the person's key traits via sensory data coupled with direct information.

First, characters must be introduced with flair. Even if your character is not dashing, a reader's first glimpse of him must somehow impress. At the very least, the reader needs to know if a character is young or old, male or female, attractive, ugly, or in-between. Whenever possible, characters—including minor and walk-on characters—are assigned at least one physical characteristic that will remain in the reader's memory.

You cannot rely on descriptions alone to create characters. You must employ your entire arsenal: possessions, appearance, dialogue, description, opinions of cast members, actions, choices, decisions, mannerisms, and gestures. Each of these character elements is made more effective by using sensory information.

Important characters are usually described when they're first introduced. It's not necessary to describe a character in the first sentence as she enters the scene, as in "Genevieve, a statuesque redhead, strode into the room, her blue eyes flashing." It's not that this approach doesn't work, it's that it lacks subtlety (see chapter fourteen for more on this topic), and you should vary your character's introductions when they show up on the page.

Avoid information dumps when you introduce characters, but introduce a character with substance and a presence that readers can experience through the senses. Here are three guidelines that will never fail you: (1) always link the information about the character to the plot and conflict, (2) use choice details, not exhaustive lists, and (3) instead of using a police blotter approach, use finely crafted language, including metaphors and comparisons.

Here's an example of a character introduction from Dennis Lehane's *Darkness, Take My Hand*:

> Diandra Warren lived in a fifth-story loft on Lewis Wharf. She had a panoramic view of the harbor, enormous bay windows that bathed the east end of the loft with soft morning sunlight, and she looked like the kind of woman who'd never wanted for a single thing her whole life.
>
> Hair the color of a peach hung in a graceful, sweeping curve over her forehead and tapered into a page boy on the sides. Her dark silk shirt and light blue jeans looked as if they'd never been worn, and the bones in her face seemed chiseled under skin so unblemished and golden it reminded me of water in a chalice.

The potency of this introduction begins with the character's name, Diandra Warren, which sounds wealthy. And although the description relies on visual cues, it is highly suggestive, describing the view and effect of the sunlight and Diandra's skin. Lehane's next paragraphs go on to describe her exquisite furnishings and accessories, depicting a woman who is privileged, tasteful, and formidable.

Lehane's example illustrates how to reflect a character's inner world and dominant traits. Notice in novels you read how characters are introduced with a few key traits, and are then fleshed out and consistently portrayed as the story continues.

If your character has thin, elegant, and expressive hands, you'll want to point them out more than once in the story. If a female character is known for her beauty or sexiness, then you can refer to her bosom, graceful legs, or porcelain skin at several places in the story. Of course you won't use the same phrases again and again, but gently remind the reader that the character is beautiful, perhaps by staging another character complimenting her.

SECONDARY CHARACTERS

Fiction that only describes main characters is similar to walking around in New York City and only noticing the businessmen wearing suits. This leaves out the doormen, cab drivers, homeless people, call girls, kids, and the teeming masses that make up New York.

But the trick lies here: Readers want to meet people they have never met before in the pages of your story. Your secondary characters should have at least one, but possibly two or three, physical characteristics or personality traits that intrigue the reader and help anchor them in your reader's mind. Think first impression or arresting characteristic, not résumé.

The same applies to minor or walk-on characters—the waiters, cab drivers, and delivery boys who are necessary to the story. We'll define minor or walk-on characters as those who don't speak or speak only one or two lines, such as "Can I take your order?" If a minor character exists for only a sentence or two, he doesn't necessarily require a description, but he still deserves a physical presence in the story. It rarely works to orchestrate a waitress appearing at your protagonist's table without including some sensory clues about this person. So, in the case of the waitress, you might briefly describe her as a tired-looking blonde, or mention that she's chewing gum when she talks, or limps away from the table as if on blistered feet. You see, it only takes a few words to make a minor character a physical presence in your story, so experiment with these small but vital inclusions.

Peter Robinson's *In a Dry Season* is part of his Alan Banks series. The book has three viewpoint characters and, like most mysteries, a large cast of walk-on characters, witnesses, suspects, and police officers. To prevent a mob scene, Robinson carefully delineates his characters, adds layers and qualities to his main characters as the story and the series progress, and makes certain that each minor character has at least one distinctive attribute that lands in the reader's brain. Robinson introduces Inspector Harmond, a secondary character, like this:

> Annie sat. Harmond's was a plain office, with only his merit awards on the wall for decoration, and framed photos of his wife and children on his desk. In his early fifties, he seemed perfectly content to be a rural inspector for the rest of his working life. His head was too large for his gangly frame, and Annie always worried it might fall off if he tilted it too far to one side. It never had; not yet. He had a pleasant round, open face. The features were a bit coarse, and a few black hairs grew out of the end of his misshapen potato nose, but it was the kind of face you could trust. If eyes really were the windows of the soul, then Inspector Harmond had a decent soul.

Notice how easily Robinson slipped in details of the inspector's office, how it bespeaks an uncomplicated, decent sort of person. Notice also how by the time Harmond's unfortunate nose is described, you want to meet the guy. Perhaps pop around to a pub for an ale, and chat with him about the folks in those family photos.

Notice, too, Robinson's technique of using setting details to characterize Harmond. A person's home or workplace is extremely revealing. The things a reader spots—or perhaps smells, if a detective is prone to eating Krispy Kremes or pizza at his desk—can whisper volumes about his mental health, habits, and efficiency. Perhaps there is a bottle of whiskey or some girlie magazines stashed in a lower desk drawer. Or maybe it's a place of sterile, orderly perfection. Pens aligned in spooky precision, not a paper out of place, not a speck of dust. Excessive neatness is always a curious, if not unfortunate, trait in any person. (We'll discuss this technique in greater detail later in the chapter.)

Robinson likewise lavishes care on minor characters who will only occupy a few pages or appear for a brief role. Here he introduces a witness, Mrs. Ketering, and uses her description to tug at the reader's sympathies:

> Mrs. Ketering was wearing a red baseball cap, a loose yellow smock and baggy white shorts down to her knees. Below them, her legs were pale as lard, mottled

185

red and marbled with varicose veins. On her feet she wore a pair of black pimsolls without laces. Though a little stooped, she looked sturdy enough for her age.

Writers often hate to describe secondary or walk-on characters, but consider this: If your minor characters are mere cardboard cutouts, the story does not lift off the page and the characters all start to sort of meld in the reader's mind, creating confusion. Secondary characters need to be distinctive, and they provide an opportunity to introduce eccentrics, oddballs, humor, and pathos.

PHYSICALITY AND A CHARACTER'S INNER WORLD

It is especially important for a reader to feel the physicality of a character, which includes bodily sensations, pain, and emotions. Because a character's inner world always reflects some sort of suffering, you have many options for depicting your characters' torments.

Capturing a character's physicality and inner world requires fresh language, inventive metaphors, and engaging sensory detail. In the short story "Wolf Winter," by Maxine O'Callaghan, protagonist Allie Reems is suffering from chronic migraine headaches in the 1880s before migraine remedies existed. These migraines are so severe that she plunges into madness and ultimately commits murder. Cleverly, O'Callaghan places a wolf in the story as the main device, paralleling the wolf's primal instincts with Allie's pain and desperation.

Throughout the story, the descriptions of the migraines, told via all the senses, convince the reader of their torments. In an early scene, for example, the pioneer family visits a town, and sensory details reveal how seemingly benign objects can trigger a migraine:

> But the light that day seemed abnormally bright, reflecting off all the windows and the shiny tin washtubs that hung outside the general store, and her head rang with the clatter of wagon wheels, the cries of children and the terrible, crashing gong of the blacksmith's mallet striking iron.
>
> She needed no urging from Cyrus to visit the doctor. There, the closed warmth of the tiny office and the smell of iodine and camphor intensified the pain so that by the time she had to suffer his questions and his touch, his face swam in spangled light and her head pulsed with agony.

As the story progresses, everything in Allie's environment becomes a source of agony. The author describes Allie's husband's nightly snoring as a "drill boring deep into Allie's skull," and we learn that:

Mostly she would hear the pain that gnawed inside her brain, eating away at the pulpy pink lobes.

In "Wolf Winter," descriptions of Allie's headache are depicted through all the senses, and the author uses an array of potent nouns and verbs to describe the migraines: *gnawing, boring, gleaming blade, sunlight raying, cleaving, stoking.* These all add up to unimaginable pain. Another principle that can be learned from "Wolf Winter" is that a writer should depict suffering for a reason—it pushes the character to some kind of action, often fueled by desperation or fear.

CHARACTERS AND EMOTIONS

Writers artfully choose details that imply characters' emotions and moods. For example, Daniel Lyons's short story "The First Snow" is an explosive drama about how a father's homosexual activities tear his family apart. Told from the viewpoint of the teenage son, the story is about betrayal and the rage and grief that accompany it. The details of the story underscore these emotions.

As the reality of the dissolution of his family begins to dawn on Henry, the oldest son, the reader is given a dark description of the father:

He sits at the kitchen table. He looks like a guy in a Vietnam movie mumbling about all his dead friends, too shell-shocked to think straight.

There is a temptation when describing characters to focus on physical details like hair color, but such descriptions of major characters are empty without emotions to support them. Look for places where you can depict both a character's physicality and emotions at the same time.

One trick to rendering emotions with authenticity is to make sure that your details are in sync with the story world and with the voice of the narrator or viewpoint character. When sensory surround is wrapped in the character's particular vision, it adds to the impact. For example, in Amy Bloom's short story "Silver Water," the narrator's older sister, Rose, is a schizophrenic. When Rose is fifteen, her mother realizes that she is clearly no longer herself. Her father, a psychiatrist, is called in to evaluate Rose, who sits there "licking the hairs on her forearm, first one way, then the other."

You, too, can follow Bloom's example of using a highly unusual behavior to convey emotion, even if your story does not contain a mentally ill character. Any character who exhibits bizarre or uncharacteristic emotions or actions will grab the reader's attention, but the character must be well drawn. A teenager who cuts her own skin is sending out her own stress signal with this coping mechanism. Perhaps a character thrusts his fist through glass, or tosses a television set out the window, or performs some action that the reader will never forget. Unusual actions are not the same as melodrama. They are used expressly to convey that something has shifted within the character and that he is likely heading toward trouble.

As in Lyons's "The First Snow," there is inherent power and credibility when a child describes a parent's emotions, state of mind, or essential nature. However, you don't need a parent-child relationship to make this work. The credibility is expressed through the level of knowledge and intimacy one character holds for another. If your characters don't possess this ability to observe and extrapolate meaning, then your story might feel distant and indistinct to your readers.

Novels With Great Description

The Confessions of Nat Turner, William Styron

All the King's Men, Robert Penn Warren

Their Eyes Were Watching God, Zora Neale Hurston

The Call of the Wild, Jack London

The Prince of Tides, Pat Conroy

Wuthering Heights, Emily Brontë

Moby Dick, Herman Melville

Heart of Darkness, Joseph Conrad

Doctor Zhivago, Boris Pasternak

Ethan Frome, *The House of Mirth*, Edith Wharton

A Thousand Acres, Jane Smiley

The Name of the Rose, Umberto Eco

Sensory Details and Poignant Pauses

Using sensory aspects is also a helpful technique when you need to pause the story for a moment of significance. Fiction moves along at a varying pace as it unfolds toward the climax. (For more information, see chapter nine.) There are times where you want the reader to pause to notice that the story has slowed for a momentous development, a turning point, a shift in the protagonist's character arc, or an epiphany or moment of realization. At places where you want the reader to pay special attention, sensory details are the tools that work.

In Robert B. Parker's *Stone Cold*, the protagonist, Jesse Stone, is the chief of police in Paradise, Massachusetts. Stone's backstory is a bit tangled. He was once a married cop in Los Angeles, but he became a bottomed-out drunk with self-destructive tendencies. Trying to salvage what was left of his life and career, he moved east to start over. Then a random series of murders sets him on the trail of a male-female team that uses the thrill of murder as sexual foreplay.

After Stone's ex-lover is murdered, he realizes that the tables have been turned and the hunter has become the hunted. This is a turning point in the story, and Parker, who usually crafts novels with minimal description, stages the turning point by showing Stone walking alone along the ocean shore. Parker uses sensory information to pause the scene for significance. (The key sensory phrases have been italicized.)

> The day was not windy, and the ocean's movement was gently rounded, with only an occasional crest of the waves. *There was something about oceans.* The day he left LA he went to Santa Monica and looked at the Pacific. *Despite their perpetual movement there was a stillness about oceans. Despite the sound of the waves, there was great silence. The empty beach and limitless ocean hinted at the vast secret of things.*

Stone mulls over the case, visits his regrets over the woman who was recently killed, and contemplates his own vulnerability to the serial killers. The line "There was something about oceans" is especially poignant because it equates oceans with stillness, an unusual observation. Without spelling out his decisions, Stone quits drinking after the walk. This is a dramatic change in his character arc, and clear-headed now, he tracks down the killers.

Find a dramatic moment, such as a major change in the protagonist's character arc, in your own work, and underline the moment with sensory details. The details don't need to be directly about the character or the change. Your story might feature a memory impregnated with sensory data; perhaps the character will observe a scenario or art that can be described with sensory details. These objects or scenarios are the vehicles or devices that make the pause more significant.

SENSORY DETAILS AND CRUCIAL SCENES

The more intimate and important the scene, the more carefully you must choose your words. Sometimes a scene will require broad strokes, such as when your character walks into a courtroom. Since many of us are familiar with courtrooms from real life or from watching films and television, create an outline that captures the reality, then focus on a few details that make it specific to your story. Perhaps it's 1930 and the jury is mostly farmers and shopkeepers. You might want to depict the farmers' rugged faces and bib overalls, or the slight scent of manure that clings to them.

Then there are times where the reader wants to walk into a character's bedroom and be part of a private or intimate moment. These moments require nuance and a deeper level of detail. Notice the fine brush strokes Barbara Kingsolver uses in this passage from *Prodigal Summer*. It is the morning after Deanna, one of the viewpoint characters, has made love with a younger man. Kingsolver lavishes description here because the lovemaking is an awakening for Deanna, and part of her character arc:

> Her own nakedness startled her even; she normally slept in several layers. Awake in the early light with the wood thrushes, feeling the texture of the cool sheet against her skin, she felt as jarred and disjunct as a butterfly molted extravagantly from a dun-colored larva and with no clue where to fly. …
>
> His presence filled her tiny cabin, so she felt distracted trying to cook breakfast. Slamming cupboards, looking for things in the wrong places, she wasn't used to company here. She had only a single ladderback chair, plus the old bedraggled armchair out on the porch with holes in its arms from which phoebes pulled white shreds of stuffing to line their nests. That was all. She pulled the ladderback chair away from the table, set its tall back against the logs of the opposite wall, and asked him to sit, just to get a little space around her as she stood at the propane stove scrambling powdered eggs and boiling water for the grits. Off to his right stood her iron-framed cot with its wildly disheveled mattress, the night table piled with her books and field journals, and the kerosene lantern they'd nearly knocked over last night in some mad haste to burn themselves down.

Notice how this segment ends with the suggestion of fire, connoting passion. Notice, too, how the reader is privy to a detailed "morning after" scene, something not used much by writers, which in this case reveals the enormity of their act.

Writer Anton Chekhov once advised writers to "seize upon the little particulars, grouping them in such a way that, in reading, when you shut your eyes, you get a picture." Kingsolver's morning-after scene is filled with particulars, such as when Deanna looks into the wrong cupboards for breakfast supplies. These sorts of details convey how she is flustered and off center from the sexual encounter.

Her single ladderback chair is also revealing: It speaks volumes about her solitary life and causes the reader to wonder what is going to happen now that her lonely existence has been so dramatically changed. Will she make room in her life for her lover?

In your own stories, look for places where the place and mood can permeate and render a compelling world.

NATURE, WEATHER, AND THE OUTDOORS

Put weather in it is a mantra worth repeating because it's a simple but important means of creating proofs of the fictional world. The real world is framed by weather day after day. We experience weather in all its seasons through all our senses. It's layered into our memories and it influences each day, but often in fiction it's added as an afterthought or, worse yet, left out of stories.

In stories, weather can influence events, create mood, cause catastrophes, conceal evidence in a crime, or free children from school for a snow day. It's especially helpful for creating texture and mood. Weather can transform a scene so that it becomes an experience that can be seen, heard, felt, tasted, and smelled.

In *The Body*, which was discussed earlier in this chapter, Stephen King uses all the senses to underscore the tragedy of a young boy's death. But weather plays a central role as well.

King lavishes sensory description on the body, but the horror and drama of the discovery reverberates when King adds a storm to the scenes. The storm, especially powerful because it comes after a long, dry summer, sets the stage for the climax, shows time passing, and drives the character's emotions to a shrill crescendo. Here is the buildup of weather that begins just as the main characters spot Ray Brower's hand:

> The breeze was now a wind—harsh and jerky, coming at us from no particular direction, jumping and whirling, slapping at our sweaty skins and open pores.

King spends the rest of the paragraph describing the boy's hand, which is exposed, white, and looks like the hand of drowned boy. Then he intersperses more weather to heighten the intensity of the discovery:

> Lightning flickered and stroked. Thunder ripped in behind each stroke as if a drag race had started over our heads.

After this brief weather report, King returns to the action, while depicting how the weather affects the characters.

Sometimes writers add weather to scenes, but then don't portray the affect on the characters. For instance, a blizzard rages in a story, but then characters don't shovel the sidewalk, slip on ice, or become chilled when outdoors. The furnace never fails and the pipes never freeze. Or, it rains in a scene, but no one becomes drenched, jumps around puddles, or turns on the windshield wipers.

King knows better, and when he uses weather in a scene, we notice how his characters are affected by it, as when wind whips Teddy's greasy, long hair away from his damaged ears. Then, King slips even more force and spookiness into the scene via the weather:

> A great whispering noise began to rise in the woods on either side of the tracks, as if the forest had just noticed we were there and was commenting on it. The rain had started.
>
> Dime-sized drops fell on my head and arms. They struck the embankment, turning the fill dark for a moment—and then the color changed back again as the greedy dry ground sucked the moisture up.
>
> Those big drops fell for maybe five seconds and then they stopped. I looked at Chris and he blinked back at me.
>
> Then the storm came all at once, as if a shower chain had been pulled in the sky. The whispering sound changed to loud contention. It was as if we were being rebuked for our discovery, and it was frightening.

When the narrator suggests that it felt like the weather was rebuking them for their discovery, it reminds the reader of the power inherent in severe weather, such as when thunderstorms, hurricanes, and tornadoes crash through.

The Body is a good example of the effective weaving of action, sensory details, and the narrator's inner thoughts and realizations. This sort of orchestration makes the overall impact of the scene more powerful.

The weather at this point has provided the soundtrack and heightened the emotions in the scene, but King also uses it to obscure the looming danger of a rival gang sneaking into the area:

> The roaring downpour and the accompanying thunder had completely covered the sound of cars approaching along the Back Harlow Road, which lay bare yards beyond this boggy tangle. It likewise covered the crackle-crunch of the underbrush as they blundered through it from the dead end where they had parked.

In the final moments of the scene, a fierce hailstorm adds to the drama and again interacts with events:

> His eyes had filled up with round white hailstones. Now they were melting and the water ran down his cheeks as if he were weeping for his own grotesque position— a tatty prize to be fought over by two bunches of stupid hick kids. His clothes were also white with hail. He seemed to be lying in his own shroud.

Obviously King is pulling out all the stops here. A scene that contains a dead body and the intense conflict between two gangs warrants this approach. Use your weather for your most dramatic scenes, as a backdrop for quieter scenes, and to instill a sensory surround in your fiction world.

{ * }

Since evocative description begins with the writer, you cannot insert compelling details into your stories or prose unless you're a person who notices these details in your own life. Train yourself to observe without judgment. Go through your days with a keen awareness, noticing the complexity and nuances of the world around you. Develop a poet's eye for detail—noticing objects, shifting cloud patterns, and how the quality of light and bird song changes throughout the day. Ask questions, and watch people wherever you go. Notice personality traits, quirky behaviors, gestures, and body movements. Remember or record conversations, jokes, and quips. Make notes on memorable meals, as well as on concerts and performances that move you. Then stir these sensory details into your stories.

chapter **13**
Subplots

{ *A novel is not only longer than a short story, it's wider.*
—Donna Levin

ubplots are miniature stories woven into the main story, complete and intriguing in their own right, serving to contrast, reinforce, or divert attention from the main plot. These mini-plots contain beginnings, middles, and ends, and support the protagonist's emotional growth, further the dramatic action, and reflect or echo the significance of theme and premise.

Subplots can be centered around main characters in actions that fall outside of the main story line, or they can be centered around secondary characters. Sometimes a combination of both is used. These stories within stories can run the entire length of the plot and be resolved near or in the climax, or they can have a short run and end long before the climax.

They can also serve as magnifying glasses, underlining the actions of the main plot or providing relief from it when, for example, a story has violence, tragedy, or other elements that can seem relentless. Generally speaking, short stories do not contain subplots, while novels can have one to four or more weaving through the main plot. Novels without subplots are thin and read more like a long short story than an evocative and poignant involvement in characters' lives.

In the graph on the next page, notice how subplots are triggered by inciting incidents just as the main story line is, and how subplots overlap with the central plot.

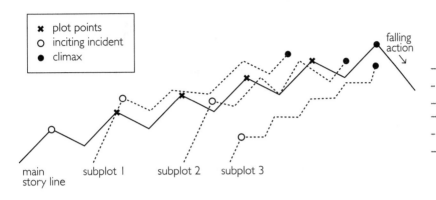

REASONS FOR USING SUBPLOTS

Subplots are often so intricately embedded into the main events that you don't even notice they're there. But if you dissect some of your favorite novels, you'll likely discover how the subplots expanded the scope, provided extra highs and lows, and created verisimilitude. In the best stories, the characters appear rich, the action is weighted with thematic significance, and the whole is sprinkled with magic. Subplots, which are based on issues, concerns, or characters' agendas, can add to all these elements by:

- proving that your protagonist's life and the story world are complicated and teeming
- weaving in the stories of two or three secondary characters into the protagonist's situation, thus revealing sides of the protagonist that cannot always be shown in the main action
- taking the pressure off the main story line so that it does not become relentless, gloomy, or exhausting
- introducing comic relief and hilarity (when appropriate to the story)
- adding tangles to the story by introducing complications, problems, and more decisions and choices to be made
- revealing the growth and change in the protagonist
- fleshing out the story and building the fictional world between plot points
- providing social and political context
- enhancing theme and proving the premise
- adding to tension or suspense
- keeping the main plot from being resolved too soon, by sidetracking the protagonist or events from time to time

- revealing characters' opinions on things happening in the world—values and philosophies not connected to the main plot
- driving the story forward with questions that need answering and events and consequences that need resolution

THE SUBPLOT LITMUS TEST

Because readers want to believe in your fictional world and the situations that exist there, subplots serve a vital role. The events, diversions, and brief interludes found in subplots make fiction feel true to life, and keep a plot from being too predictable. Here is a litmus test of sorts to help you decide if a given subplot is necessary to your story: If a subplot can be removed without creating a hole in the story, it is not needed.

Writers often discover that subplots evolve as they develop the story, as if the characters are whispering suggestions. If your subplot evolves naturally from the main story and is not gratuitous or an afterthought, it will be more believable.

Subplots can revolve around everyday actions like shopping trips, phone calls, intimate moments, and displays of friendship. For example, Robert B. Parker's Spenser series features a large, gruff, and macho detective with an equally masculine sidekick, Hawk. The men work out together and hang out at elegant bars and restaurants, where they drink-top shelf champagne or imported beers. Spenser is a gourmet cook and has a lover, Susan, who is an elegant psychiatrist, while Hawk dates equally educated and fabulous women. These activities and relationships prevent them from becoming stereotypes and provide respite, moments to discuss the case, and opportunities to interject humor.

CREATING COMPLICATIONS

While conflict drives fiction, complications are necessary to entangle the character in ever-more-vexing dilemmas, difficulties, and situations. Complications are actions that enter the story world and change the course of the story. The most notable complication is the one associated with the inciting incident, the first change that opens the story, sets it into motion, and causes imbalance. As your story moves along, things keep getting worse for your protagonist, and often these worsening situations are created by complication-based subplots.

The best complications are unexpected but realistic, and somehow expand the story. They can be positive or negative; can thwart either the protagonist or antagonist; can stem from other characters, events, or discoveries; and can be based on anything from mistakes and misunderstandings to bad weather and physical threats.

Negative complications create problems for the protagonist and supporting characters, and make solving the main conflict more difficult, by providing new obstacles that must be overcome along the way. Complications create a dizzying effect and add nail-biting moments to fiction.

If you've ever watched a daytime soap opera, you've noticed that there is no one single plot line. Instead, there many interconnections, complications, and linking story lines. In television dramas that feature an ensemble cast, such as *The West Wing, ER,* or *The Sopranos,* the story lines are so interwoven with subplots that it is sometimes difficult to separate out the main story. In these dramas, the characters also deal with issues with family members, personal health problems, romances that bloom and die, troubled children, competition, or strife among coworkers. That list is only a beginning—the subplot possibilities for a large cast are endless.

If you watch television dramas, you might want to spend a week or so keeping track of subplots in your favorite shows. Then number and name the subplots, and notice which ones last for an entire season or throughout the series. This small exercise proves the importance of secondary actions in making the whole complicated and captivating.

ENLARGING THE STORY WORLD

Authors most often use subplots to enlarge the world of the story. Without subplots, a novel reminds us of the South Pole, where only penguins are able to survive—a vast, white, harsh environment with only a single species to focus on. You need other creatures—especially predators—for conflict, interest, and variety.

In chapter six, we looked at Elinor Lipman's *Isabel's Bed* for its structure and use of flashbacks to convey backstory, but the book also includes a number of subplots that enhance the scope of the story world. The main story centers on Harriet, who moves to Cape Cod to ghostwrite Isabel's scandalous life story. One of the subplots traces Harriet's and Isabel's attempts to find and understand true love. Another subplot is about women's friendships and how beautiful women relate to other women. Yet another hilarious subplot focuses on writing groups, casting a satiric eye on these sometimes dysfunctional gatherings of scribes.

Jane Smiley's *Good Faith* is about the real estate industry during the Reagan administration. The main story line follows the rise and fall of the fortunes of forty-year-old Joe Stratford, who's divorced and lives alone.

The main plot follows the classic "stranger comes to town" scenario. The stranger is Marcus Burns, a former IRS agent who now works as an investment counselor and who pulls Joe into a business deal. A number of subplots reflect the era and paint a picture of the real estate industry and other interests that intersect with it. One subplot reflects the implosion of the unregulated savings and loan industry, while another looks at the dangers of day trading and gold speculating. Smiley's forte is transforming her research into readable drama; her subplots, even if they teach how golf courses are built and land development works, never feel like instruction, but like part of a large, entertaining world.

ENTWINING LIVES

Some novels are written with an ensemble cast, and in these stories there is a single connecting thread—a family, a place, an event, a company, a war—that holds together a complicated series of ongoing subplots running alongside the main story line. Best-selling Irish author Maeve Binchy has made this sort of novel her staple. Her novels are especially noted for well-rounded secondary characters, complexity, cleverly entwined subplots, and characters that combine to create a fully realized world. One such novel is *Scarlet Feather*, which follows one year in a start-up catering business in Dublin.

The main story centers around the business, starting on New Year's Eve when partners Tom Feather and Cathy Scarlet discover a location for their operation and buy the building. The business gets off to a roaring start, but that doesn't last, and their personal lives also begin to fall apart. Written in an omniscient viewpoint, with each chapter a single month, events in the catering business serve as the main thread and include a fairy-tale wedding, party disasters, a robbery, slow-paying customers, and cooking on a live television show. These events move forward, intricately woven among subplots that simmer along with the gourmet meals. These subplots include:

- Cathy's husband, Neil, is a workaholic lawyer who doesn't really support her.
- Neil's interfering mother doesn't think Cathy's good enough for him.
- Cathy's mother was once Neil's mother's maid.
- Tom's relationship with the beautiful Marcella is floundering.
- Muttie Scarlet, Cathy's father, has good and bad luck betting on the horses.
- Marcella longs to be a model, but she's too old for high fashion.
- Tom's father ends up in the hospital with a heart attack.
- Cathy becomes pregnant and then suffers a miscarriage.
- Neil's cousins, eight-year-old twins who continually wreck havoc, disappear.

Binchy pulls off complicated story structure by using many half scenes, flipping from place to place and character to character with few explanations and transitions, relying heavily on dialogue, using minimal setting details, and keeping most fully realized scenes short. Because the viewpoint is omniscient, she slips into many of the characters' thoughts while zigzagging among dozens of characters' lives.

This sort of novel would be difficult for most beginning writers to attempt, but still can be instructive to examine, especially if you yearn to write in depth about a huge cast of characters. Notice Binchy's scene cuts and how quickly she moves in and out of scenes. Also note that her dialogue contains a liberal dose of subtext, every character has an agenda, her protagonists are sympathetically drawn, and she knows enough about the food business to make the main story line convincing.

SUBPLOTS IN ACTION

Almost any issue, concern, or agenda can become a subplot, and some—like historical events such as major wars—are used to set your plot in a larger reality. Here is a list of commonly occurring subplots, but it is by no means exhaustive. Many of these works have more than one subplot, and, of course, this list could soar into the hundreds.

- Academia: *Lucky Jim*, Kingsley Amis; *The Prime of Miss Jean Brodie*, Muriel Spark
- Addiction: *Infinite Jest*, David Foster Wallace; *Under the Volcano*, Malcolm Lowry
- Backstory/Character Histories: *Sophie's Choice*, William Styron
- Domestic Abuse: *The Color Purple*, Alice Walker; *Them*, Joyce Carol Oates

199

- Family Relationships: *Little Women*, Louisa May Alcott; *Sons and Lovers*, D.H. Lawrence; *The House of Mirth*, Edith Wharton
- Historical Significance/Consequences of War: *Stones From the River*, Ursula Hegi; *Sophie's Choice*, William Styron; *The Game* and *O Jerusalem*, Laurie R. King
- Hobbies/Sports: *The Natural*, Bernard Malamud
- Job/Career/Coworkers: *Glengarry Glen Ross*, David Mamet (play); Janet Evanovich's Stephanie Plum series; Peter Robinson's Alan Banks series
- Mental Illness: *One Flew Over the Cuckoo's Nest*, Ken Kesey
- Nature/Environment: *The Call of the Wild*, Jack London; *Robinson Crusoe*, Daniel Defoe; *Out of Africa*, Isak Dinesen
- Politics: *The Handmaid's Tale*, Margaret Atwood
- Racial Heritage/Culture: *The Woman Warrior* and *China Men*, Maxine Hong Kingston; *The Joy Luck Club*, Amy Tan
- Racial Relations/Politics: *A Passage to India*, E.M. Forster; *Beloved*, Toni Morrison; *The Color Purple*, Alice Walker
- Romance: *Cold Mountain*, Charles Frazier; *Doctor Zhivago*, Boris Pasternak
- Sexual Abuse: *Me & Emma*, Elizabeth Flock
- Small-Town Life: *The Adventures of Tom Sawyer*, Mark Twain; *To Kill a Mockingbird*, Harper Lee
- Spirituality/Religious Practices: *The Secret Life of Bees* and *The Mermaid Chair*, Sue Monk Kidd
- Social Conventions: *A Room With a View*, E.M. Forster
- Social Mores and Values: *To Kill a Mockingbird*, Harper Lee; *The Time Machine*, H.G. Wells; *Kim*, Rudyard Kipling

CREATING SUBPLOTS THAT MATTER

Subplots are not tossed into a story willy-nilly as if you're sowing grass seed. Some might appear in your imagination along with the main story line, while others will develop as you get to know your characters.

To help yourself imagine the intertwining events, people, and relationships, draw a diagram of your story line and the intertwined subplots. While there are many options for creating this diagram, and you might want to create more than one diagram, here's a fairly simple way to begin: Write your protagonist's name in bold letters in the center of a piece of paper. From this name, create a web or wheel with spokes, connecting your protagonist to everyone else in the story. Begin by placing your antagonist on the page, then add secondary characters and sketch a line to connect them to the protagonist. Be sure to connect each relationship in the story by calling out significant subplots and conflicts.

In addition to or instead of creating a web, you can write a brief outline that summarizes a subplot. For example, suppose your main story line surrounds Jennifer's search for her sister, Brenda, who disappeared from her college dorm. Meanwhile, a romance subplot is woven in to complicate matters. Your subplot outline can be fairly simple, such as:

A few weeks after Brenda disappears, Sam and Jennifer meet at a party and discover they both have a passion for microbrews and mah-jongg. The two start spending time together, but then Sam has a family emergency and travels to Pennsylvania without contacting Jennifer before he leaves. While he's away, Jennifer, feeling rejected, confused, and angry, starts dating her old boyfriend, Justin, who promises to help her with her search. Justin begins pressing her to marry him. As strange clues about Jennifer's sister's whereabouts pile up, Sam returns; he and Jennifer argue about the state of their relationship and decide to call it quits.

Sam and Jennifer meet three months later at a mah-jongg tournament, where they are teamed together and beat all their rivals. Jennifer is wearing an engagement ring, so their banter is forced. Later, during a celebration, Sam observes Jennifer with Justin and can tell that he's not right for her. In a bold move, Sam tells her this.

In the main story line, Jennifer discovers that her sister was murdered and, realizing that life is fragile and remembering how her sister always took risks, she breaks off her engagement and resumes a relationship with Sam.

If your subplots are based on your protagonist, begin the most important one in the early chapters after you have the main story line launched. If you have a subplot that involves a secondary character, it's often best to delay starting it until the reader is familiar with the main characters and the milieu of the story, and understands the story question. The main story line must be established with a firm foundation before these subplots take off, so that the reader isn't confused.

When constructing your plot, envision the plot and subplot more as a web or maze than as parallel lines like a railroad track. The best plots zigzag back and forth between main story and subplot. You don't write the main plot, then stop it to write the subplot, then drop out of that sequence to return to the main plot. Instead, the subplots *intersect* with the main story line, and vice versa.

Subplots are most easily devised from the characters nearest the protagonist. Thus, when you look for subplots, you don't need to look far. In Janet Evanovich's Stephanie Plum series, Stephanie's on-again, off-again romance with Joe Morelli and her dangerous attraction to Ranger provide the main subplot. But the protagonist's wacky family also provides subplots and comic relief.

Here's a tip on using people close to your protagonist: The closer the emotional ties between the subplot character and your protagonist, the greater depth your story will have.

SUBPLOT MISSTEPS TO AVOID

Finding a balance between your main story line and your subplots requires balance. You might face tough choices and decisions about what to include and what to leave out. Here are a few warnings about incorporating subplots.

- **Don't dangle subplots like loose threads.** If there is more than one subplot, it works best not to resolve them all at the same time or in the climax. Tying up too many loose endings in the climax tends to be messy and steals the focus from the main ending.

- **Don't follow a subplot with the same focus and word count that you devote to the main story.** Pay attention to proportion when devising subplots. Generally, subplots will never take up more scenes than main plots.

- **Never toss a subplot into a story to take up space or add to the word count.** They should always be specific to the story and highlight some aspect of character, story line, theme, or premise.

- **Don't forget to provide your subplots with rising and falling action.** Subplots are based on actions and events that cause your characters to shape new behaviors, actions, emotions, or thoughts. As in the main story line, the most significant events are those which result in a character's emotional change.

- **Don't let your subplots weaken the main story line.** In novels, when you use multiple viewpoints or alternating time frames, the story will split off and widen into separate segments. The same problem can happen with subplots— they can send the story skittering off on a tangent, and that tangent, unless well crafted, can be distracting or seem extraneous.

{ * }

Subplots are a powerful tool for plotting, but require forethought and planning. Since a single plot line cannot carry enough interest in a novel, you have exciting choices to make when you devise your crowded, fascinating world. Choose wisely with your theme and premise in mind, and, when possible, merge your subplots in with your protagonist's main actions.

chapter 14

Subtlety

{

If you would be pungent, be brief; for it is as with words as with sunbeams. The more they are condensed, the deeper they burn.

—Robert Southey

n old writing maxim that resonates with common sense is *Less is more.* Subtlety is needed on all levels: in diction, style, voice, and grammar, as well as in plot and characterization. A lack of subtlety leads to redundancy and overstatement, too-obvious characters, overblown dialogue, scenes that carry on or explode instead of delivering dramatic moments, and plots and subplots that take off like runaway trains.

Subtlety is difficult to explain, but when it is present in fiction the writing whispers and contains a poignancy that lingers far longer than obvious ploys such as shouting, pratfalls, curses, and winks. Since readers are not usually looking for subtlety, an author's subtler techniques can go unnoticed.

TWO APPROACHES: OVER AND UNDER

Writers tend to fall into two broad camps: those who overwrite and those who underwrite. And, while a novelist may be able to get away with writing a *spare* story, a *thin* story will never ignite the reader's imagination. A spare story is one in which the writer deliberately chooses to pare down every element, using a small cast of characters, only one or two subplots, and little exposition and description.

A well-crafted, yet spare story can work when every word counts and there is enough information to take the reader on a fictional journey. Ernest Hemingway usually wrote spare stories, but readers still feel immersed in his stories and understand the ramifications of the plot on the lives of the characters.

A thin story, on the other hand, is not based on deliberate choices, but rather on inexperience. In a thin story, the writer does not supply enough sensory data, creating a story line that can't be followed with confidence because of a lack of needed information. Spare stories spark the reader's imagination, but thin stories do not have enough data to do so, leaving the reader confused. In these anemic offerings, the reader is often adrift, longing for a setting detail to place him in the scene, a hint about the themes or deeper meanings, or any doorway into the writer's intentions.

The opposite problem occurs when a novel is overwritten, because if it is crowded with too many descriptions, characters, subplots, and themes, the story line becomes choked and muddled. The overachievers smother their sentences under purple prose and convoluted clauses.

Overwritten stories stop for many a scenic detour, and the characters are often breathing heavily with hearts pounding, exclaiming angst, heartbreak, and worry. Descriptions of windowsills, sunsets, cowboy hats, and barren landscapes go on and on, but don't quite add up to resonance, mood, or meaning.

Not only does an overwritten story never soar, it leaves the reader weary. This is where the real danger lies, because exaggerated characters, a convoluted plot, and too much dull detail can blunt the reader's senses, just as too much chocolate can ruin your appetite. Overwriting is most common in beginning writers. Nervous and unsure of their skills, they often keep piling on details and subplots, certain that this equals storytelling. Or, beginning writers sometimes believe that it's the *reader's* job to discern the story buried under the excess. This is not the case. Your job as a writer is to cause fiction to lift off the page and into the reader.

TRUST YOUR READER

It can take years to hone your discernment, to be able to judge your work and know when you're being subtle or when your writing is over the top. Excess and gimmickry stem from inexperience and a distrust of the reader. Each reader brings her own frame of reference and understanding of human behavior to your pages. If you leave out minor details or don't describe every sunrise or searing kiss, the reader can fill in the gaps with her imagination. This does not mean that the reader is doing your job for you. Instead, she is an active participant in your story, knowing what your character knows and feeling what he feels.

Contemporary readers, accustomed to the sights and sounds of a multi-media world, come to your story with a vast storehouse of images, memories, and information. Your job is to remind them of what is in their storehouse, not to serve as a nonstop tour guide who points out the highlights as well as every stop sign and crack in the sidewalk. The exceptions to this guideline are historical novels, fantasy, and science fiction, where your job is to build an intricate story world so that the reader not only imagines it, but also understands its history, laws, and culture.

This advice may seem confusing when you note the success of authors who are often not subtle, particularly literary writers such as Charles Dickens, Herman Melville, John Updike, Joyce Carol Oates, and the like. Their plots wander and tangle, and pages are drenched in imagery, metaphor, and symbolism. Also, genre authors such as mystery writers P.D. James, Elizabeth George, and Laurie R. King write sprawling tales featuring large casts and descriptions that ramble on for pages. But these authors, while laudable, aren't necessarily whom you should emulate if you're a beginning writer. Start writing at your current skill level, creating the sort of story that you most love to read, based on a character or an idea that just won't let you go. You might not be ready to write a generational saga that skips across four continents. Instead, focus on telling a manageable tale and building it scene by scene with clarity and grace, rather than on embroidering with complicated subplots and twists.

Writers make many solitary choices as they practice their craft, deciding what to include and what to leave out. Writing is a tightrope walk of guiding the reader to an experience while somehow staying out of his way. Your decisions about when to be bold and when to hold back stem from understanding when a story needs to slow down, when it should whisper, and when it needs to create blood-boiling intensity. As you write, constantly ask yourself "What effect am I going for here? What are my characters feeling?" Not every scene can have the same emotional impact, and not every dialogue exchange can disintegrate into a shouting match.

SETTING, CHARACTER, AND SUBTLETY

As writers become more practiced, they realize that there are times to state and inform, and times to suggest or hint. In a setting, you might want to suggest menace, danger, or a disaster looming. So if your story is set in a sleepy resort town, you might depict the waters as turbulent or endlessly deep to foreshadow future events.

If a character has murderous intentions or dangerous secrets, you'll want to include some mysterious note about him. Perhaps your character has a way of evading answers, or is vague about his past. Or, perhaps we first meet him in a setting that strikes an odd note. Most characters, particularly antagonists and villains, must be unmasked over time, until their pasts and secrets are exposed in the climatic moments. If a character is somehow unbalanced, but you don't want the reader to realize it when he first appears in the story, you can toss in little oddities—maybe the way he arranges food on his plate so that the carrots don't touch the meat loaf or mashed potatoes.

Let's say your character, a traditional Southern woman, appears gracious and charming, but has a will of steel. This characteristic is important to the overall story, so you might depict her running her household like a well-oiled machine, setting up the Ladies Aide meeting, and setting behavioral standards for her family that would make a Marine Corps drill sergeant proud. You could also show her in the kitchen, after the family finishes dinner, with a cleanup routine that whisks the leftovers out of sight and restores the kitchen to sparkling perfection. Her movements are practiced, efficient, and orderly.

Now, you might be thinking that this is a small aspect of characterization, but it is not. If she was the type who retired to the porch with an after-dinner drink to watch the night sky while the leftovers congealed on the serving platters and the dirty dishes attracted flies, this would imply a vastly different character, perhaps one who is dreamy, or simply relaxed about housekeeping. Your character, on the other hand, has a steel backbone for a reason. Perhaps her children will rebel against her nature, longing for a mother who is more flexible and easy. Or perhaps after a lifetime of self-control a tragedy will shake her to her core and all her self-control will crumble, exposing the woman beneath the steel façade.

The point in adding details is to find a select few that murmur volumes, rather than creating travelogues and catalogues. Allow readers to interpret how and why a person operates in her world by providing subtle details, choices, and characteristics.

207

SUBTLETY IN CHARACTER DESCRIPTIONS

Fictional characters are bigger than life, with huge appetites, passions, longings, and goals made visible through actions. Recall some of literature's memorable characters—Tom Sawyer, Huck Finn, James Bond, Sherlock Holmes, Jo March, Scarlett O'Hara, Frankenstein, Hannibal Lecter, Atticus Finch. While Atticus epitomizes a Southern liberal and intellectual, this is not a subtle bunch.

In many stories, the protagonist serves as the reader's alter ego, standing up to bad guys when they'd cower or run, and making love to the woman or man they'd be afraid to approach. Protagonists in many genres have heroic qualities and are proactive, although occasionally stories are written about a more passive character.

Yet even larger-than-life characters need moments of normalcy, nuance, and subtle gestures. If they're caterwauling, rampaging, and lusting every moment of every page, it wearies a reader. Fiction seesaws between obvious action and more delicate shadings of emotion. There are intense scenes, but also quiet moments and reflection, which are often built into scene sequels.

When you need to be direct, slip into a viewpoint character's thoughts, but don't spend so much time there that the reflective moment overshadows the action. Endless ruminating wears on the reader and can be static. The reader doesn't need access to all the character's thoughts: Save these explorations for the more explosive or painful realizations, difficult decisions, and haunting or painful memories.

The story in Dai Sijie's novel *Balzac and the Little Chinese Seamstress* centers on two young men from the city who are exiled to a remote mountain village for reeducation during China's Cultural Revolution. Their discovery and subsequent theft of a stash of banned Western classics, along with a flirtation with a tailor's daughter, keep them sane in their bleak surroundings. Here is how the little seamstress is first described in the opening of the second chapter:

> The princess of Phoenix mountain wore pale pink canvas shoes, which were both sturdy and supple and through which you could see her flexing her toes as she worked the treadle of her sewing machine. There was nothing out of the ordinary about the cheap, homemade shoes, and yet, in a place where nearly everyone went barefoot, they caught the eye, seeming delicate and sophisticated. The fine shape of her feet and ankles was set off by white nylon socks. . . .

When she leaned over her sewing machine, the shiny metal base mirrored
the collar of her white blouse, her oval face and the sparkle in her eyes—without
doubt the loveliest pair of eyes in the district of Yong Jing, if not the entire region.

Notice how the chapter begins by calling her a princess and describing her pink
shoes, because an arresting detail about a character creates intrigue. Remember to
remind the reader of these qualities from time to time after they are introduced.

More carefully drawn details of the seamstress's beauty and sensibilities are
inserted, and then this bit of setting:

The room served as shop, workplace and dining room all at once. The floorboards
were grimy and streaked with yellow-and-black gobs of dried spittle left by her
clients. You could tell they were not washed down daily. There were hangers with
finished garments suspended on a string across the middle of the room. The corners were piled high with bolts of material and folded clothes, which were under
siege from an army of ants. The place lacked any sense of order or aesthetics, and
exuded an atmosphere of complete informality.

This paragraph introduces conflict in the story by describing the unwashed floor.
Because the young men are from educated and professional families, they are at
odds with the villagers. Since the seamstress is not of their class, her presence is
disruptive, but because she is intelligent, curious, and exceptional, she will also
broaden their beliefs about females of her class. When appropriate, include a
character who challenges your protagonist's beliefs, because these characters can
serve as catalysts for change.

CONVEYING EMOTIONS

John Gardner called details the lifeblood of fiction, but some writers consider it
to be emotion. Emotions energize characters, and thus stories and readers. Your
deep understanding of the emotions and psychology of your characters brings
them to life. And if you want to write drama instead of melodrama, it is in character emotions that subtlety is especially needed.

Emotions flood through us at differing intensities, some lasting a long time, some
passing quickly. Emotions trigger increased blood flow to the brain and a release of
hormones that affect many physical systems. In real life, a person's emotions flicker

across her face. Research has shown that the basic emotions are anger, disgust, sadness, contempt, happiness, fear, and surprise, with many variations of each.

As a writer, make certain that you're working with these basic emotions and their variations, and that your characters' emotions are exhibited physically. Emotions are individual—they're what make people so fascinating and mimes so annoying. After all, the caricatures of emotions created by the person in white face are broad strokes and exaggerations.

Fictional characters are multi-dimensional, and their layers must be revealed gradually and proven via the series of changes they undergo. A character's beliefs and philosophy create his attitudes and approach to life. They influence his decisions and choices, and also cause him to react and behave in distinctive ways, displaying specific emotions. Some people react to crisis or change with hysteria, and some people are stoic. Some people react to challenges with anger, bitterness, or resentment.

A character's emotional life will predispose him to act and react in certain ways, all of which are influenced by his past. As your characters respond to story events, so do your readers. In all this, remember that often the deepest or strongest emotions are the most difficult to render realistically and subtly. Use the following techniques to create believable, nuanced emotional expressions for your characters:

- Rid your text of clichés and generic markers, such as "blinking back tears," or "pounding heartbeats." Instead, find fresh depictions of emotions through images and language.

- Find eccentric or specialized ways in which people or characters reveal emotions. Your character's emotional core supplies the reactions, but then you can make choices based on his interests and the accoutrements of the setting.

- Analyze emotions in plays and films, noticing when they are underplayed.

- Know what your characters fear the most. Is it illness, poverty, loss of love, death? Is the fear rational? How will they avoid their fears? What will they do anything to avoid? How far will they go to achieve their desires?

- Generally avoid stating emotions in ways like "Mary felt miserable." Sometimes a simple declaration is necessary, but emotions should be proven in your characters' actions and reactions.

- Make the emotions significant and motivating. Greed, love, hate, jealousy, and guilt cause things to happen.

- Give your characters emotional choices and have them regret these choices at times. Not taking action can also be a choice with consequences.

- Pay attention to when your characters are simmering and when they're operating at full boil. If your character reacts with the same level of rage to spilling coffee on his clean shirt, getting cut off in traffic, and his girlfriend dumping him, you've created a psychopath, not a believable, knowable human.

CREATING AN EMOTIONAL BALANCE

Make certain that characters react with emotional consistency. In real life, dealing with a person who overreacts or reacts with inappropriate emotions can be extremely difficult. Generally, children and teens are prone to disproportionate reactions and people learn to modulate themselves as they mature. Similarly, characters' reactions to events must be age-appropriate and reveal their emotional health. Perhaps an unbalanced character will react with a vicious outburst when a waiter doesn't immediately appear at his table after he's seated in a crowded restaurant. A more stable character, on the other hand, will look around the room and notice that the waiter is extremely busy with six other tables, and will chat with his dinner companion. (Note that characters in a scene who are experiencing contrasting emotions—one person enraged at a waiter's incompetence while another is nonplussed—can be dynamically juxtaposed.)

All characters, whether they are considered normal or deviant, need to exhibit consistency in their reactions. A bizarre or troubled character will react in ways that make sane people cross the street to avoid him. Readers don't expect a deranged character to act normally and will be disappointed when he does. For example, an unstable character that gets dumped by his girlfriend will respond by deluging her with e-mails, phone calls, and pleas for her return, or perhaps will slash her tires or perform some other vengeful act.

A normal character will wish the ex-girlfriend well, then head to the corner bar, where he'll nurse a few beers and commiserate with his friends. Normal characters cope and act within a consistent range that befits their level of sanity and maturity.

Troubled characters also react within a consistent range, but remember that a few choice actions, such as returning all the gifts the ex-girlfriend gave him or phoning her at 3 A.M. every night until she changes her phone number, are better than a whole range of reactions.

SUBTEXT

What is left unsaid is often more potent than what is expressed. Subtext, the underlying level of emotions, can create layers of tension, symbolism, and meaning in any story or scene. In fact, subtext is perhaps your most useful tool for subtlety. In *Creating Unforgettable Characters*, Linda Seger, an author and Hollywood script doctor, defines subtext as "what the character is really saying beneath and between the lines."

Much of what happens to people in the real world is experienced subliminally or is communicated nonverbally. Experts in human communication claim that 97 percent of all communication is nonverbal. You might chat with your office mate and take in her crossed arms and the dark circles beneath her eyes, and although these details are not discussed, they are still communicated. As a result, you might draw the conclusions that she has not slept well, isn't feeling comfortable, or is being defensive.

Because in real life subtext often comes in body language or small clues, fiction writers resort to slyness to depict it. In *Creating Unforgettable Characters*, Seger explains:

> Often, characters don't understand themselves. They're often not direct and don't say what they mean. We might say that the subtext is all the underlying drives and meanings that are not apparent to the character, but that are apparent to the audience or reader.

With this in mind, look for places where a character is in denial or feeling vulnerable or confused. Perhaps she's afraid or unable to display tenderness. Perhaps she cannot admit to her fears or worries, or is hiding a secret or desire. Often, subtext suggests something counter to a character's action. In the aftermath of violence, for example, a ruthless gang member might reveal his tenderness toward his girlfriend and infant son, which would seem at odds with his cold-blooded approach to protecting his gang's territory.

$\mathscr{T}$RUTHS · $\mathscr{A}$BOUT · $\mathscr{S}$UBTEXT

- People often don't or can't express what they mean.
- People often act the opposite of how they intend to or in opposition to their true feelings.
- People often have feelings/emotions that they find repugnant.
- Despite attempts to hide our true feelings, they are often obvious to other people.
- Subtext is revealed in how people speak differently to friends and strangers.
- Drama or humor can come from the disparity between text and subtext.
- Subtext can reveal backstory, since a character acts as he does because of influences from his past.

PROPERLY PLACING SUBTEXT

The amount of subtext found in novels is often dependent on the genre. The best romances, for example, use subtext to enhance the tension and suspense in the story, and also to make the interactions between the lovers less obvious and thus more interesting. Generally speaking, however, more subtext is found in literary fiction than in genre fiction.

Subtext can be found in any element of fiction, from scene content and setting details to metaphors and how characters dress. In the film *American Beauty*, a middle-aged couple, played by Kevin Spacey and Annette Bening, are in a loveless, sexless marriage. While this isn't overtly discussed, an opening scene depicts the husband masturbating in the shower, indicating his sexual frustration. As he roars through a full-blown midlife crisis, his daughter's friend, portrayed amid clouds of soft, red rose petals, becomes the object of his desire, while his wife tends to rose bushes, with their thorns and manicured beauty symbolic of her harshness and inaccessibility.

213

When a woman wears a red, low-cut blouse on a first date, her choice of garment communicates something. When you create your character's home or office, the belongings can communicate aspects of his personality. Belongings can also communicate wealth, status, interests, and much more. If your character's home is filled with family photos, it might indicate sentimentality, a close-knit family, or parents that live chiefly for nurturing their children. On the other hand, a home without photos or with few personal items communicates other aspects of character.

A character's car can also contain subtext. There's a big difference between a man who drives a battered, mud-spattered Ford pickup truck and one who drives a spotless Porsche convertible, or between a character who has an oil change every three months and one who drives his car until it falls apart.

Taking subtext further, bright colors can indicate energy; red and fire, passion; children and some animals, innocence or purity; blue skies, optimism; and birds, freedom. Of course, all these objects can also hold other meanings, but your job as writer is to invest objects with meaning. Look for small ways to slip coded references or subtext into your stories.

From time to time, give your characters props or tasks to occupy them and reveal emotion. Cigarettes and alcoholic beverages have long been used to reveal emotion, but characters who are upset can also be portrayed in a kitchen whacking at vegetables, driving a car with hands gripped on the wheel, straightening or cleaning obsessively, yanking weeds out of the garden, or ordering their children around. Or, a character can snuggle with a child to diffuse a situation, or start petting the family collie as a way of soothing herself.

Intense scenes that stage sex or violence can be kept in check by using subtext. Without subtext, the violence can be gratuitous and the sexual interlude can be lurid or melodramatic. Subtext shows the emotions in the scene that cannot be stated, and reveals the humanity, motivations, drives, and desires behind the actions, giving them meaning.

NOVELS WITH GREAT SUBTEXT

Jane Austen's novels

Stephanie Plum series, Janet Evanovich

Broken for You, Stephanie Kallos

The Jane Austen Book Club, Karen Joy Fowler

Spenser series, Robert B. Parker

The Secret Life of Bees, Sue Monk Kidd

Girl With a Pearl Earring, Tracy Chevalier

A Good House, Bonnie Burnard

Blessings, Anna Quindlen

The Remains of the Day, Kazuo Ishiguro

The English Patient, Michael Ondaatje

The Book of Ruth, Jane Hamilton

Talk Before Sleep, Elizabeth Berg

What We Keep, Elizabeth Berg

The Starlite Drive-in, Marjorie Reynolds

The Accidental Tourist, Anne Tyler

My Dream of You, Nuala O'Faolain

SUBTEXT IN DIALOGUE

Powerful dialogue should simmer with subtext. These invisible words lurk below the surface, filtering into the atmosphere in a scene. Subtext can expose internal conflict and can reveal when a character's declarations ("Of course I love you, why do you ask?") are at odds with his true feelings. In real life, children often blurt out whatever comes to mind, but as we age, social graces take over, and we learn that we cannot say everything that occurs to us. This restraint leads to subtext in life, which can be imitated in fiction.

Another reason for using subtext is that characters who always say exactly what they mean are overbearing or dull. In screenwriting and playwriting, this kind of dialogue is called "on the nose," and if used exclusively becomes boring and flat. Beginning writers often use on-the-nose dialogue and are confused when readers don't warm to it.

Subtext is the opposite of on-the-nose dialogue, lacing conversations with innuendo, insinuation, and nonverbal clues. It is most often used when the speaker has something at stake emotionally. A screenwriter friend of mine calls subtext "the river of emotion that flows beneath the words, illuminating what the character thinks and feels but does not say."

Subtext is a terrific tool for when your characters have secrets, or cannot speak the truth for various reasons. For example, men dread hearing a woman ask, "Do I look fat in this?" Often what she really means is: "Do you still find me attractive? Do you still love me? Can you still see in me the girl you fell in love with twenty years ago?"

Subtext is also a way of using indirection instead of dealing with the real issue at stake. For example, a couple might argue about taking out the garbage, or engage in small power struggles about money or a child's grades when they're really arguing about more intimate aspects of their relationship.

Avoidance and evasion are other aspects of subtext: When a character remains silent instead of answering, it's a certain clue that something is wrong. Or, a character might change the subject or answer a question with a question. Intonations such as sarcasm or a tremor in the voice also communicate emotion. If your character is prone to humorous jibes instead of straight answers, that too can be subtext.

WHEN ON-THE-NOSE IS ON TARGET

There are times when on-the-nose dialogue is called for, and these are generally times when your character feels safe. These safety zones occur when:

- your character chats with a close or trusted friend
- your character talks to a baby, child, or pet

- your character speaks with a priest, therapist, or mentor
- the truth has been "earned," as in the climax
- the subject requires a simple, to-the-point approach

AVOIDING MELODRAMA

Some aspects of fiction are designed to shock, and some scenes depict a knock-down fight or a passionate culmination of lust. While some genres or stories require graphic violence, it's usually when the reader is allowed to imagine the worst outcomes that the story unsettles him the most. Further, it is often when emotions and actions are the most intense that you, the writer, must pull back instead of exploiting the scene. For example, in Ron McLarty's *The Memory of Running*, the story's inciting incident is a car accident in which Smithy Ide's parents are severely injured: They later die in separate hospitals. The reader is taken into the quiet but infinitely sad moment of his mother's death, drawn with aching subtlety:

Mom looked the same, except, like Dr. Deni told me, I could hear her little breaths. Puffs, really. Her eyes were still open a little, but I knew she couldn't hear me. I pushed her thin hair onto the pillow with my fingers.

"There," I said.

I concentrated on Mom's breathing and told myself that they were small but powerful breaths. Small and powerful like Mom, and when she got home, I would tell everyone how this Indian doctor had told me she was going to die, but her breathing got more and more powerful, and her body cooled right down, and she lived.

But she stopped breathing. I never felt so stupid, Mom. I went to the nurses' station.

"I think my mom has stopped breathing."

Toni and another nurse, an older man, walked into the room, and I followed them. They closed Mom's eyes, took out the IV, and left. All of the engines and monitors were off. I stood, then sat, then remembered my dead pop and how I had lied to her about him. It was reasonable to lie, because Mom was so tiny and that news was so big, but I have learned that you don't want to lie to your mother at the moment of her death. It seems to never stop bothering a person. A lie like

217

that is one of the main reasons I talk out loud when I'm alone. I say, "Mom, Pop died over at Portland General, but everything's still okay."

A person doesn't get over a family.

Sometimes things happen that make a person feel like standing up is just too much. It's the knees then. Legs. Heart. I put my face under Mom's until I could stand up.

The death of a character, especially the protagonist's sweet mother, could easily be an occasion for melodrama or overkill. McLarty could have aimed his camera at the mother's chest and revealed her final gasps and the buzzing of the monitors. But notice how the simple gesture of Smithy smoothing his mother's hair and saying "There" speaks so poignantly about tenderness and what she meant to him. Notice how he managed to describe guilt, an emotion that is often involved when people die, but rarely spoken of. But note also how, when less is said, when the author selects a few choice declarations and movements, they speak with an eloquence that can't be matched by hysterics and theatrics.

Subtle Style

While all writing requires music, at times it's necessary to simplify the tune. For example, repetition is a terrific technique that can be used to underline and emphasize, but when used too often, the reader wearies of it.

MODIFIERS, QUALIFIERS, AND INTENSIFIERS

Subtle style requires that you pay attention to modifiers: Overuse is a sure sign of a novice. In all your sentences, nouns and verbs are the most important words, and they—not modifiers—should receive top billing. Precise and powerful nouns make a sentence visual and clear, while verbs are the engines that propel sentences forward with force or cause them to limp and sputter.

An abundance of modifiers often means that you're adding props or decorations to your writing, shoring up wimpy nouns and weak verbs, when instead you need a few lean, clean words to form a clear sentence. Examine every adjective and adverb, and ask yourself if it truly adds to the meaning of the sentence. You need to be able to justify a modifier's existence in a sentence.

Adjectives modify nouns, pronouns, and gerunds (verbs with an -*ing* suffix that work as nouns). Get rid of obvious and redundant modifiers: *green* grass, *tall* trees, *blue* sky, *little* babies, *sweet* puppies, *cheerful* grins. Instead, choose adjectives that are unusual, that bring the subject into a clearer focus, and that add to voice and meaning.

Adverbs are rarely needed in a sentence. Like adjectives, adverbs have a place in our writing, but they shouldn't be the *first* words you reach for when strong nouns and verbs will suffice. Adverbs modify everything except nouns and pronouns, so they are dangerous creatures that can sneak in anywhere.

The worst adverbs are attached as an afterthought to a wimpy verb, usually with an *-ly* suffix. Instead of writing "Allison ate quickly," "Allison ate hungrily," or "Allison ate slowly," write "Allison wolfed the pie," or "Allison dawdled over her pie." Instead of *move quickly*, use *race, lope, bolt, scurry, hustle, scramble,* or *dash*. The best verbs create pictures in the reader's mind and sound like what they mean.

Another adverb problem is found in inserting attributions. Attributions are the "he said"/"she said" parts of writing that describe dialogue, and we generally strive to make them invisible. Adverbs are rarely needed to describe the dialogue. Its tone, meaning, and vigor should be contained within the exchange, not explained in the attribution.

Qualifiers and intensifiers are two more categories of adverbs that demand weeding. Here is a short list of intensifiers: *very, quite, absolutely, completely, truly, basically, really, extremely, totally, naturally, so, particularly, perfectly, actually.* Intensifiers are sown into sentences to give weight and importance. Writers use them when trying to express that something is extraordinary or unusual, but again, intensifiers rob sentences of freshness and power. For instance, why write that someone is *very weak* when you could describe the person as *fragile, feeble,* or *frail*? Why write *really hungry* when *ravenous* is the appropriate word? How about *hilarious* instead of *very funny*? Instead of *extremely happy*, how about *ecstatic*?

Qualifiers are adverbs that qualify how we feel about a subject. They give writers wiggle room, but remember that good writing isn't slippery—it's definite, clear, and rich. Intensifiers include: *somewhat, rather, often, mostly, pretty, a little, sort of, kind of, quite, very, a bit, too, usually, probably, ordinarily, mostly, mainly, generally, as a rule.*

Why does this matter? Because as writers we're delivering a lush and vivid world, not a place that's kind of nice or sort of real. Don't write about a character who is "rather handsome" or "kind of smart." Either a man is attractive or he isn't. He's intelligent or he's not. Don't hide behind vagueness. Be specific, be sure, be powerful. It's the only way to write.

PURPLE PROSE

This term describes prose that is heightened, flowery, and overdone. The culprits of purple prose are usually modifiers that make your writing wordy, overwrought, distracting, and even silly. You might say that Hemingway's prose is the opposite of purple prose.

There are times to heighten a passage, such as when you want the reader to slow down and notice, or when you want a scene to be lush and sensuous. Lush descriptions and moments can be effectively used before, during, and after an emotional scene. The trick is to keep language proportionate and appropriate. Use language with a specific purpose in mind, not because you love writing descriptively. In purple prose, skin is always creamy, eyelashes always glistening, heroes always brooding, and sunrises always magical. Purple prose also features an abundance of metaphors and figurative language, long sentences, and abstractions.

Find nouns and verbs that are precise, and trust that they'll perform their job in the sentence. Vary your sentence lengths and use long sentences with a specific intention. Use abstract diction with care ("She was born sad"), and back up these statements with proof. Strive for variety and style, especially when describing emotions and emotional moments.

Reserve heightened language for important moments in the story, especially turning points or times when you're revealing your character undergoing change. That way the reader will pay attention to the significance of what is happening. One last caution: Beginning writers tend to end short stories and novels in a wash of purple prose, thinking this underscores the emotions of the climax. However, there are dozens of means to end a piece, and sometimes understatement, a short dialogue exchange, or a simple poignant image can convey more meaning than a contrived and flowery ending.

WORD CHOICE

Examine your word choices and ask yourself if you're showing off. Sometimes a writer's education gets in the way of his voice, and he strews fancy, multi-syllabic words that sound important but usually don't deliver in sentences. Remember this simple tip: Short words are generally better than long words. The simpler the language, the broader your audience. After all, the best writing makes complex subjects clear and easily understood.

Scrutinize your vocabulary and replace *correspondence* with *letter, compensate* with *pay, indicate* with *show, purchase* with *buy, implement* with *do, visualize* with *see, informed* with *told, numerous* with *many, initial* with *first, commence* with *begin, sufficient* with *enough*. Why, you ask? Your writing voice will depend on the narrator or viewpoint character. You want to achieve a voice that is in harmony with his cultural and class roots and that reflects his education. However, remember that in most cases an accessible voice is conversational and natural. It sounds like most of us talk, not like the lecture of a college professor or the elocution of congressmen grandstanding before national media. Does this mean you can never use words like *elocution?* No, of course not. Just use them with awareness, with judiciousness, and when you need to sound formal or solemn—not to prove something about your education.

After you've eliminated your overly formal words, remove cluttered expressions and little word pileups. It's simple: Wordy is boring. Again, these rascals sneak into our writing and we don't even know that they are there. For example, instead of writing *at this point in time,* write *today* or *now.* Instead of writing *in the vicinity of,* write *near.* Instead of *make an adjustment,* write *adjust.* Instead of *in the opinion of the group,* write *we think.* Instead of *in the near future,* write *soon.* Instead of *a large percentage of,* write *many.* Instead of *put in an appearance,* write *appeared.*

What you're probably noticing in this section is that I'm talking about subtraction and not addition. Writers, especially beginning writers, often try to fix their stories by adding more words, more descriptions, and longer scenes. But as the late Gary Provost explained in *Make Your Words Work,* every word in every sentence must perform a job. If it doesn't, give it the pink slip. Words matter, and each one should be sparkling and weighty. The only way to make your writing subtle yet powerful is to choose precisely the word that is needed for meaning and connotation. Finally, every sentence that does not push the story forward and deepen the reader's understanding is unnecessary. Developing your skills at cutting excess is one of the most important things you can do as a writer.

TIPS FOR WRITING WITH SUBTLETY

We've been discussing ridding your stories of padding and shrillness, while at the same time inserting subtext and other whispers. In using these techniques, your goal is to create stories that are free from too much description, overwrought emotions, and melodrama. Here are some parting tips for writing with subtlety:

- Readers will remember a single, poignant image rather than a complicated description.

- Don't explain unless it's necessary for a deep understanding of some major element. Most fiction attempts to distill human experience, not create a recipe for it.

- Practice writing poetry. The brief descriptions and images in poems, often stunningly understated, teach us to capture moments, people, and places in a few words.

- Be sparing when using unexpected words and phrases. The best writing doesn't show off or call attention to itself. Jargon, as well as unusual, invented, archaic, or onomatopoetic words, should also be inserted with care.

- Don't force-feed information to your readers. Describe or show characters in action. Don't explain why they do what they do or how they are feeling.

- Big truths are found in the smallest moments. Seek them out and use them as a kind of shorthand.

{ * }

Find ways to insert subtext—the unspoken, the innuendo, the nuanced moments that are not directly represented, and the actions that speak of feelings that are too volatile to express out loud. Also, look for times in your story to pull back, to allow the reader to bring her own understanding of human nature into your story.

chapter 15
Suspense

{
There is no terror in the bang, only in the anticipation of it.
—**Alfred Hitchcock**

Fiction isn't written to make readers happy. Its purpose is to jangle their nerves, make their hearts race, give them goose bumps, and disturb their sleep. A complacent reader, after all, is one who nods off instead of turning the pages until dawn. The urge to keep reading comes from many factors, but mostly from suspense. Suspense is a technique that requires sleight of hand and is tied to readers' primal instincts and fears. Your job is to unsettle your readers, whether or not being sneaky or sly comes naturally to you. Here is how it is done.

SUSPENSE 101

Suspense as a fiction technique has evolved from a long literary tradition and can be found in everything from Edgar Allan Poe's stories to *The Moonstone* by Wilkie Collins to *Jane Eyre* by Charlotte Brontë to *The Picture of Dorian Gray* by Oscar Wilde. Suspense is a major factor in mystery novels and horror fiction, and emphasizes both the immediate danger to a vulnerable character and the potency of his adversary. However, suspense belongs in *all* fiction and does not require Gothic settings, supernatural beings, or murder. Think of suspense this way: If conflict is the engine of fiction, then suspense is the fuel that makes it run.

A recipe for suspense is made up of curiosity, uncertainty, and anxiety. Suspense creates apprehension and a dread of approaching events, especially the climax. It also comes in many shades, from inquisitiveness to expectation to actual fear as a character faces danger. When done correctly, suspense is embedded into the setting and enhanced by the mood or atmosphere of the story. It stems from the protagonist's challenges and dilemmas, and is activated by events in the plot. Woven into every scene, it makes the world of make-believe captivating.

Laying the Groundwork for Suspense

Once your reader becomes trapped under the spell of the story, suspense happens in ever-building increments. Your job as a writer is to seduce the reader via the opening scenes, then, once she's involved in the protagonist's life, to disturb her and force her to speculate about upcoming events and results.

Suspense is a stimulus, appealing to our primitive fight-or-flight response as well as our rational need to solve problems. Suspense operates on a pain-and-pleasure principle as well. It hurts so good to be afraid, as anyone who has ever been buckled into a roller coaster knows. The reader derives pleasure from solving the puzzle of the unfolding plot, but also is enthralled when solutions dangle just beyond reach. Suspense requires that the reader form a hypothesis about what is going to happen, even though she may be unaware of doing so.

Creating suspense involves withholding information and prolonging crises. This is accomplished by slowly developing your characters and making careful structural choices. Suspense increases when you eliminate extraneous information and when the reader longs for something that doesn't happen, whether it be some relief, release, or a confrontation.

Prolonging Dread: The Calculated Insertion

Suspense teases the reader by creating anticipation. Think about anticipation as a striptease act. When a stripper walks onto the stage wearing her cowgirl outfit, she doesn't begin by stripping down to her G-string and holster. No, she twirls her lasso and prances around, tantalizing the audience, perhaps leaning over to expose a bit—or a lot—of cleavage. She milks the moment. Then the music picks up and she gets down to the serious business of peeling off her costume, but one item at a time, perhaps starting with a glove, drawing out the final moment.

Likewise, you can stretch out your suspense by using insertions. These devices, built from various elements of storytelling, sidetrack the story, stall the danger, and prolong the moment as your reader longs for a conclusion. Insertions can come anywhere in the story, but they are especially effective in a scene where the protagonist is heading toward a goal or objective. An insertion hinders his progress or the outcome.

Insertions vary in their intensity, sometimes causing irritation, sometimes causing outright danger. But no matter their degree, they always create suspense because the reader's gratification is delayed. Insertions can be built from description, setting, dialogue, thoughts, backstory, emotions, interruptions, another character's unexpected arrival, and action in a subplot.

In *The Lovely Bones,* author Alice Sebold draws out the suspense in her opening scenes by using a combination of insertions. The second sentence of the novel reveals that fourteen-year-old Susie, who narrates the story from heaven, is dead, and the pages that follow describe her murder at the hands of her neighbor, Mr. Harvey.

And because the reader knows that Susie is already dead, Sebold draws out her murder to create suspense, empathy, and haunting horror. The scene begins on a late December afternoon. It is snowing as Susie takes a shortcut home through a cornfield. Suddenly, her neighbor, Mr. Harvey, appears:

"Don't let me startle you," Mr. Harvey said.

Of course, in a cornfield, in the dark, I was startled. After I was dead I thought about how there had been the light scent of cologne in the air but that I had not been paying attention, or thought it was coming from one of the houses up ahead.

"Mr. Harvey," I said.

"You're the older Salmon girl, right?"

"Yes."

"How are your folks?"

Although the eldest in the family and good at acing a science quiz, I had never felt comfortable with adults.

"Fine," I said. I was cold, but the natural authority of his age, and the added fact that he was a neighbor and had talked to my father about fertilizer, rooted me to the spot.

225

"I've built something back here," he said. "Would you like to see?"

"I'm sort of cold, Mr. Harvey, and my mom likes me home before dark."

"It's after dark, Susie," he said.

The reader can feel the trap being set and wants to shriek at Susie to get the heck out of there. Instead he trails Mr. Harvey and Susie to the trap. Sebold spends seven paragraphs drawing out the scene, describing Susie's family dynamics, slipping into the future, when Mr. Harvey speaks to her mother about her murder, and showing Susie complaining to Franny, her intake counselor in heaven. This interlude evokes more sympathy for Susie and her parents, and illustrates the dastardly machinations of the child-murderer.

As Susie follows Mr. Harvey deeper into the cornfield, the author describes the corn and includes a brief flashback where Susie's mother explains that the corn is grown for horses, not humans. So again, Sebold stretches the moment before taking the reader into Mr. Harvey's hideout:

"I've made a little hiding place," said Mr. Harvey.

He stopped and turned to me.

"I don't see anything," I said. I was aware that Mr. Harvey was looking at me strangely. I'd had older men look at me that way since I'd lost my baby fat, but they usually didn't lose their marbles over me when I was wearing my royal blue parka and yellow elephant bell-bottoms. His glasses were small and round with gold frames and his eyes looked over them and at me.

"You should be more observant, Susie," he said.

By now the reader is convinced that Mr. Harvey's just uttered the understatement of the century. The next page prolongs the reader's agony as Susie reflects on her gullibility (with Franny chiming in) and tells the reader that her ears were freezing because she'd refused to wear a silly cap that her mother had made her one Christmas.

They reach a trap door, and Susie confesses that by now she's curious, yet a little concerned. The details and observations draw out the scene, creating more empathy for Susie because the reader is struck by her youth and naïveté. The details about her rape are heartrending and further prolong the outcome:

Mr. Harvey made me lie still underneath him and listen to the beating of his heart and the beating of mine. How mine skipped like a rabbit, and how his thudded, a hammer against cloth. We lay there with our bodies touching, and, as I shook, a powerful knowledge took hold. He had done this thing to me and I had lived. That was all. I was still breathing. I heard his heart. I smelled his breath. The dark earth surrounding us smelled like what it was, moist dirt where worms and animals lived their daily lives. I could have yelled for hours.

I knew he was going to kill me. I did not realize then that I was an animal already dying.

"Why don't you get up?" Mr. Harvey said as he rolled to the side and then crouched over me.

His voice was gentle, encouraging, a lover's voice on a late morning. A suggestion, not a command.

I could not move. I could not get up.

When I would not—was it only that, only that I would not follow his suggestion?—he leaned to the side and felt, over his head, across the ledge where his razor and shaving cream sat. He brought back a knife. Unsheathed, it smiled at me, curving up in a grin.

He took the hat from my mouth.

"Tell me you love me," he said.

Gently, I did.

The end came anyway.

So that's how it's done. You might want to read the complete chapter to note how Sebold draws out the scene by moving in and out of the immediate action, slipping in description, backstory, and future events. Notice also how she doesn't describe the murder in detail, but rather allows the reader to imagine Susie's end. Often this sort of understatement is more potent than a blow-by-blow depiction of violence because the reader's imagination, fueled by suspense, fills in the details.

SET PIECES: BUILDING SUSPENSE ONE SCENE AT A TIME

The important scenes, where the emotional payoffs occur, should be scattered throughout the course of your story. These scenes are called set pieces, a term borrowed from screenwriting, and they include the climax. The events in set pieces explode the drama, and, depending on the needs of the scene, can escalate suspense via increased jeopardy, release the reader from built-up tension and suspense, or both.

227

In a set piece (usually there are about a half-dozen in a novel), the stakes are high and the drama is turned up a notch. (Think back to our earlier discussion of set pieces in chapter seven.) Scenes and events leading up to the set piece build tension. If you're writing a political thriller, a set piece is an action scene where the hero chases the villain through a dangerous neighborhood while bullets fly. A set piece might also be a showdown or fight, a natural calamity such as a hurricane, or a couple severing a romance. We rely on set pieces because they are staged via action, explode in the now, and cause readers to worry and fret. As in films, set pieces are intended to be remembered weeks after the reader finishes the story, as in *Jurassic Park*, when the raptors are chasing the children in the kitchen.

When a novel begins with a set piece, this highly dramatic opening salvo must put questions in the reader's mind, create suspense, and set the story in motion. Nick Hornby's *A Long Way Down* begins with four characters of various backgrounds and circumstances meeting on New Year's Eve at a London high-rise, all with the intent to commit suicide. The reader immediately wonders what has happened to these characters that forced them into such desperate frames of mind. And if they're not going to kill themselves, what will happen next? Will they change their minds or resolve their personal conflicts?

Most writers choose not to open with a set piece, instead sprinkling set pieces throughout the story line to keep the tension boiling. A potentially perilous outcome is always worrying to the reader, so if along the way you plant a series of failures and losses both large and small, the reader will worry that even worse losses and catastrophes will happen next. The next time you read a novel and feel gripped by suspense, list all the unanswered questions in the story and note if the author answered the questions in set piece scenes.

SUSPENSE AND CHARACTERS: TAKING ADVANTAGE OF FEARS AND FLAWS

Fiction is about characters that readers are intimately involved with and worried about. Readers dread what might happen to them and anticipate good and bad events that will influence their situations. Characters are imperfect, and their imperfections also create suspense for the reader.

Whenever you create a major fictional character, you're devising a person who can be unmasked over time. When a reader first meets your character, she will take note of the dominant traits that serve as the foundation for the character. When readers meet Jo March of *Little Women*, they find her outspoken, plucky, witty, and willful. Your character's dominant traits will remain constant in the story and will be revealed by the plot events.

Once the dominant traits are established, you can reveal your character's fears, weaknesses, and flaws. Typically, in a romance, both characters have strong reasons for *not* falling in love, ranging from a workaholic personality to nursing a broken heart. Romances often feature antagonists, such as a meddling mother-in-law or a third party vying for the heroine's affections. Whatever the characters' reasons for not giving in to love, they are tied to their flaws, sometimes called fatal flaws, which must be overcome in order for love to bloom.

Romance authors use flaws, a series of missed communications and misunderstandings, and setting to keep the protagonists apart until the last possible moment. Tension is stretched taut in a romance and often stems from information that a protagonist is not privy to, unrealistic expectations, or false assumptions.

No matter the genre, most plots are designed around your protagonist's greatest fear. In fact, if you don't know your protagonist's greatest fear, you don't know your protagonist. His fear, coupled with backstory, will propel his motivations, often with disastrous results. Once you identify this fear, you'll be able to design a plot and individual scenes to play it out. In *Little Women*, Jo March is afraid for her father, who is serving in the Civil War, but she is also afraid of feeling vulnerable to love. Both these fears are brought into play in the novel. Once the reader sympathizes and empathizes with a character, knowing her flaws and fears, suspense is introduced and then escalated as danger unfolds in the story.

EMBRACE VULNERABILITIES

If you're driving down the street and spot a puppy about to run in front of traffic, you'll slam on your brakes and perhaps jump out of your car to rescue him. You know a puppy is vulnerable and doesn't understand the dangers of traffic. Similarly, when a reader is aware of a character's vulnerabilities (created by his fears and flaws), she is more tuned-in when dangers occur, and this awareness increases suspense.

After the inciting incident tosses the first volley at the protagonist, he'll be thrown off center; then, as the story proceeds, he'll become weakened and weary. Yet despite not playing in top form, despite vulnerabilities, the protagonist will persevere.

It's important to note that protagonists are often heroic, but never perfect. Dean Koontz, author of dozens of novels, suggests that writers should never create protagonists who are unafraid of danger. To do so is a huge misstep because characters that are invulnerable sap suspense from the story. So when you're creating your protagonist, decide on her dominant personality traits and physical characteristics while remembering that flaws and weaknesses create suspense.

Colin Harrison's *The Havana Room* is a psychological thriller with a protagonist riddled with flaws. Bill Wyeth is a successful lawyer who returns from a business trip to his apartment in Manhattan. He arrives home late and finds his wife asleep, as well as their son and eight boys, who are guests at a sleepover birthday party. Hungry, he orders Thai food from a takeout place, eats it, and retreats to his den.

Then he hears footsteps in the hall. Wilson, one of the guests, is thirsty, so Wyeth pours the boy a glass of milk and then tucks him back into his sleeping bag.

In the morning, the boys arise for breakfast … except for Wilson. Wilson isn't sleeping late; Wilson is dead. He suffered from a severe allergy to peanuts, and the Thai food Wyeth ate contained peanuts. Wyeth's hands contaminated the boy's milk. In this moment, Wyeth's old life ends and his downfall begins:

> Judith stood rapidly, hand to her mouth. She rushed from the room in horror, and as our lives fell away minute by minute—the arriving EMTs, the police, the call to Wilson's parents, the other boys, now traumatized, crying or chattering nervously, the retrieval of the murderous empty glass (the peanut oil still on its lip, still smellable as the intensified essence of peanuts), the arrival of the other parents—as all that we had known about ourselves crumbled into oblivion, I could not help but recall that drink of milk—the cool glass beaded with condensation, the surface of the milk itself curved upward where it clung to the glass, the satisfying incarnation of liquid love, almost tasteable from arm's length, ample and full, safe and clean. Who would have thought it, who would've thought that I, Bill Wyeth, dependable, taxpaying minivan-man, respected partner in a top law firm, would kill an eight-year-old boy with a glass of milk?

230

Then I recalled that Wilson was one of the boys I'd wanted invited, for his father was Wilson Dean Sr., a managing partner in one of the city's major investment banks, itself one of my firm's largest clients, a company with offices in 126 countries. His boy had choked to death on my ambition—you could see it that way, you really could.

Thus, we see that Wyeth's ambition, greed, and ego have cost him dearly. Once considered a rising star in the legal community, he becomes a pariah and loses his job, his wife and son, and even his apartment.

Mistakes, large and small, shape believable characters and cause the reader to worry about the outcome of the story. Often, a character's actions and mistakes create more troubles as he tumbles deeper and deeper into a mess of his own making. With this in mind, make certain that your protagonist's flaws cause disasters until he makes the choice to face them, as in *The Havana Room.*

PROBE YOUR CHARACTERS' EMOTIONAL DEPTHS

Whether characters will meet salvation or ruin is the fulcrum upon which suspense is built. As you shape the characters' experiences into suspense, you'll probe their emotional depths and give interesting, complicated characters difficult problems to overcome.

As characters bumble around struggling to solve problems, new emotions stemming from the unfolding story events and old emotional baggage (such as the guilt and anguish that Bill Wyeth carries with him in *The Havana Room*) will emerge. Emotional baggage guarantees that problems will be doubly difficult to deal with, push aside, or ignore.

When fiction heats up, characters react with varying intensity of emotions—sometimes they'll freeze, sometimes they'll fly into a rage, sometimes they'll be annoyed, frustrated, or pugnacious, or perhaps become icy, controlled, and calm.

Emotional intensity also stems from motivation, the inner engine that drives the plot. There's external motivation (the character's need to solve problems) and internal motivation (the character's raw emotional needs). The deeper the character's desire, the greater the suspense.

Motivations and emotional intensity must be recognizable and in sync with a character's dominant traits. A superspy doesn't become hysterical under fire, while a teenager likely will. The reader longs to share a commonality of experi-

231

ence with characters and to filter the character's experiences through his own. When your character feels guilty about letting down a friend, many readers can relate to that emotion. They can also understand when a character drinks too much, blurts out a stupid statement, or is somehow self-destructive. Likewise, readers relate to emotions that arise from the need to protect another vulnerable person, the needs for love and acceptance, fear of the unknown and change, a desire to avoid conflict, and a need for revenge or justice.

SECRETS AND REVELATIONS

Readers enjoy unraveling secrets and watching as revelations are brought to light. Interesting characters hold suppressed tendencies, secrets, and complicated desires, all of which create suspense by teasing the reader with bits of a character's inner world. A character's inner world is depicted through backstory, motivations, and goals, but it's dramatized in scenes. (More information on this topic is found in chapter five.)

For example, *Blessings*, by Anna Quindlen, begins in the first paragraph with a secret—a young couple drops off a baby at a country estate in the middle of the night. The obvious questions that loom over the story are *Who are the baby's parents?* and *Will they want her back?* But deeper secrets lie at the heart of the story, and they track back decades to when the owner of the estate, Lydia Blessing, now in her eighties, was a young woman.

Me & Emma, by Elizabeth Flock, is constructed around two secrets. Told through the eyes of eight-year-old Carrie, *Me & Emma* tells a harrowing story of abuse by an alcoholic stepfather and an emotionally absent mother. Carrie has been shaped by the loss of her beloved father, but the truth of her father's death is only one of the story's secrets. The other secret, which doesn't explode until the final pages of the book, provides a surprise readers will never forget. Both secrets, when revealed, cast a light back on all the events that came before, and tie the story together.

Relevance is crucial when using secrets and revelations to construct characters and plots. For example, in *Blessings*, the secrets in Lydia's past affect her major life decisions and how she interacts with people many years later. In *Me & Emma*, the secrets *are* the plot. Secrets force the reader to lean closer to the story events and devise theories about what is happening and what is hidden. Secrets stir the sleuth and busybody in all of us.

MORAL AND UNBEARABLE CHOICES

Characters become known to readers by their decisions and choices. John Gardner once said that all true suspense is based on the "anguish of moral choices." Moral choices require courage and present a painful dilemma for the character involved. This is where a character's core values, passions, and fears are laid bare. In *On Moral Fiction,* Gardner explains this further:

> … suspense, rightly understood, is a serious business: one presents the moral problem—the character's admirable or unadmirable intent and the pressures of situation working for and against him (what other characters in the fiction feel and need, what imperatives nature and custom urge)—and rather than moving at once to the effect, one tortures the reader with alternative possibilities, translating to metaphor the alternatives the writer has himself considered. Superficially, the delay makes the decision—the climactic action—more thrilling; but essentially the delay makes the decision philosophically significant.

Perhaps the best-known example of an unbearable choice was created by William Styron in *Sophie's Choice.* Set against the backdrops of pre-war Poland, post-war New York, and the Holocaust, it depicts the fatal consequences of guilt and madness.

Stingo, a writer and the story's narrator, learns that his neighbors Sophie and Nathan are both beset by separate but dangerous demons. In a series of flashbacks, the reader learns that Sophie was imprisoned in Auschwitz-Birkenau and was forced to choose between saving her son or daughter. After choosing her son, she ultimately lost both children and now cannot live with the guilt, grief, and depression brought on by her impossible choice.

Often characters are forced to choose between right and wrong, and, in doing so, find that morality has many shadings of grey. As in real life, the consequences of a choice must be momentous to create suspense. If your character is struggling to decide between vanilla and chocolate, the reader won't care. But if the question she wrestles with will bring down ruin on her best friend, or destroy a person's reputation, then things get interesting.

VILLAINS: CRAFTING SUSPENSE THROUGH ADVERSITY

Conflict in fiction creates the stress, opposition, and adversity that push at the protagonist. And while conflict can come in many forms, the usual means of heaping misery on your protagonist is to create an antagonist or villain for him to butt up against. If readers believe danger or evil lurks in your story in the form of a character, then you've got immediate suspense. Readers have been trained from early childhood experiences with cartoons and fairy tales to recognize the jeopardy created by an antagonist, and jeopardy always translates into suspense.

Modern novels, television series, and movies too often take the easy route by depicting antagonists and villains who are as stereotyped as the black hats they wear. Crooked cops, psychotic killers, deranged outlaws, mad scientists—they enter the story with all the panache of cardboard cutouts, their only ambition to be evil or greedy, although we never know why.

These one-dimensional bad guys sap the emotional impact from the story, because readers don't understand them. Like protagonists, the best antagonists are motivated by powerful forces that stem from their complicated pasts. These motivations, along with their actions, must have a certain, understandable logic. So, while readers may not agree with an antagonist's motives and ethics, they should understand how the antagonist or villain justifies them.

Just as the terms *hero* and *protagonist* are incorrectly assumed to mean the same thing, the terms *villain* and *antagonist* are also used incorrectly. A protagonist is the main character in the story and will be most changed by the events of the story. While he can be a likeable person, he doesn't necessarily need to be heroic and can be an antihero, such as Holden Caulfield in *The Catcher in the Rye*. A hero is a main character who has traits that the reader would like to emulate, such as intelligence, bravery, tenacity, or a commanding presence. James Bond and Sherlock Holmes are well-known heroes.

The word *villain* originally came from the Middle Ages (*villein*), and described a feudal serf. Because serfs worked the land, they were in the lowest class and were considered uncouth, boorish, and brutish. Over time, the term has also come to indicate evil and often depravity.

The word *antagonist*, on the other hand, is derived from Greek and is a force or person that someone struggles against. An antagonist is an adversary, and his job is to thwart your main character, perhaps by competition, perhaps by dangling a goal or object that he desires, or perhaps by creating a problem he needs to overcome. The antagonist's main role is to force the protagonist to triumph over his real or perceived flaws in order to win the prize. The villain represents evil and is always a greater threat than an antagonist, and usually the threat is physical.

The best villains are complicated, unforgettable, and intensely motivated. Villains are as formidable as the story's hero, like Sherlock Holmes's nemesis, Professor Moriarty, who, with his keen mind and shadowy crime syndicate, has been described as "like crime itself." Then there is Darth Vader, another villain with a complicated backstory—not to mention creepy cyborg implants and other enhancements. J.K. Rowling created the ultimate villain in the dark wizard Lord Voldemort, chilling her young readers with his evil ways, and creating a worthy adversary for Harry Potter and Professor Dumbledore.

As creator of the antagonist or villain, it's necessary for you to creep into his psyche, to know him intimately, and to see him sympathetically. If your antagonist or villain has a strongly developed set of beliefs, a solid self-concept (however deluded), and a logic for his actions, you'll naturally increase suspense. Since many of us cannot always acknowledge our own weaknesses or dark sides, it can work to imbue your antagonist with a similar myopia.

THE ROLE OF THE INNOCENT BYSTANDER

The late filmmaker Alfred Hitchcock, called the master of suspense, often tossed innocent bystanders into the midst of bizarre or dangerous events and then forced them to cope with and survive a situation that they hadn't expected. The capriciousness or randomness of this device creates suspense because a reader or movie viewer can easily imagine how frustrated and terrified she would feel if something similar happened to her.

In *The Birds*, adapted from Daphne Du Maurier's novel, socialite Melanie Daniels innocently arrives at a small coastal town to deliver a pair of love birds to a man that she was rude to, hoping to make amends. Unbeknownst to her, the town isn't what it seems, and she walks into a nightmare beyond her control. When you yank a character from her ordinary life and plunk her into a terrible scenario not of her own making, you've created a situation in which suspense is at full boil.

There's also another way to utilize the role of innocent bystander. In *The Birds*, Hitchcock kills off the likeable teacher Annie Hayworth, making her a *sacrificial* innocent bystander. Her death ups the ante by illustrating the danger for all the characters, and adds emotional trauma when Annie's student witnesses her gruesome death. While you don't necessarily need to kill off an innocent bystander, putting minor and vulnerable characters such as children in jeopardy along with the major characters increases suspense.

An innocent bystander stirs a reader's empathy and creates suspense because he doesn't deserve the mess he's fallen into. Hitchcock understood that the innocent bystander device works because it implies that life's random events can easily plummet a person into peril and tragedy.

AMBUSHED: MAKING THE SNEAK ATTACK WORK

While the best suspense comes from a steady and constant pressure on the reader's nerves, this pressure can also be interspersed with peak moments and sinister actions that further increase suspense. A sudden disaster or surprise adds to the story and makes the reader edgy. Such developments expose characters when they are unprepared and thus doubly vulnerable, and this causes the reader to evaluate circumstances in a new light. For example, if a character reacts with cowardice or panic to the surprise, then the reader will worry about her ability to handle further pressures.

These sudden events come in many shapes and sizes, and prove that life can bushwhack or ambush us, and that we are never safe. They prove, too, that tragedies and terrible consequences often come packaged with these sneak attacks. In Larry McMurtry's *Lonesome Dove*, the body count mounts as the cowboys head north on the cattle drive. Disasters are planted along the way, as when Deets, the scout, is killed by an Indian's arrow; an Irish immigrant is overtaken by a swarm of water moccasins during a river crossing; and Blue Duck sneaks up on a boy and a deputy and slits their throats. These events prove that death can be random and unreasonable.

Disasters such as fires, explosions, and burglaries all ratchet up suspense and capitalize on a reader's belief that life can be dangerous or violence random. Primitive fears and vulnerabilities stimulate emotions and suspense.

Since suspense is usually tied to a reader's anticipation, disasters must be used sparingly and be linked to the scope and genre of the novel. Readers of thrillers and Westerns expect a body count. Suspense readers expect a murder or two, along with violence and danger to the person tracking down the murderer. But disasters, like surprises, dull the reader's senses when overused.

Depending on the needs of the story, varying amounts of foreshadowing will set up the surprise or disaster. If you choose not to foreshadow the surprise, it must stem from something plausible—an element of nature, a character's motivation, or circumstances of the story world, such as two groups feuding over the same land.

Many short or average-length novels (60,000–80,000 words) contain only one or two surprises. If you insert a series of blitzes into the story, the reader will feel played with. The bottom line is that surprises of all sorts must be handled with utmost care. Surprises often work best at the end of a scene or chapter, as cliffhangers.

PLANT CLUES, NOT BOMBS

While surprises can increase suspense, sometimes scenes that are finely crafted via foreshadowing, clues, and delaying events can create more suspense than exploding surprises. When a reader is prepped for a disaster, when he's in on the game, he's involved and worried.

Imagine this scenario: A family reunion has been staged at a lovely park. The reunion is going well when suddenly a mother calls out to her child, a darling five-year-old moppet with golden curls. After the child doesn't answer, the mother starts searching and cannot find her. She becomes worried, then frantic as she draws others into the search, until the gathering is in an uproar of worry-etched faces and frantic calls. She's gone.

Now that's a bombshell surprise, and it's fine as far as it goes, but it contains no suspense, and the impact of the surprise doesn't last long. Now imagine scenario two. It's the same reunion, but from time to time, the reader glimpses little Samantha, eyes the color of the summer sky, golden curls as soft as cashmere. The reader sees her plant a kiss on her grandmother's cheek and giggle as she chases bubbles and slips down the slide. The reader then watches as her cousin, Jason, teases her and reduces her to tears by thrusting a squirming frog in her face. After she runs in tears to her mother and is admonished to be a big girl and quit tattling, Mom gives her a brownie and suggests that she go and enjoy her treat. Samantha hides behind the sturdy trunk of an elm to regain her composure and sulk.

But the reader spies something else lurking within camera range: a man, who at first was sitting quietly in his car, watching, but who is now drawing closer. His breathing is slightly ragged as his eyes follow the tiny blonde girl. He approaches the child behind the tree as she nibbles on her brownie, tears still glistening on her cheeks when she looks up at him:

> "That looks yummy," he says, kneeling down to her level.
>
> "Want a bite?" she asks, forgetting in the moment all her mother's warnings about stranger danger.
>
> "Sure." He accepts a chocolate morsel and puts it in his mouth.
>
> They chew in silence.
>
> "I saw that boy chase you with that frog. I'd never do that to my sister."
>
> "He's not my brother. He's my stupid cousin."
>
> "He's big enough to know better."
>
> She nods in agreement.

Cut back to the reunion, where adults are starting to pack the food and paraphernalia. As she's storing leftover hot dog buns and potato salad, Samantha's mother looks around for her daughter and doesn't see her among the children.

Adding the child molester to the story surprises the reader, because at a reunion the worst thing the reader expects to happen is for Uncle George to drink too much and tell off-color jokes. Instead, the reader finds herself plunging into a parent's nightmare. By setting up the scene, the reader knows things that the characters don't know: that a villain is lurking nearby, that a child is feeling vulnerable, and that the villain knows how to manipulate children to earn their trust before he pounces.

The writer could also choose not to depict the villain meeting Samantha, but instead introduce him in a scene previous to the reunion. In this scene, he stakes out another victim or engages in another deviant or criminal activity. Then, after Samantha disappears, we cut to a scene where he and Samantha are back at his lair.

Yet another option would be for the writer to build suspense by portraying the pedophile in the park scene *and* by introducing him beforehand. This early introduction could up the creep factor by showing the villain's environment—perhaps a collection of kiddy porn or some object that appears benign but is not, like a small room with the lock on the outside of the door, or a trophy barrette from a previous victim.

There's always a temptation to explode bombs in your stories, but remember that your reader wants to see the hardware attached to the bomb, the timing device ticking off the seconds one by one. The reader also needs to know the people in the bomb's vicinity and perhaps the terrorist who is setting the bomb. By planting clues, building suspense in increments, foreshadowing, and prolonging events, you will appeal to your reader's instincts.

The Haunted-House Effect

As children, many of us visited a haunted house or carnival fun house. In these places of fright, you creep along corridors and into rooms where at any moment a ghost might appear, a ghoul might pop out screeching, a skeleton might clatter in with bones rattling, or a coffin might creak open, revealing a gruesome corpse. As you creep along, eerie organ music suggests a manic touch at the keyboard. The air smells of fear, and just when your nerves are stretched taut, blood starts dripping from the ceiling and a shriek that sounds straight from the grave splits the gloom.

It is not so much the sight of these horrors that terrifies, it is the prolonged agony of dreading and fearing what might be around the corner. No matter how you brace yourself for what is to come, the haunted house is built to inflict suffering via a series of stressors. In fiction, unbearable tension can be applied in many ways. Let's say you're writing a scene where a heroine is confronted with a rapist in her apartment. Your first choice is to decide if the reader knows beforehand about the rapist or if this information will be withheld. If you opt for letting the reader in on the secret, we will watch him use a glass cutter to slip into the heroine's bedroom, then crouch in her closet with his bag of horrors—duct tape, gloves, a straight razor, and a camera, since he likes to photograph his victims.

Next, your heroine comes home. It's likely that you'll choose to portray her as vulnerable, perhaps exhausted after a long day at the office or emotionally drained because a date didn't go well. Or, in contrast to the emotions that occur during her attack, she might enter the apartment in high spirits. She turns the key in the lock, and then steps into the apartment. After slipping off her jacket and putting on the tea kettle, she finally steps into the bedroom, where the rapist lurks. Just as she reaches for the closet door, the phone rings. Her boss is calling with another demand; her best friend wants to know how the date went; her mother is calling from Florida, complaining about her ailments. And meanwhile, the rapist is waiting, trying to decide how to maximize the terror in his victim. The suspense intensifies and the reader practically holds his breath to see how the nightmare will unfold.

As a writer, it can be helpful to think back to childhood nightmares and terrors. Were you sure monsters lurked in your shadowy closet? Were you afraid of an abandoned house or graveyard? Did you ever see ghosts or encounter something or someone who was evil?

Key in to your feelings of childhood dread and terror; then, with your memories firmly in mind, look for places in your story where you can exploit and prolong these emotions. When a reader enters these scenes, he will feel apprehension and disquiet. Employ the haunted-house effect to make readers uneasy, or better yet, struck by the heebie-jeebies.

Scene Setups: Enhancing Atmospheric Pressure

Suspense is enhanced by atmosphere and mood. Because you'll be employing a variety of techniques to create the mood and ambience for a scene, sometimes you'll dab in only a few suggestive details, and sometimes you'll provide a full-fledged description of a place. The more complicated the scene, the more complicated the setup.

Here is a key scene setup from Ray Bradbury's *Something Wicked This Way Comes*. Notice how sensory and unsettling this description of the carnival is, how, instead of describing cotton candy, clowns, and toddlers giggling, Bradbury creates an atmosphere as disturbing as a fingernail scraping down a blackboard. (Italics are used to emphasize the sensory information, specific nouns, and potent verbs that contribute to Bradbury's atmosphere of fright.)

> A carnival should be all *growls, roars* like timberlands *stacked, bundled, rolled* and *crashed*, great *explosions of lion dust*, men ablaze with working anger, pop bottles jangling, *horse buckles shivering*, engines and elephants in full stampede through *rains of sweat* while zebras neighed and *trembled* like cage trapped in cage.
>
> But this was like old movies, the silent theater *haunted* with black-and-white ghosts, *silvery mouths* opening to let moonlight smoke out, gestures made in *silence so hushed* you could hear the wind fizz the hair on your cheeks.
>
> More *shadows rustled* from the train, passing the animal cages where *darkness prowled with unlit eyes* and the calliope stood mute save for the faintest idiot tune the breeze piped wandering up the flues.

As the reader enters the carnival, he's no longer expecting to find teddy bears and gooey happiness. He's going to be tiptoeing into the place, neck prickling, on guard. In your own work, use language, imagery, and metaphor to heighten the mood and atmosphere in scenes. If you suspect that your word power doesn't enhance suspense, examine an author like Dean Koontz, who is known for using language and metaphor to build an extra layer of fright and unease.

WORD BY WORD

Every word in every scene communicates something and can create atmospheric pressure, as illustrated in the Bradbury excerpt. Whenever possible, choose words for their emotional connotations, and sometimes for their fright factor. *Shriek* or *screech* contains more of a fright factor than *yell* or *holler*. Someone can *break out* in nervous laughter or *squeal* with nervous laughter. In the following excerpt from Bram Stoker's *Dracula*, Jonathan is approaching Dracula's castle. Notice how Stoker applies language that is as precise and sharp as a scalpel. Again, key words have been italicized.

At last there came a time when the driver went further afield than he had yet done, and during his absence the horses began to *tremble* worse than ever and to *snort* and *scream with fright*. I could not see any cause for it, for the *howling* of the wolves had ceased altogether; but just then the moon, sailing through the *black* clouds, appeared behind the *jagged* crest of a beetling, pine-clad rock, and by its light I saw around us a ring of wolves, with *white teeth* and *lolling red tongues*, with *long, sinewy limbs* and *shaggy hair*. They were a hundred times more *terrible* in the *grim silence* which held them than even when they *howled*. For myself, I felt a sort of *paralysis of fear*. It is only when a man feels himself face to face with such *horrors* that he can understand their true import.

It's clear from Stoker's word choices in this description that the reader is approaching a place of nightmares, not lollipops. The technique here is to adjust the language to the needs of the scene. If a quiet scene is about to unfold, then the language should be quiet and simple. If you're working to create worry or dread, then the language needs to prickle and slip under the reader's skin as in the above excerpt.

241

Sleight of Hand: The McGuffin Technique

The McGuffin, a common plot device also used frequently in films, is when the reader's attention is drawn to an action, object, effect, or information that has no other purpose than to advance the story. While the reader can become distracted by and/or concerned with the McGuffin, and the entire story can be built around it, the McGuffin itself is not the story, as it does not cause or explain the ending of the story. Instead it's essentially a distracting device. Once the McGuffin is introduced, the reader will keep trying to figure out its significance because the characters seem to believe in its significance. Meanwhile, the *real* plot will be heating up.

In Colin Harrison's *The Havana Room*, for instance, the mysterious room below the steak house is the McGuffin. It appears that what happens in this chamber of secrets lies at the heart of the novel, but in reality the story is built around real estate deals, swindles, and another character's past.

It is believed that Alfred Hitchcock first coined the term McGuffin, and many of his films contain the device. In Hitchcock's *North by Northwest*, government secrets seem to motivate characters and events. After being kidnapped, the protagonist, Roger Thornhill, is mistaken for an undercover agent by foreign spies and then is implicated falsely in the murder of a U.N. official. With this accusation against him, he must run from the foreign spies, the FBI, and the police. However, no government secrets are revealed at the story's end, and they don't drive the plot. Instead, the story centers on uncovering the real murderer.

Quentin Tarantino planted a McGuffin in *Pulp Fiction* in the form of the mysterious briefcase with glowing contents owned by crime boss Marsellus Wallace. In the film, there are actually four story lines that are interwoven and track back and forth in time. However, the main story follows two hit men, Vincent and Jules, as they take care of business for Wallace. The briefcase is considered a McGuffin because its contents are never revealed and the other plot events overshadow it completely.

Suspense Fumbles and Blunders

We've been discussing the techniques that make suspense seethe in your story. They require finesse and proper proportions to work. Here's a list of suspense gaffes that can ruin a scene or dilute suspense:

- **Bait and switch.** This occurs when an author devotes attention to a specific aspect of the story, such as an emotional argument with the character's mother (bait), and then substitutes or jumps (switches) to a set piece, an action scene, or violence that is unrelated to the previous development but contains the same players. Readers will lose trust if you don't connect the dots between scenes and payoffs.

- **Chrome.** This term stems from the chrome on the cars of yesteryear. Think of the Cadillacs and Buicks driven by mobsters, or the 1960 Chevy your grandfather owned. Chrome in fiction means that the author has spent too much time and words describing settings or details that don't affect the plot, stimulate the reader's emotions, or push the story ahead.

- **Circuit breakers.** Imagine this: The tension in the scene has reached an almost unbearable peak—as when a couple is about to make love, a woman is about to give birth, or a detective is about to make an accusation—when suddenly the author pulls the plug by leaving the scene for another event or locale that is not as interesting or emotionally charged. Or, just as the scene is about to take off into the emotional stratosphere with a show-down or declaration of lasting love, the writer describes the scene secondhand afterward rather than staging it in front of the reader.

- **Exposition dumps.** It's easy to dump exposition into a complex novel. After all, there is so much that needs explaining. Exposition that runs for several paragraphs can sometimes work if it describes a complicated setting, situation, or character, or if it creates a spooky atmosphere. There are no hard and fast rules about how long exposition should be. However, exposition is considered a dump when it is so long that it stalls the story, contains information that a reader doesn't necessarily need to know, and is not interwoven into the story. The worst of this ilk sounds like an encyclopedia entry.

- **Too much foreshadowing.** Foreshadowing is used to make future events logical and to weave elements of the story together. When a child plays with a jack-in-the-box, he winds the crank and a familiar tune plays. The tune and the act of turning the crank create anticipation, foreshadowing the event: the clown popping out of the box. Without foreshadowing, the clown would pop out arbitrarily.

Foreshadowing proves that events are not arbitrary, but are causally related. When foreshadowing is done right, it increases tension and suspense; when it is overdone, there is no surprise or intrigue.

- **Gorilla in the room.** A gorilla in the room destroys suspense by diminishing credibility. Here's the scenario: The gorilla is marauding about, wreaking havoc, but for some implausible or bizarre reason, the characters cannot see the gorilla, or they believe that since he's furry, he's not dangerous—an inappropriate reaction to jeopardy. Children in the town are disappearing or acting strangely, but no one is alarmed; if the protagonist is trying to figure out what is happening to the kids, no one listens to his warnings. If you've planted a gorilla in your story, characters need to run shrieking when it appears.

- **Idiot at large.** Idiot at large is a problem of plausibility and credibility. Imagine this: It's the proverbial dark and stormy night in your scene. The electricity flickers, then dies, with only lightening flashes and candles to illuminate the gloom. Since a jailbreak at a nearby maximum-security prison earlier in the week, Maytown has been swarming with search parties, yet the escaped prisoner, a former Special Forces operative, seems able to disappear like a ghost.

  The protagonist, who is home alone with a bad cold, hears a rustling sound from the lower floor and, instead of dialing 911 or acting logically to the danger, sets off to investigate the darkened basement with a butter knife. At this point, your reader starts groaning out loud. Don't send your character into danger without a thought to the consequences; instead, make certain that she takes appropriate action. Perhaps she attempts to dial for help, but discovers that the criminal has cut the phone wires. Or, she can attempt to escape, but then suddenly he's looming at the door, blocking her way. The lesson here is that when the going gets tough, a protagonist fights back to the best of her ability.

- **Rush jobs.** Beginning writers fail to set up big scenes because they're in a hurry to explode the bomb or push a character off the cliff. But a reader needs a before so that he can truly appreciate the after. When you rush through the setup information, the scene will lack texture and believability, and the emotional payoff will fall flat.

- **Stall tactics.** While prolonging suspense is necessary, stalling it is deadly. If the author knows that he's got a big scene or set piece coming up and puts it off by inserting backstory or an unnecessary flashback, or by including too much exposition or setting, the reader will grow impatient and skip past the details to reach the action.

- **Superman syndrome.** Flaws cause suspense, and, unlike diamonds, characters with flaws are more interesting, endearing, and fascinating. If you've created a Superman type and underplayed his flaws, realize that this sort of emphasis dilutes suspense and veers toward melodrama.

- **Transition disasters.** Spending too much time and ink moving your character from scene to scene kills suspense. In our modern world, most readers understand how characters walk across rooms, drive across town, or fly from Los Angeles to New York. Now, if a terrorist boards the plane at LAX, readers want to be on the plane with the protagonist, but in general, the to-and-fro should be kept to a minimum.

{ * }

Suspense in all its forms works best when what is at stake in the story matters to the protagonist *and* to the reader. Suspense needles the reader with anxiety and places her in the dark, groping for a way out.

Suspense requires that you dig deep into your bag of tricks to arouse curiosity and dread, and then sustain them. Bring in a character's old fears, unfinished business, enemies, or ghosts to complicate the current situation. Add subplots that also instigate discomfort, such as decisions that need to be made, actions that must be taken, and problems that need to be solved. Use place to crank up the tensions—a lawless border town in the Old West, the onset of a violent thunder storm, the gray, joyless days of deep winter. And don't forget your basic sleight-of-hand device to build suspense: Reveal information or resolve troubles at the last possible moment.

chapter 16

Tension

{

When in doubt, have a man come through the door with a gun in his hand.
—Raymond Chandler

ension is part curiosity, part unease, and part dread. It is linked to every aspect of your story, is found on every page, and creates a vivid fictional world that seethes with trouble and causes your reader to fret and worry. Tension, along with suspense, jabs at the reader's senses with haunting questions, uneasy situations, and shifting circumstances that must be unraveled.

Before we go further, let's pause to distinguish tension from suspense. Suspense, as discussed in the previous chapter, is created by withholding information and prolonging outcomes. When you create suspense, tension is also naturally created, but they are not the same thing. Tension is a sense of disquiet that permeates every possible moment in the story. Where suspense creates apprehension and anxiety, tension is the constant unease that lurks beneath the surface of the story, eating at the reader's nerves, making him feel fidgety and even rattled. It is palatable and literally makes the reader tense his body while turning pages.

Tension varies in degrees throughout a story, depending on the needs of a specific scene. It works with conflict to bring the emotional level from a simmer to a boil, then back again. Tension is also felt on pages that don't portray direct conflict. It is created on a word-by-word basis because the fictional world is an unsettling place, and tension agitates and involves the reader. Author Gary Provost explained in *Make Your Words Work* that tension can't be limited to a single scene:

> Tension is not just something that you put into your dramatic last scene when the ax murderer is hiding in the closet. It is a cord, or series of cords, that stretch across every paragraph that you write. And tension is not always a matter of life or death. "Will he kiss her?" is tension. "Will she slap his face or melt in his arms?" That is tension.

Fiction is designed to cause a reader's emotions and mood to go up and down with every turn of the page. Unlike real life, where people usually avoid conflict and misery, in fiction, the best parts of the story are where the characters are in the worst trouble. Readers love to suffer along with characters, perhaps because they're removed from these miseries, perhaps because they're escaping their own miseries while reading comfortably in their homes or airplane seats.

Because large and small outcomes are always uncertain, tension stems from the structure of a story and its individual scenes. Scenes are designed around a simple construction: A protagonist desires something, and someone or some force in the scene will thwart, grant, or stall this desire. Tension increases when the outcome is in doubt and the reader wants the protagonist to succeed. Readers simply must keep reading to discover how things work out.

While tension is created by uncertainty, it is also as omnipresent as the sky. As you sit near a window, step outdoors and water your garden, walk to your car, or tour the Grand Canyon, the sky is the backdrop in all its striations and moods. It's a huge aspect of your day-to-day reality. It affects your mood and outlook, and it dictates your activities. Similarly, tension surrounds all aspects of fiction and affects the mood in every scene.

INTRODUCING TENSION IN YOUR FIRST SCENES

The first infusion of tension in your story stems from introducing a story question in the opening scenes. All openings must pique curiosity, which then becomes uneasiness and then escalates to worry. Fiction begins with a threatening change to the protagonist's status quo that starts the story action and causes the reader to wonder what will happen next and how things will be resolved.

The opening paragraph of Flannery O'Connor's novel *The Violent Bear It Away* depicts a bizarre situation and a story question that makes the reader wonder about what comes next:

> Francis Marion Tarwater's uncle had been dead for only half a day when the boy got too drunk to finish digging his grave and a Negro named Buford Munson, who had come to get a jug filled, had to finish it and drag the body from the breakfast table where it was still sitting and bury it in a decent and Christian way, with the sign of its Saviour at the head of the grave and enough dirt on top to keep the dogs from digging it up. Buford had come along about noon and when he left at sundown, the boy, Tarwater, had never returned from the still.

This opening salvo leaves the reader wanting to know who the uncle was, how he died, and how his nephew handles his death.

In *The Postman Always Rings Twice*, by James M. Cain, the first sentence is a setup for the story question: "They threw me off the hay truck about noon." The reader immediately wants to know what sort of person is tossed off a vehicle and why. The reader soon learns the narrator had been in Tijuana and was catching up on sleep in the back of the truck. By the second paragraph, the narrator has arrived at Twin Oaks Tavern, a roadside café, and is swiftly being served a huge breakfast that he cannot pay for.

The reader is immediately uneasy because it's clear that the narrator is a drifter who sneaked onto the hay wagon and now is conning the Twin Oaks owner out of a meal. Then, in the middle of his con, he's offered a job by the owner. The speed of the scene, aided by pared-down language and spare details, also makes the reader tense. But then Cain adds the coup de grâce—the owner's wife steps into the scene:

> Then I saw her. She had been out back, in the kitchen, but she came in to gather up my dishes. Except for the shape, she really wasn't any raving beauty, but she had a sulky look to her, and her lips stuck out in a way that made me want to mash them in for her.

All these details add up to an uneasy situation certain to veer toward trouble, and trouble always creates tension and suspense.

Now that we've looked at several examples, you can create your own tense openings by using the following guidelines:

- Introduce your protagonist as soon as possible. The reader's first glimpse of your protagonist should be unforgettable and create curiosity and a longing to know her better.

- Begin your story with a change that plunges your protagonist into action. This change must create an immediate goal for the character and have an uncertain outcome.

- Craft this first change so that it causes the protagonist to begin to tilt off center. Fiction isn't about protagonists who are grounded and stable and fully functioning. Instead, they are off-balance, struggling, and often desperate, and these states in turn create tension.

- In your opening, hint at the protagonist's backstory rather than revealing it.

- Although structures vary, generally avoid premature flashbacks in your opening. Make the reader worry about the present situation before you introduce the past.

- Don't bog down your opening with so many characters that the reader will have difficulty keeping track of your cast.

- If you open with description instead of a scene, make certain that the description piques the reader's interest and creates unease.

- Opening with tension doesn't mean that you should resort to melodrama or blazing gun battles. Trust in your reader and use slight actions and small torments for the characters. Violence isn't necessary to create tension.

- Analyze the verbs in your first pages and see if you can replace passive verbs or dull verbs like *see, look, get, put,* and *walk* with more sensory verbs that jab at the reader.

MAINTAINING TENSION THROUGHOUT THE MIDDLE

The middle is the longest segment of the novel and is a bridge between the opening and ending. The opening of your story shows that change is inevitable, and your middle proves it. Because of its length, this portion often suffers from lagging

249

tension and action that drifts away from the main conflict. Many problems that are common to middles can be solved via structure and careful plotting.

Induce tension in the middle by staging a major turning point or reversal about midway in the story. Examples might be the hunter becoming the hunted, the death of a character, an unexpected betrayal, or an event that veers out of control and turns into a disaster. In a mystery novel, the detective might spend the opening chapters following a certain line of inquiry or honing in on a single suspect. In the middle, the suspect might be murdered, or another major event might occur that changes the story's direction.

In the middle, the protagonist needs to face a drastically altered playing field, one that is constantly changing. In the middle of Michael Crichton's *Jurassic Park*, a fierce storm descends, the power is shut off, and the dinosaurs escape while the main computer is rebooted. These changes create new threats, intensify already-brewing conflict, reveal a protagonist reacting to threats, and increase the stakes. In the middle, what a protagonist fears most is often brought into play, or the dangers he has been avoiding grow closer and closer:

Here are some guidelines to keep tension boiling through the important middle.

- Make sure the conflict changes and the intensity of the conflict increases.

- Each time you introduce a new snag or crisis, be sure it creates an unanswered question.

- If there is a villain or antagonist in the story, use the middle to reveal what he is capable of.

- Use the middle to reveal and exacerbate the protagonist's internal conflict.

- If the story line warrants it, make sure time is running out—a patient will die, a true love will get away, a criminal will go free, etc.

- Have the crises in the middle cause the protagonist to confront his flaws and weaknesses, which of course isn't easy.

- Make the middle a point of no return—the protagonist is now forced to continue until the conflict is resolved.

- Use the middle to prove that the protagonist is capable of change.

ENDING WITH TENSION

The ending is the payoff for all the events that preceded it. If it fails, then the novel fails. An ending must contain tension to increase its effectiveness. Endings depict events where the conflict is resolved and nothing will ever be the same again. In action stories, the ending is usually a final, physical confrontation between the protagonist and antagonist. In a literary novel, the protagonist is often forced into a decision, an action, a discovery about himself, or a recognition of some insight. The ending releases the reader from the story events, closing the door on them and allowing the reader to look back at the significance of everything that happened.

Because endings have a huge burden to carry in the story and because writers want to end with a bang, they often go overboard when creating endings. Endings must be tense, intense, and true to the story. It's also important to remember that the events in the ending must be *proportional* to what preceded them. Here's a great tip from writing guru Jerome Stern's *Making Shapely Fiction*:

> Writers of novels sometimes feel the ending must be very emotional or violent, and go for melodramatic effects. They fear that if there is no physical confrontation, no grand scene, readers will say, "Is that all? Have you taken me all the way for this?" But if the journey's been worth going on you don't need an earthquake to make it interesting. Many "spectacular" endings seem false to the landscape of the rest of the book. It might be best to stay true to the terms of the fictional world you made.

Here are a few guidelines to make certain that your endings don't fizzle, but instead cause the reader to close the book with great regret at leaving your story world:

- Tense endings force a protagonist to act in ways that the reader would be afraid to—confronting the antagonist, running into the burning building, or escaping the murderer's clutches. The ending supplies the most vicarious thrills and action in certain genres.

- In a literary novel with less dramatic action, the protagonist on a journey of self-discovery chooses a difficult course of action—leaving the stifling marriage, stepping out of corporate life, or confronting her past head-on. Quieter endings require that the reader see the protagonist and her situation in a new light.

251

- To focus tension, endings contained in a single scene work best. These scenes can culminate from various preceding forces, but boil the drama in a single pot.

- Short story endings are often low-key or muted, but must always prove that something important has happened in the life of the protagonist.

- If the ending contains revelations such as the identity of a murderer, delay them until the last possible moment.

- Avoid spelling out every aspect of the ending or its implications. Trust the reader to interpret meanings.

- Once you have answered the story question, tied up the subplots, and/or resolved the main conflict, resist the urge to linger. Get off the stage as quickly and gracefully as possible.

- If the ending is shocking, violent, or abrupt, you might want to include an epilogue that reveals the consequences of the plot. Epilogues are used when the fate of the characters is not spelled out in the climax and thus the ending is too ambiguous or unsettling without them. But remember, not every minor character or issue can be accounted for in complex fiction—sometimes readers must imagine the outcomes.

DON'T FORGET TO BREATHE

While fiction is imbued with tension and suspense, it requires ebbs and flows to vary the level of tension. The solution is to intersperse breathers throughout the story, where you turn down the tension a notch. The number of breathers you will use depends on your story needs and genre.

A romance has more breathers than other genres because it is centered on characters' emotions and inner conflict, and the reader wants to spend time exploring these emotions. These breathers might take the form of dialogue with a trusted confidant, character thoughts, or sequel scenes. Thrillers keep the tension ratcheted up, but transitions to change locations or relay important data provide breathers.

The best breathers appear natural to the story line and the character's personality, and might include eating a meal, walking the dog, straightening the office, or attending a party. Since fiction contains peaks and valleys, make sure the lulls of the story don't stop the momentum, but instead provide a pause or turn the drama down a notch or two. Sometimes these lulls are the calm before the storm, so make the action that follows doubly intense.

TOOLS FOR CONVEYING TENSION

There are a number of handy tools in the fiction writing toolbox that can be used to induce and manipulate tension.

CHANGE AS AN INSTRUMENT OF TENSION

Here's an easy equation for maintaining tension throughout your story: Change equals tension. A novel is a record of a character being threatened and transformed by a series of changes, and as the story progresses these changes become increasingly threatening. As noted earlier, the first change—created by the inciting incident—introduces the first dose of tension, but you can never let up pressure on your character.

When a character is threatened by a change, she often reacts badly or with desperation, which in turn creates more tension. Change comes into play when new locales, characters, and circumstances are introduced, and issues from the past invade the present. Of course, stories can also evolve around changes in the protagonist's inner world that force her to confront her weaknesses, flaws, and fears.

The best changes throw the protagonist off balance, while the ensuing changes keep her tilting further off as she struggles to right herself, but never quite succeeds. If the change tips toward a positive outcome, it needs to eventually turn sour. You might want to keep another formula in mind: Change equals torment. Torment your characters, and tension *must* result.

It can be helpful when plotting your novel to create a list of changes that you're planning to inflict on your protagonist. As you orchestrate scenes dramatizing the changes, ask yourself what the worst possible outcome for your protagonist is. Often a character's worst fears will be the subject of a novel or short story, and these fears can be reduced to a single word: change.

TWISTS

Stories are constructed around a series of surprises and twists. The unexpected unsettles readers, keeps the story from lagging, and gives the story line a series of peaks that inject tension and keep the reader's interest. In *The Wizard of Oz*, when Dorothy and her pals finally reach the Emerald City to visit the wizard and ask for help, he yanks the rug out from under them and demands that they bring back the witch's broomstick. In *Romancing the Stone*, after Joan Wilder and Jack Colton find the sought-after emerald deep in the cave and escape the bad guys, they become separated by a river, and she is forced to confront her worst fears about him and face her sister's kidnappers alone.

When you insert these mini-shocks, naturally tension is introduced. The reader stays involved because he wonders about the ramifications of these surprises. But some stories aren't structured around surprises. Some stories offer a subtler unfolding, and some (like frame stories) have their endings revealed in the opening. From there, the plot unravels, illuminating how the ending came about. In these cases, the tension must stem from within the character, from motivations or sources that push her to act in certain ways.

RAISING THE STAKES

This leads to another point: The stakes in fiction matter because stakes create tension. The protagonist's ultimate happiness, perhaps even his life, depends on the outcome. If the stakes in the story are low, then tension will be weak. The stakes are often linked to inner conflict, as the protagonist wonders if what is at stake is worth it. In these situations, the story line forces him to reconsider his beliefs and values.

It's easy to recognize the increasing stakes in Ernest Hemingway's *The Old Man and the Sea*. In the first scenes, the stakes are centered on Santiago's ability to catch a fish and, by doing so, restore his reputation. The stakes go up as Santiago struggles to land the biggest fish he's ever encountered. Will he land the fish? Will the fish drag him too far out to sea? Finally, the stakes go up again as he struggles to survive his ordeal at sea, especially when sharks are drawn to his boat by blood lust.

Hemingway didn't craft the story around a young man who was at the top of his game and at peak physical prowess. A fisherman with unwavering confidence and rippling muscles would not inspire the same kind of stakes (and thus tension) as an older man with so much to prove and gain or lose.

Analyze the escalating stakes in published novels, particularly ones that are similar to your story. Diagram or outline a novel, noting the series or events that crank up the stakes. Then, scrutinize your own plot. If the published novel has ten key events that escalate the stakes, and your story has three or four, that information illustrates the weakness in your plot.

DIALOGUE

Dialogue is not conversation, it's conversation's greatest hits. Dialogue is often a power struggle, and this exchange demands that one person loses. It's also loaded with subtext, the river of emotion that flows beneath the words but remains unspoken, and subtext creates tension. Dialogue is a natural place for conflict to play out: Perhaps one character is trying to placate an aggrieved character and failing. Dialogue can feature arguments, wheedling, whining, refusals, and head games.

While some dialogue strictly dispenses information, most is an exchange where tension is palpable. Tense dialogue is a tight, more intense version of real-life speech. When you're editing your own tense dialogue, examine the visual impact of your dialogue sections. Tense dialogue contains lots of short sentences, fragments, and white space. If your dialogue is rehashing events that have already happened or is commenting on events that are happening instead of showing them, then it will dilute tension.

If your dialogue goes on for pages without pause, it will lack tension, no matter the subject. If your dialogue contains chit-chat, comments on the weather, greetings, compliments, and other niceties, it will also lack tension. Exchange discussions for confrontations, arguments, teasing, and misunderstandings.

If a large portion of your dialogue is staged as experts or sages conveying information, rethink your strategy. While genres such as thrillers and mysteries require experts to convey important data, try to keep these exchanges as brief as possible, include visual elements in the scene, give the characters with distinctive voices,

255

and add occasional humor to lighten the scene. Your other option is to reveal this information in exposition, which is sometimes better suited for imparting facts.

Carl Hiaasen is known for suspense novels that are offbeat and driven by hilarious, edgy dialogue. *Skinny Dip* evolves around Chaz Perrone, a marine biologist who's in the midst of an environmental scam. Because he fears that his wife, Joey, has caught on to his shenanigans, he decides to toss her overboard into the Atlantic while they're on a cruise ship, forgetting that she was a former champion swimmer. She manages to cling to a bale of Jamaican marijuana and is plucked from the water by Mike Stranahan. Joey decides to play dead for a while, and Stranahan helps her taunt Perrone while they figure out just how far to push him. Their mischief includes Stranahan making a series of phone calls designed to rattle Perrone:

Mike Stranahan phoned Charles Perrone at 5:42 A.M.

"Good morning, dipshit," he said, this time doing Jerry Lewis. The Mexican writer who owned the island adored *The Nutty Professor*, and Stranahan had watched it often on the VCR. There were worse ways to get through a tropical depression.

At the other end of the line, Joey Perrone's husband needed a few moments to rouse himself. "Are you the same guy who called yesterday?"

"That's riiii-ghht."

Chaz Perrone said, "We should get together, you and me."

"Why?"

"To talk."

"We're talking now," Stranahan said. "You tossed your beloved into the Atlantic Ocean. I'm curious to hear an explanation."

"I didn't push her. She fell."

"That's not what I saw."

"Listen to me," Perrone pleaded, but his voice trailed away.

"Yoo-hoo? Chaz?"

"We should do this in person."

"Do what? There's eighteen hundred dollars in your checking account," Stranahan said. "That's pitiful."

"I can get more," Perrone blurted. Then, warily: "How'd you know what I have in the bank?"

"Pity-full."

256

"Don't hang up. Don't!"

Stranahan said, "How would you ever get enough money?"

"People owe me."

Stranahan laughed. "Are you a biologist or a loan shark?"

"Okay, Rolvaag. Tell me how much you want."

Again with the "Rolvaag" stuff, thought Stranahan. "I haven't decided on an amount," he said.

"Okay, when can we get together? I'm serious."

"Bye-bye, Chaz."

"Wait," Perrone said, "I've gotta ask—that voice you're doing? "

"Yeah?"

"Jim Carrey, right?"

Stranahan said, "Mister, my price just doubled."

Notice how Hiaasen's dialogue is as lively as a Wimbledon match, conveyed by colorful characters using humor, fragments, and short exchanges, without thoughts, and with few speech tags. Notice too how the final words linger, creating an extra dose of tension and pushing the reader into the next scene.

REVELATIONS

All fiction evolves around revelations, which are discussed in chapter five. When a reader first meets your protagonist, the reader knows nothing about him. Like meeting a stranger at a party; the character is a blank slate. After you chat for a few minutes, you learn he's a stockbroker or a journalist or a barista at Starbucks. You discover his age or approximate age, whether he's clever or dull, educated or illiterate, witty or serious, single or married, happy or depressed, calm or agitated. When you first walked into the party, he was just a guy sipping a beer in the living room, but after discussing the hostess's remodeled kitchen, the buffet items, and politics, you have enough information to form judgments about this person.

When a reader encounters your protagonist, Jed, he's a stranger to her, but once she comes to know his dominant personality traits, she will be able to form opinions based on Jed's dialogue and thoughts and actions. With each page, the reader discovers the character's flaws and strengths, his self-concept and desires, the influences from his past, and, most of all, his secrets. And as each detail, each secret, is exposed, the tension mounts, as does the reader's vested interested in Jed.

257

The most interesting characters have secrets or some intrigue that they don't want people to know about. Perhaps Jed cheated on his wife and the subsequent divorce was his fault. Perhaps Jed's father abandoned the family when he was five, and he's never been able to recover from that loss. Perhaps Jed suffers from a deep loneliness. Perhaps he is ashamed of his loneliness. Or he could be ashamed of his sexual fantasies, a childhood trauma, or his need to be mothered by women.

This is not to say that all characters are, at their core, troubled personalities. The point is that perfect people are boring and lack tension. Characters must have emotional needs, wounds, and skeletons in the closet. These factors cause tension and keep the reader interested. Readers are nosy; they want to delve into a character's private affairs, rummage through his trash bin. In the real world, we're rarely able to snoop to our heart's content. In fiction, we have a license to look around, to open up the secret drawers and hiding places.

Exploit Your Story Type

There are three main categories of fiction: character-driven stories, idea-driven stories, and plot-driven stories. In a character-driven story, the inner world of the protagonist, what she thinks and feels, along with her interactions with other characters, are more important than the events in the plot. The reader is allowed to see deep into the protagonist's heart and soul. Most literary fiction and all romances are character driven. The tension in a character-driven story stems from reader identification and empathy. The more a reader cares, the more he worries. These stories can also center on families, friendships, and communities.

An idea-driven story is based on a thought-provoking idea or question, or a group of intriguing, related concepts. The characters and events in the plot are orchestrated to feature the idea and are affected by it. Science fiction stories, like H.G. Wells's *The Time Machine*, are often idea-driven stories. Another, more contemporary example is Robert J. Sawyer's *Mindscan*, which explores the ramifications of humans adopting android bodies when their human bodies wear out. The tension in idea-driven stories comes from the impact of the idea on mankind—often the technology (or whatever concept is explored) can be mishandled, exploited, or deadly.

A plot-driven story features the intricacies of events as the central focus. While such a story relies on characters and setting to propel the events, both play second fiddle to the actions. Mysteries and thrillers are typically plot driven, and feature a high proportion of action. Plot-driven stories need a large dose of tension and forward momentum. The danger of writing such stories is that the plots can seem formulaic and the characters one-dimensional because they exist to create actions that make readers worry. Tension can be increased with reader identification, so you need to create sympathetic, interesting characters in grave jeopardy.

It's important to realize that, in fiction writing, there is often a blurring or combining of these categories. You're not required to stick to a single type, because often by combining them you will create the best story. However, when you're working with a combination, make one element dominant and feature the other element as secondary. For example, Ruth Rendell writes psychological mysteries that probe deep into the psyches and motivations of her characters. However, her stories are still mysteries, and tracking down the killer is still paramount.

There seems to be a supposition that character-driven fiction is somehow superior to plot-driven fiction, but it takes as much craft to create a plot-driven story as a character-driven story, especially one in which the reader cares about what happens to the characters. Trying to rate the approaches is like comparing apples to oranges: Each type has its unique appeal. Thus, it's senseless to compare a plot-driven story such as David Morrell's *First Blood*, which is the novel on which the Rambo films were based, to Anne Tyler's *The Accidental Tourist*, which explores a couple's grief after the murder of their son. What you can do, however, is examine how each of these authors manages to convey tension and a sense of forward movement, then emulate his or her methods.

Out of Sync: Maintaining Constant Tension

Tension must be intricately woven throughout a story, not just appear in moments of distress or while a character strives for a goal. A great trick for inducing a constant underlying tension is to portray your protagonist as uneasy, uncomfortable, or somehow at odds in each scene. She can be hot, cold, bored, nervous, lonely, hungry, tired, aching, or craving a drink or smoke. The point is, she is rarely at ease, rarely happy, and rarely comfortable.

As a writer, you should constantly look for opportunities to make your character feel out of sync with her surroundings. You send a rookie cop to a grisly crime scene. You force an introvert to attend a party. You place a character who is struggling financially in an environment of wealth. Because you're striving to use tension as an underlying factor in every scene, rarely feature your character alone in a scene. The reason is simple: A character alone can be static. If you're tempted to create these protagonist-alone scenes, it's helpful to imagine your character on a stage alone and immobile. Sit in the audience and observe her, and ask yourself what you can add to make the scene sizzle with tension.

If you're forced to create scenes where a character is alone, find ways to introduce tension. Perhaps while alone the protagonist recalls a painful memory, and thus the scene segues into a flashback. Or, she could be deliberating over difficult choices or thinking back to previous events in the story. In a transitional scene where the character is driving or walking to the next locale, she can be dreading what is about to happen, fighting traffic or a downpour, or in some way interacting with the environment.

WORD BY WORD

You can also embed tension in your story with word choice, especially by choosing verbs that amp up the wattage of your sentences. You want readers waiting, worrying, and twisting, so your words should evoke frustration and longing. Refer to dangers, weapons, and pain in all its agonizing forms.

Language must evoke fear and convey emotion. Do your characters want to hide, flee, fight, rejoice, despair? Are they filled with rage or lust or both? Emotions need to simmer, boil, and explode. Characters need to bleed, faint, shiver, sweat, suffer.

Choose words for their suggestiveness, connotations, and associations. A terrific example comes from the first line of Peter Robinson's *Innocent Graves*:

> The night it all began, a thick fog rolled down the dale and enfolded the town of Eastvale in its shroud.

Notice how *shroud*, a word that shivers with connotations of graves, burials, and death, ends the sentence on a note of menace that also foreshadows.

Another technique that can be learned from this example is, whenever possible, to place solid nouns that evoke tension and suspense at the end of sentences and paragraphs, because emphasis belongs in final notes.

SOUND EFFECTS AND HIGH-VOLTAGE WORDS

Don't underestimate the sound of your words: Sound can communicate a tension all its own. Collect a vocabulary of tense sounds to shatter your reader's nerves. The second sentence in Peter Robinson's *Innocent Graves* shows how sound causes quivers:

> Fog in the market square, creeping in the cracks between the cobbles; fog muffling the sound of laughter from the Queen's Arms and muting the light through its red and amber panes; fog rubbing and licking against cool glass in curtained windows and insinuating its way through tiny gaps under the doors.

The author is making deliberate word choices to create unease, suggest danger, and form a cohesive world. Robinson could have written about fog *slipping* in the cracks, but *creeping* insinuates something more sinister, as does *muffle*, *mute*, *rub*, and *lick*. Tension comes from using high-voltage words when they're needed.

Scrutinize the sounds in your sentences and use hard consonants; for example, use *claws* instead of *talons*, *nails*, or *paws* because *claws* sounds more dangerous. Hard *k* or *g* sounds often express pain or menace as in *kill*, *crush*, *crunch*, *con*, *connive*, *gripe*, *gall*, *grate*, *grind*, *crack*, *kick*, and *kickback*. Menace is what tension is all about.

EDITING FOR TENSION

Tense fiction is pared down to the essentials, with every word in every sentence having a distinct purpose, every sentence in every paragraph being necessary to the whole, and every scene contributing to the story line. Every writer has a different approach to editing, but generally it's best to edit in stages, examining separate elements or effects in each stage of editing.

No matter your system, decide what is essential and what is gratuitous or a digression. Cast an eye at overall flow and pacing, which are linked to tension. Consider these questions:

- Have you begun the story at the last possible moment?
- Does the opening create intense curiosity?
- Is there a single dramatic question that focuses the story?
- Is the story overpopulated?

- Does the story locale contribute to tension?
- Are the subplots a source of tension?
- Do the flashbacks contain tension, or do they meander backward in time?
- Is there a major reversal or surprise midway?
- Is there too little or too much foreshadowing?
- Have you withheld information from the reader until the last moment?
- Are the stakes high in the story and the consequences for failure dreadful?

{ * }

Tension is never a bit player in fiction; instead, it is linked to every aspect of storytelling. It helps turn the setting into not just a place where the story occurs, but an intriguing and somehow unsettling place. It transforms dialogue into meaningful encounters rather than banal exchanges. It infiltrates scenes so that they prick the reader's sense of dread, and it turns the most virtuous reader into a snoop, desperate to delve into the hidden corners of your characters and their world.

chapter 17
Theme & Premise

> Though many writers like to think of themselves primarily as storytellers, yarn spinners, and fabulists, themes and ideas are inevitable. Every work raises questions, examines possibilities, and imagines the consequences of actions. You can't avoid making meaning if you want to.
>
> —Jerome Stern

$\mathcal{P}$erhaps you have a friend who claims that he never reads fiction. Implying that it is somehow beneath him, this person perhaps decries fiction as frivolous or meaningless. It is all you can do to restrain yourself from responding to this remark by shaking him. Hard.

You and I, lovers of fiction, know the pleasures and power of narrative. We know that the best fiction illuminates life and often elevates it. We read fiction for the delicious escape it affords, but we read it also to find ourselves, to discover truths, to untangle the knots of human mischief, to answer questions and explain possibilities—in other words, to cast a light on what it means to be human, and to explore the implications and truths of what it means to inhabit this spinning planet.

This light is cast by the means of theme and premise.

Theme is a fairly simple concept to grasp: It is what your story is about. This central idea or insight serves as a unifying element, a connecting thread woven into the story, creating cohesion.

Theme simmers beneath the narrative and, like other elements, often whispers. The best themes infiltrate the reader's consciousness rather than being ladled from the story like a thick stew. They lend significance to the events in fiction and reflect larger meanings. Human weakness, fallibility, vulnerability, and imperfections are rich territories to explore in your themes. Basic instincts like fear, greed, and jealousy can also be tied into themes.

Themes emerge from all that you, as the writer, have observed in a lifetime of watching people stumble, suffer, survive, and, of course, triumph. Understanding the theme of your story will help you focus on what is important in the story and what you can leave out, which is especially useful during the editing process. Ronald Tobias, author of *Theme and Strategy*, explains it this way:

> Theme is your internal guidance system. It directs your decisions about which path to take, which choice is right for the story and which choice isn't. As we write, we only start to understand the meaning of the work, but with theme, we actually structure the work on a *concept* that guides us from the start.
>
> The idea of theme shouldn't be some fuzzy, in-the-back-of-your-mind idea, but a viable, working pattern. … The idea of theme comes from what we may call priority of technique. Almost every work contains the major elements of storytelling: plot, character, style, idea, and mood, or emotional effect. These five elements do not always have the same priority in the work. Sometimes plot is more important than character, and sometimes character is more important than plot. Any one of the five elements of plot, character, mood, style, or idea can dominate the others. The element that does dominate the work is said to be the work's *theme*.

Let's keep Tobias's concept of an internal guidance system in mind, since it seems like a highly practical device. In fact, wouldn't it be great if it squawked or wailed a high-pitched alarm every time we veered off track in our writing? Think of the time it would save you in crafting fiction.

WHAT THEME IS NOT

A lot of writers start stammering when asked about the themes in their fiction. I believe much of this discomfort or confusion stems from unpleasant memories from high school or college lit courses where they were forced to write papers on the themes found in *Beowulf* or *The Grapes of Wrath*. If you have been confused by theme in the past, take heart. It is not necessarily the concept touted by academics and it is not difficult to discern in the works of your favorite authors or in your own writing.

Theme is not the message of your story, nor is theme a moral as stated in Aesop's Fables. Instead, it is the central concern of the story and it gives the story a focus.

Let's clarify further that the theme of a story is not the same thing as its subject. In a romance, the subject is a relationship. In a mystery, the subject is often a murder or the solving of a crime, and neither of these are themes. Sometimes a mystery is about a missing persons case or an insurance fraud, but again these subjects are not the themes.

In a romance, if one of the protagonists is grieving for a dead spouse and cannot allow intimacy back into her life, then the theme might be the tenacity of grief. Or it might be fear of passion or the need to always be in control. In a mystery or suspense story, the theme might simply be justice, or it might be the price of greed, power, or corporate corruption.

Themes can often be expressed in one word or a simple phrase. If you were asked to express the theme of spring it could be hope or renewal or rebirth. If we were to express the theme of Memorial Day we might describe it as duty, honoring sacrifice, honoring the dead, and remembering the brave who have fallen. Fourth of July themes are independence and freedom. Gratitude is the theme for Thanksgiving, while mischief is the theme for April Fool's Day.

In fiction, themes are often about desire, denial, corruption, guilt, and other key but relatively simple concepts that link the story elements together.

The Tangibility of Theme

Theme is often tangible, *felt* by the reader and reflected in language, setting, and voice. In *The Old Man and the Sea*, perhaps one of the most analyzed stories in all of literature, Ernest Hemingway taps into themes that echo throughout his body of work and reflect his ideals of heroism, masculinity, and resilience. Santiago, the fisherman, looks deep within himself for the courage, will, and perseverance to triumph over terrible odds. Santiago persists with honor and grace, and, echoing Hemingway's themes, asserts that "man is not made for defeat … [a] man can be destroyed but not defeated."

Stephen King's novella *The Body* is a coming-of-age story layered with a tragic theme: Life is not fair. This is evidenced by the accidental death of a young boy, by the brutality of the older gang, by Teddy's abusive father, by the death of the narrator's brother, and by his parents' lack of compassion and interest in his life once their favorite son is gone. Another theme is the inescapable influence of family and childhood on every adult.

In William Styron's novel *Sophie's Choice,* the theme is guilt and the crippling hold it can have on a person. In fact, both Sophie, who feels responsible for the deaths of her children at the hands of the Nazis, and Nathan, who feels guilty for his family's slaveholding past, wrestle with it.

Margaret Mitchell's *Gone With the Wind* is, on the surface, a romance, but the story's memorable characters, layers of conflict, underlying themes, and scope have turned it into a classic. Several themes are woven throughout: resilience, war's sweeping destruction, the importance and endurance of land (Tara), and Southern traditions and ways of life before and after the Civil War. *Gone With the Wind* and other epics, such as Herman Wouk's nine-hundred-page *Winds of War*, are often inlaid with more than one theme. The trick to achieving thematic coherence in epics is to choose themes that complement, rather than contradict, each other.

Enhancing Your Theme

If you're worried that your fiction doesn't contain themes, or if you're questioning whether it does, that too can be solved. A flatness or thinness in a story can indicate a lack of theme. If your plot veers in several directions but lacks coherence or a sense of connectedness, or if you've included random events or characters who act in ways that are not quite believable, then you may also have theme problems. Imagine theme as an invisible thread that links the disparate elements of a story together.

The reason writers concern themselves with theme is that theme lends a work resonance and significance. Without theme, you have a collection of events that don't reveal anything important about human nature. Your fiction will be strictly episodic, meaning that one thing happens after another, but the events don't create a lasting impact.

If you write stories that are framed by your concerns, beliefs, and values, then your unique slant will filter into the story and create theme. So begin by writing about ideas that fascinate and bother you, or by creating characters who care about things that you can relate to. Or, you can take the opposite tack and write about characters who represent values quite opposed to your own. The point is, with theme you have an opportunity to allow your passions and opinions to shine through your characters' actions.

Dennis Lehane, *New York Times* best-selling author of *Mystic River*, writes crime dramas populated with tarnished heroes who make us think about themes we'd sometimes rather not think about. His stories are artfully crafted, yet astonishingly violent, populated with more sociopaths, psychopaths, and screwballs than your most terrifying nightmares. The themes he explores are innocence lost, corruption, vengeance, and why people hurt other people.

In *Mystic River*, the main theme is loyalty, specifically family loyalty and the bond between husband and wife. When Dave's wife betrays him and turns him over to Jimmy Markum and his thugs, it's a turning point in the story. Lehane himself once said of the scene:

> It's a huge moment. That's the culture I come from—Irish-American working class—loyalty is the attribute that's valued more than anything. It has its great side, something I'm very much in love with. The thing that I look for in people, and if I don't find it, if your word is not your bond, then your word is shit, thus you are shit. It's the philosophy I grew up with and I pretty much took it into the world with me. But I think there's a bad side to that too. It leads to Nazism. It leads to the Mafia.

Taking a cue from Lehane, ask yourself what you see in life. Themes often come from the intersections of human behaviors and vulnerabilities. Notice the cost of things such as loyalty, fame, and independence. Notice too ideas that won't let go, small moments or life events that haunt you years after they happen.

CHICKEN OR THE EGG: DOES THEME COME BEFORE STORY?

Two schools of thought exist when it comes to writing with a theme in mind. The first is that a theme (or themes) evolves organically as it emerges from the character's actions; and the second is that theme is the basis from which you write.

Following the first school depends largely on whether you have an intimate knowledge of your characters. If you understand your cast members—especially your protagonist—and why they do what they do in your story, you can trust that their actions will create a theme.

The second school of thought dictates that, since theme is the glue that holds the story together, you must understand your theme in order for your story to unfold correctly. Theme will help you make decisions about the story and about why characters act as they do. Theme serves as a compass, a generous influence over all you write.

If your approach doesn't fall strictly within either camp, don't worry. Like all fiction techniques, working with a theme will become easier as you deepen your understanding of the underpinnings of fiction and its more subtle aspects. The truth is that writing fiction requires a great deal of thoughtfulness and analysis, and yet necessitates surrendering to the world of your story. As you slip into your characters' mind-sets and explore their lives, you'll start to discover the important connections in the story. What I'm saying here is that you need to spend a lot of time thinking about your story, allowing it to speak or perhaps whisper to you.

So, while either approach for devising a theme might work for you, I have noticed while working with many writers over the years that theme generally evolves and becomes refined as the story progresses. You cannot write by basing every plot point or character decision on theme, but neither can you ignore it, particularly in your final draft. Keep this in mind: The plot, characters, dialogue, setting, voice, and everything else are all vessels for the theme.

But there is a larger issue to consider: Working with a predetermined theme might close off options for your plot and constrain the story.

Focusing on theme can hinder your imagination and brain processes. The right brain is associative and finds connections between images and ideas—it is the garden where you harvest inspiration. The right brain needs room to roam, to play with ideas and images. If you focus too hard on milking the theme, the magic that happens when writing fiction might fail. You want to walk amid your story world with your characters confiding in you, suggesting additions to your scenes. If you're too focused on themes, your characters cannot speak to you and take up residence in your imagination.

Chance also plays a role in writing fiction. You might walk down the street and spot an intriguing-looking person and then decide to insert her into the story. Or you might be reminded of an incident from your past and let that too wend its way into your story. Writers need to allow for all sorts of influences (within reason) to slip into their stories, so an excessive focus on theme might shut out these options.

PUTTING THEMES TO WORK

Five hundred years after Shakespeare's death, his plays are read, analyzed, and performed because his themes resonate with enduring significance. Shakespeare knew that themes in fiction are based on timeless power struggles and deeply held emotions. His body of work, which consists of 38 plays, 154 sonnets, and 2 epic narrative poems, is the most studied in history. The range of themes he covered is too vast to list, but his works continue to influence us because the themes he explored were timeless and connected to human nature.

There is something else to be learned from Shakespeare and other great playwrights, like Arthur Miller, Edward Albee, and Terrence McNally: the need to balance theme with drama. If your story is based on moral principles, it's important that you restrain yourself from preaching. Instead, allow the theme to evolve naturally via your characters' dilemmas. Don't tell yourself that you're going to write a novel about greed. Instead, explore a character who wants too much or who believes that happiness lies in accumulating property, and then explore the lengths he'll go to to acquire things or power. Then reveal what happens when his possessions (or power) are threatened.

Theme often comments on basic human struggles and the triumph or failure of the human spirit. In the *Rocky* film series, we see Rocky Balboa representing both the everyman and the underdog. Rocky is a hero who grapples to maintain his dignity, self-worth, and humanity while engaging in brutal battles. Rocky follows in the footsteps of Hercules and Zeus, as does Rambo, another hero who looks within himself to find the strength to persevere when the odds seem insurmountable. Rocky and Rambo represent heroes who are not the strongest, smartest, or surest, but who prove that within each person lies the heart of a hero.

Themes can also comment on the wrongs of society, as in John Steinbeck's *The Grapes of Wrath*, which follows impoverished, displaced farmers as they become migrant workers laboring to survive. In Margaret Atwood's *The Handmaid's Tale*, the author describes a government corrupted by misogyny and religious fundamentalism, and shows what happens to women who have their rights and freedoms stripped away.

Themes can describe the peculiar alchemy of families, sometimes constructed of equal parts love, duty, and dysfunction, as in *Ordinary People*, by Judith Guest;

Terms of Endearment, by Larry McMurty; *Amy and Isabelle*, by Elizabeth Strout; and *Songs in Ordinary Time*, by Mary McGarry Morris.

Themes can also comment on the power, destructiveness, and grandeur of nature and how man is elevated or diminished by it, as in *Jaws*, *The Perfect Storm*, and *The Old Man and the Sea*.

THEME VS. PREMISE

Now that you have a working understanding of theme, let's define premise and explain how it is linked to theme. Both theme and premise provide foundations for building your story, but premise is linked most specifically to the story's conclusion. Like theme, premise influences and is influenced by several aspects of a story: (1) the truth and understanding arrived at by the story's end, (2) the protagonist's character arc, and (3) the conflict. Premise differs from theme in that it comments on cause and effect.

For our purposes, then, premise can be defined as a truth or conclusion—usually but not always about human nature—that is proven by the story's events and ending. It often reflects the protagonist's journey of understanding and the ramifications of the character's actions. Most often, premise can be summed up in a simple statement, such as "True love never dies."

It's important to note here that premise is sometimes confused with story concept, which is basically a one- or two-line summary. For example, a writer might be asked what his story premise is and reply, "It's about a wild bachelor living the good life in Manhattan whose life changes overnight when his sister dies and he becomes the guardian of his niece and nephew, ages four and six." This response qualifies as a story concept, not a premise.

THE TRUTH CONNECTION

The chief role of a premise is to prove or provide important understandings about human nature. When fiction does not comment on or reveal human nature, it can be baseless and silly. It comes down to a simple idea: All good story tellers have something to say about *why* people act as they do.

Sometimes it is said that if there is no premise, there is no story. This is because premise proves a hypothesis postulated by the story about life or the human

270

condition, and without it all you have are characters moving around in scenes, unaffected by the outcome. Tied to a story's resolution or outcome, premise is the end of the road, the destination, and the consequences (both good and bad) of surviving the conflict and the obstacles in the story.

A premise is a truth that the story proves, and helps reader extrapolate meaning from the story events. A romance generally proves the premise that love conquers all, but, of course, a romance can have any number of variations on that premise. Many war stories often prove the premise that war comes at too high a cost. While there are many variations, a war novel features a story where the main action takes place amid a battle, or is about preparing for or recovering from battle. War novels have been around since Homer wrote *The Iliad,* and demonstrate their tragic premise by killing off sympathetic characters, depicting human suffering and loss of all kinds, and questioning the necessity of war.

On the other hand, novels that feature heart-warming endings—such as the novels in Jan Karon's Mitford series, which follows Father Timothy Kavanagh, an Episcopal rector, and his flock—prove "in life there is always hope" or "people are essentially good," or a similar premise about goodness and spirituality.

In *Jurassic Park*, the themes of the story are greed and arrogance, while the truth that is proven in the premise is that man should not try to manipulate nature for his own ends. This premise is proven by the deaths of multiple characters, the near deaths of other innocent characters, and the general havoc that is unleashed through the resurrection of a long-extinct species.

Scott B. Smith's novel *A Simple Plan,* which was made into a film directed by Sam Raimi, proves the premise that greed corrupts. The story follows two brothers and a friend who find four million dollars in a downed airplane. They devise a scheme for keeping the money, but, like with all simple plans, soon everything goes wrong. The ending reveals a damaged marriage and a series of cold-blooded murders that prove the premise.

Like theme, premise brings meaning to fiction, and illuminates and makes sense of life. Readers turn to fiction to understand life's costs and blessings, and, often, for the hope of redemption. Our real world can dole out large doses of chaos, tragedy, and misery interwoven with capricious fate and simple unfairness; fiction is a place to sort it out and make sense of it all, and to restore order and justice to those who have been wronged.

271

Both premises and themes serve as filters or sorting devices for writers and keep the story from meandering, so in this way they can be considered the perimeters of a story. If characters or subplots or scenes don't relate to your theme and premise, you can sometimes discard them.

In *Sophie's Choice*, the premise, proven by the double suicide of the main characters, is that you cannot escape your past and your demons. In this case, Sophie's and Nathan's demons were guilt and mental illness. (The theme, as you may recall from page 266, is the powerful effect intense guilt can have on a person.)

THE CHARACTER ARC CONNECTION

The premise also connects to the character arc, because at least one main character must be changed by what the premise proves. As has been mentioned in earlier chapters, character arc is the transformation or change that occurs in characters over the course of a story or novel. A character can demonstrate an upward or downward arc, and is often seen in new light as a result of the arc.

In *A Simple Plan*, Hank Mitchell, the protagonist, demonstrates a downward character arc. In the beginning of the story he seems like a well-adjusted, decent fellow living a simple life in the town where he grew up. By the novel's ending he has blood on his hands, has lost his brother, doubts everything about himself, and wonders if he can ever repair his marriage, which was forever changed by greed.

Character arc is most revealed in the choices a character makes—especially difficult moral choices—and when he lies, cheats, steals or kills in order to gain. In James Dickey's *Deliverance*, a novel about four middle-aged Southern men on a perilous canoe trip down a Georgia river, the premise first appears to be that man cannot tame the wilderness. (The themes are manhood, courage, and the power of nature.) However, as the story progresses, readers realize that the premise is actually tied to the character arc, and that the development of the character arc for each of the main characters comes at a high price. The survivors of the river trip are tested by the story events, especially by the murder of their friend Drew.

The premise of *Deliverance* is that adversity reveals things that we'd rather not know about ourselves. The story's remote setting and violent actions force the premise into the light and reveal the men's brutal self-discovery. Especially illuminating is how all the men face life-or-death moral dilemmas in the story, and will never be the same again.

THE CONFLICT CONNECTION

As we discussed earlier in this chapter, premise leads to understanding and truth, and this understanding is always dramatized by the story's conflict. Conflict—something or someone opposing your protagonist's goal—is what fuels the story action, propels it toward resolution, and proves the premise. Conflict always has an outcome of win, lose, or draw, and the end of conflict brings with it a sort of body count—either literally as in *Deliverance* and *A Simple Plan*, or figuratively, as in most romance novels. When this reckoning takes place, the premise is crystallizes.

In some stories, the premise is dramatized with your protagonist on one side of the conflict, taking up the sword to champion the premise, and your antagonist on the opposing side. In screenwriting circles, this opposition is called the counterpremise, which we'll look at later in the chapter on pages 274 through 276.

Think of premise as a mathematical equation with three parts: protagonist, antagonist, and conflict. For example, the premise of *Romeo and Juliet* is that petty feuds have innocent victims. In *The Grapes of Wrath*, the premise is that the American Dream is not possible for all who live in this country.

Another example of conflict linked to premise is seen in *Kramer vs. Kramer*, a novel by Avery Corman about a divorcing couple locked in a bitter custody dispute. Protagonist Ted Kramer is a workaholic ad exec, and antagonist Joanna Kramer is a stay-at-home mom. When Joanna leaves, Ted is forced to reevaluate his priorities and bond with his son. Joanna eventually returns, and a custody battle ensues. The themes of the story are self-involvement and the search for identity. In the end, both parents put their son's needs first, which proves the premise that family is more important than individual needs.

Here is the trick to remember: When you create the central conflict for your story, make certain that the premise exposes an underlying truth or some form of enlightenment by the story's end. The premise and the ending of the conflict should always reinforce each other.

The premise also helps to reveal the inner conflicts of your protagonist and antagonist by exposing their flaws and needs. These traits are revealed throughout the story, but must be fully exposed by the end, when the truth of the premise becomes known. In the film *Good Will Hunting*, we see a protagonist both blessed by genius and haunted by his inner conflict. He must wrestle his inner demons—a lack of self-esteem, a belief that he's unlovable, and a fear of abandonment—in order to accept love and intimacy. The premise is that facing your demons is worth it for love.

In the Star Wars movies, the powers of good in the world—embodied by Luke Skywalker and other characters—overcome evil, embodied by Darth Vader and his minions. The premise that good is more powerful than evil is proven in the films that show Luke overcoming the forces of evil.

PREMISE, LESSONS, AND FEARS

Fiction depicts a before and after in a character's life, and premise shows the after-effects of the story events. Because premise is tied to some form of understanding (often the protagonist's self understanding), it's also helpful to look at premise as the knowledge a protagonist gains as the result of the story events and resolution. This knowledge is tied to his character arc and usually is obtained throughout the story, with the greatest knowledge gained in the final scenes or chapters. In *Kramer vs. Kramer*, both central characters arrive at understandings that prove the premise. (The premise is that family is more important than individual needs.) Ted Kramer learns that family is more important than career, and Joanna Kramer learns that family is more important than personal identity.

If you are still confused about the premise in your own story, ask yourself what knowledge your protagonist has gained as a result of her growth in the story. Another trick for working with theme and premise is to understand your character's greatest fears, and then link those fears to the premise and theme. *Kramer vs. Kramer* sets up several interesting dilemmas based on characters' fears. In the opening, Joanna Kramer fears that she's never going to find herself in a world that is passing her by while she cares for her son and struggles in a marriage that has gone sour. Based on these fears, she leaves her husband and son. Ted Kramer fears that if he loses his job, he'll lose his identity and everything he's worked so hard for.

THE COUNTERPREMISE

The counterpremise is another way of defining the conflict and increasing the tension. Here is how it works: There are often, but not always, two sides to a premise. The protagonist acts as the knight or defender of the premise, and sometimes is reluctantly dragged into events to prove the premise. The counter-premise is a powerful argument against the protagonist's goal and is a means of creating conflict, involvement, and sympathy for the protagonist. The antagonist usually champions the counterpremise, although there can be a whole range of forces—not necessarily human—opposing your protagonist. The reason we add the counterpremise to our repertoire of writing skills is that the more powerful the counterpremise, the more powerful the conflict.

If this seems complicated, just think back to most arguments that you've engaged in, recalling how both sides believed strongly in their positions. Similarly, the counterpremise, the antithesis of the premise, is a strong belief or force pushing against the protagonist. Fiction and films depict a sort of tennis game, with the premise and counterpremise volleying back and forth, the antagonistic force saying "no you can't," and the protagonist responding "yes I can." The counterpremise is a way to verbalize the negative powers stacked against the protagonist; from this clash of wills, tension and suspense are created, and your climax emerges.

Going back to the *Kramer vs. Kramer* example, recall that the themes are self-involvement and the search for one's own identity, and the premise is that family is more important than anything, which is what Ted Kramer discovers by developing a real relationship with his son. However, when Joanna Kramer sues him for custody of their son, the counterpremise is that mothers are naturally the best parents for offspring. In fact, there is an actual courtroom scene where the premise and counterpremise are staged, and the father ultimately loses. However, the ending provides a reversal when Joanna grants him custody, proving the story's premise that family comes first, which now *both* parents hold true.

We've mentioned that the main theme of Dennis Lehane's *Mystic River* is loyalty. The premise is that revenge should never be dealt out by individuals or a community, but rather be left to law enforcement. The counterpremise champions the belief that personal revenge is justified when the crime is personal. There are examples of this premise and counterpremise throughout the book, as when Jimmy decides to find out who murdered his daughter and punish him before the police do, but the story's ending proves the error in Jimmy's thinking and motives.

While you can use a counterpremise in your story, the facts or details of the story should not contradict the theme or premise. Your story works to disprove the counterpremise. In *Mystic River*, the counterpremise that everyone is entitled to vengeance or justice is demonstrated to be false, and three lives are snuffed out and other lives ruined to prove its falsity.

THEME AND PREMISE: GETTING SPECIFIC

Theme and premise connect the scenes (and the dots) and keep a story from becoming episodic or rambling. They also reveal what matters deeply in your story. Fiction mirrors or is a metaphor for life. Sometimes metaphors are painted with broad strokes, and sometimes mirrors don't reflect accurately, but premises and themes are never distorted, vague, simplistic, or clichéd. For instance, statements such as "child abuse is wrong" or "war is horrific" are true, but they are too vague, trite, and indistinct to create a resonating theme or premise. Your story has to reflect a specific slant on why child abuse is wrong. For example, consider the long-term ramifications of innocence lost in Dennis Lehane's *Mystic River*, where this concern plays out as a secondary theme, or how war can scar a landscape as well as people, as in *Gone With the Wind* and *Cold Mountain*.

If you don't illustrate the theme and prove the truth of the premise by the end of the story, then the story will fall flat. Conversely, if you pile on lots of themes and more than one premise, the story will become a confusing muddle. As mentioned in other chapters, fiction is about change influencing a character or group of characters, and premise reveals how these changes affect the characters. The protagonist's decisions and choices are entwined in the premise because in the end they must prove the premise.

A note of warning here: Be wary of trying to tack themes onto the ending. The sudden emergence of a pulpit of sorts at the ending will make the ending feel contrived, when instead it needs to deliver a heavy dose of emotion wrapped in drama. Also be wary of believing that all endings must expose a profound truth or insight. Endings must be balanced, and that often means an understated or simple culmination of the plot events.

$\mathscr{W}$HAT'S THE $\mathscr{D}$IFFERENCE?

To clarify matters, here is a side-by-side description of theme and premise. One tip to keep in mind is that theme can often be expressed in a single word or phrase, while premise is often a sentence that demonstrates the writer's opinion on a subject.

Housekeeping, Marilynne Robinson

Theme: personal freedom

Premise: A person cannot be eccentric or rebellious in contemporary society without paying an enormous price.

Mystic River, Dennis Lehane

Themes: loyalty, innocence lost

Premise: No one has the right to take revenge into his own hands.

The Secret Life of Bees, Sue Monk Kidd

Theme: belonging

Premise: Family is the people who love us most.

To Build a Fire, Jack London

Theme: survival

Premise: Nature is a cruel teacher.

Fried Green Tomatoes at the Whistle Stop Café, Fannie Flagg

Theme: courage

Premise: Love, though tested, endures.

Bastard Out of Carolina, Dorothy Allison

Themes: dangerous love, the bond of family

Premise: A dysfunctional family or relationship puts children at risk.

FINDING AND ANCHORING
YOUR OWN THEME(S) AND PREMISE

The tricky part of writing with a premise and theme is that they are not part of the structure, but rather the underlying forces. If you get stuck trying to find the theme or premise for your story, don't despair. Instead, return to your characters and think about the truths they're revealing in their actions and choices, and what they come to know through the course of the story. This goes back to the tried-and-true advice to show, not tell. In other words, don't lecture your reader or suggest how he should think. Instead, slowly reveal the layers of your characters' psyches, desires, and motivations, and your themes will emerge.

Also, notice how passions and fascinations play out in your own life. Notice how your story reflects your values and beliefs, how what you've learned about love or death or greed comes through. Often these hard-won insights can focus your story. But no matter how passionately you feel about a topic, restrain yourself and your characters from editorializing, because it dilutes the magic of storytelling. Although themes can be implied or plainly stated, they are never heavy handed or shrill. So if your characters are standing around giving speeches about the theme, omit these sections or tighten them so that they're realistic exchanges. An exception is found in children's stories, where the premise is often spelled out clearly in the end.

If your theme cannot be expressed in a simple word or phrase such as *freedom*, and if your premise cannot be expressed in a simple statement such as "motherhood is a doomed existence," then you might be in trouble. Remember, you're addressing a generalization about life, or a revelation about human nature, not coming up with a formula to save mankind from itself. That said, there is no single, proper way to express or state your theme or premise. Just remember that they don't need to express conflict in an obvious way, such as "man versus nature," and you should avoid reducing your premise to a cliché such as "the early bird gets the worm."

USING SUBPLOTS TO CONVEY THEME AND PREMISE

Subplots in a novel exist for several reasons, but are mostly a means to prove that life is complicated and messy, to focus on secondary characters, to add texture

and believability to your story world, and to reveal the different sides of your protagonist. Subplots also provide a breather from the relentless arc of the main plot
and are where the writer has the opportunity for further explorations, possibly
adding the subtleties in the story line.

Subplots have their own stand-alone quality, but at the same time are gracefully woven into the plot, depicting the intersecting lives of your cast of characters,
and also reflecting or assisting the theme and premise.

While subplots are connected to the theme of the story, if you write a sprawling novel with eight subplots—all reflecting the theme—you might be treading on
dangerous ground. The reader will feel surrounded, as if you're underlining or
shrieking the themes. Fiction cannot be this obvious. Some elements of modern
culture, such as television dramas and reality shows, like to wrap up themes in
tidy packages with giant bows that demand untying. Fiction doesn't need such
pat approaches or tactics.

Subplots are a way to connect events in your story thematically. If your
subplots are rich in meaning, then there is no need to preach or lecture to your
reader. One last point about subplots: They often work to drive a protagonist
away from his goals, serving as a dangerous distraction that increases conflict
and tension. In many stories, subplots prove the difficulties of human emotions
and dilemmas. For example, they can reveal that relationships, facing the truth,
and communication are difficult.

WRITING AND EDITING
WITH AN EYE TOWARD YOUR THEME

We started this chapter by comparing theme to an inner guidance system. However, because writing fiction is often a means of self-discovery, our themes tend
to emerge as we write the story. Thematic devices are not always conscious or
easily understood. We discover truths about our characters and their journeys
as we write the early drafts.

It might seem like I'm advising you to write without your guidance system
plugged into an outlet. But as you start writing, trust that your guidance system
will click on at some point. Begin with a main character, what she wants, and why
she wants it. Then shape the protagonist's desire into a tangible goal, possibly giv-

ing her several reasons for her desire, and adding the people or forces that stand in her way. If the goals and conflict in the story matter intensely to someone, then themes and a premise will materialize. As you work on later drafts of your story, use theme and premise to keep the story from rambling. To add resonance to the whole, weight themes so that they have more impact in the final chapters.

After you've completed your first draft, print it out and read it carefully with a pen in hand. If possible, allow a few days or weeks for the draft to cool before approaching it with your editor's hat on. When reading it, you can investigate your mind at work. Patterns, motifs, images, moods, colors, and repetitions can be noticed. As you read your first draft, ask yourself:

- Can I see a setting or a character's appearance in a new light?
- Do certain ideas or scenes have more zing than others?
- Is the conflict resolved in a way that is plausible and satisfying?

In your final drafts, as you discover your theme, you might want to underline it by adding moods, symbols, or images.

If you're new to writing fiction, spend some time consciously thinking about what matters to you socially, politically, and ethically as you look at the world and the people around you. Your theme gives readers insight into what your novel is about, loops a connecting thread between the scenes, and helps move the story forward. A premise proves that the events in the story have mattered and have revealed aspects of humanity that we can all recognize.

{ * }

Human nature provides themes for our stories, while conflict, so inherent in everyday living, supplies premises. There are countless ways to play out the drama of what it means to be human. Adult readers don't open novels merely to follow characters frolicking through an adventure or series of misfortunes. They read fiction for enlightenment. Now, this doesn't mean that, Buddha-like, you impart wisdom with every loaded metaphor or character ploy. Rather, imagine that the glimmering threads of your story's tapestry will reflect on larger meanings about this complicated business of living.

chapter 18
Transitions

> The efficient and elegant writer makes each scene bear as much as it can without clutter or crowding, and moves by the smoothest, swiftest transitions possible from scene to scene.
>
> —John Gardner

Some fiction techniques are barely noticeable, but they remain as vital to our stories as joists and support beams are to a house. Transitions—the words, phrases, sentences, or paragraphs used to bridge what has been said or has happened with what is going to be said or will happen—create flow between elements in your story, although they are often barely visible.

Transitions must be consciously embedded, because readers resent feeling adrift, befuddled, or in any way disoriented in a scene or any other part of the story. Readers also hate to be jolted by sudden unconnected events or to dangle, waiting for an outcome that never arrives. Transitions connect the various paths along the character's journey and grant readers firm footing in every new scene they enter. In addition, they aid the internal logic of your story by moving readers from sentence to sentence, paragraph to paragraph, idea to idea, scene to scene, and chapter to chapter with grace and ease.

Transitions give ideas and stories fluidity, connectivity, and cohesion, but perhaps more importantly, they help readers trust in the story, allowing them to move along with its momentum while anticipating what is up ahead. While the reader anticipates what lies ahead, he also believes that all the actions, events, and meaning in the story will somehow tie together and reach a brilliant crescendo.

Transitions are like punctuation in your sentences—you employ them as a courtesy to readers so they can find their way through your story and keep the fictional dream flowing. Crafting transitions might not make you feel like a creative genius, and it doesn't qualify as one of the more captivating parts of storytelling, but it reveals your respect for your reader.

TRANSITION FUNCTIONS

Transitions are foundational elements in a story, part of the structure and organization. As stated earlier, transitions create flow and ease, but there is another important rationale for using transitions: Not every event in the story can unfold in real time. If all stories were told in real time, every novel would be eight hundred pages long or longer. There are times when it's necessary to summarize, to omit the boring parts of a character's actions, and to jump in and out of time. Transitions serve as bridges, walkways, and traffic signals as the writer manipulates time and moves events to new locales.

At the same time, it's also important to realize that you do not need to connect every element in a story. In fact, if you can leave a transition out of a sentence without causing confusion, do. Transitions are your way of showing courtesy to the reader, but do not imagine your reader is an intellectual invalid. While you should always guide the reader along in the story, there is no need to hover or announce every change. Let's look at the many purposes of transitions.

1. MOVING READERS THROUGH TIME

This is perhaps the most-often-employed use for transitions. However, not all time in fiction is equal. Sometimes we need to linger on action, sometimes the action will unfold with breathtaking speed, and sometimes we want to whisk through time quickly, dispensing only vital data. Here are transition examples that show the reader that time has passed:

> We had left the restaurant as dusk fell and were picking our way across the parking lot, Mom clinging to my elbow.

> A few moments passed, then his fingers pressed into Mom's neck, searching for a pulse, a hopeful sign.

It had been three weeks since my mother's death, and I still was not used to thinking of her as gone. When the phone rang, I half expected to hear her voice on the other end.

By the time the police car arrived, a crowd had gathered.

By the end of October, I had sorted, tossed out, and packed all my mother's belongings.

The pointer to keep in mind here is that in fiction time must always be accounted for. If six hours, six days, or six years have elapsed between scenes or chapters, you need a means to express this, and transitions are one of your tools to do so.

2. BRIDGING THE GAPS BETWEEN SCENES

Transitions are especially important in stories where the action skips around in time or moves through multiple viewpoints. Whenever a new scene starts, it's your job to quickly inform readers who is in the scene, where and when it is taking place (often also indicating how much time has elapsed since the previous scene), and how it links to the previous action.

In a well-paced and well-told story, you can get away with scene cuts, which involve leaping into a new scene and locale directly from a previous scene and locale without a pause for breath and without informing the reader where she is via a transition. Scene cuts emulate film techniques and are announced by an extra blank line to indicate a change. But if every scene jumps into a new locale without warning the reader, she will soon grow fatigued and disenchanted. You must sometimes insert clues about where the scene is taking place and how the character got there.

Here are three transition examples from P.D. James's *A Certain Justice*. Each indicates that a shift has taken place. *A Certain Justice* is a mystery that begins with a trial for murder, where a distinguished criminal lawyer, Venetia Aldridge, defends her client on charges of having brutally killed his aunt. Notice how much information James manages to slip into her transitions:

In Pawlet Court, on the western boundary of the Middle Temple, the gas lamps were glowing into light. Herbert St. John Langston, Head of Chambers, watched from his window as he had on every evening, when he had been working in chambers, for the last forty years. It was the time of the year, the time of day, that he loved best.

Slowly and with a careful avoidance of drama or obvious anxiety the court reassembled, waiting for the jury and the appearance of the judge.

He had said that he would be with her at Pelham Place by six-thirty, and by six Octavia was ready and waiting, moving restlessly from her small galley kitchen to the left of the door into the sitting-room, where she could gaze from the window up through the basement railings. It would be the first meal she had cooked for him, the first time he had entered her flat.

James's scenes are always strongly anchored by specific places and details, such as the gas lights.

As just demonstrated, transitions are often designed to accomplish several tasks in a few sentences. They are also sometimes used to reveal emotions that are the fallout from the previous scene; for example:

Dusk fell with its welcoming grace. With darkness descending, I sat alone with my fears, thinking over the events of the day, wrestling with decisions I'd rather avoid.

Or:

I was now faced with the hard facts of my life. It was over. Three years of my life swept away as if by a storm. The future not only looked lonely, it looked impossible.

These examples show that transitions can create the sequel (or aftermath) portions of fiction—the sections that happen after major scenes, where the characters react to, analyze, or reflect on what has happened, and often make decisions about the next course of action. Without sequels, the action can seem rushed or relentless.

3. COMPRESSING TIME

Drama contains high points, low points, and in-between points. If you treat every moment equally in a story, your story will seem unbalanced. Some moments need emphasis and slowing down, while others need to be compressed or summarized.

Since not every action in a story needs to happen in real time, transitions serve to compress time, and since not every moment in your story is equally important, transitions also summarize when events do not need a large amount of detail.

284

They are especially helpful when time has passed, but nothing significant has happened in the plot. For example:

> After the tumultuous events of the weekend, the following week was like an oasis of calm. Kristin's routine of heading off to work each morning and returning each evening at dusk was structured and busy—the way she preferred her life.

Compression is also helpful when a large swath of time has passed (a month, year, or decade), but events within the time frame are not vital to the plot. As a writer, you must constantly make choices and decisions about what is important in a story and what is not. Compression is your tool when you've decided that some events or periods of time are not particularly momentous but still must be accounted for. Remember, not every event or segment of time needs a blow-by-blow account, but you are required to acknowledge that time has passed.

Here's an example from Mary Lawson's novel *Crow Lake*. The inciting incident is a car accident that kills a couple, leaving their four children orphaned. The narrator, the second youngest in the family, is looking back and piecing together events of her childhood, musing about how they affected her adult self:

> I find it hard to remember much of what happened in the days immediately following the accident. Most of my memories seem to be merely images, caught in time like a photograph. The living room, for example—I remember what a mess it was. We all slept in there the first night; probably Bo wouldn't settle or I couldn't get to sleep, and in the end Luke and Matt brought Bo's cot and three mattresses into the living room.

It's a good idea, when you compress information, to focus on a few poignant details such as the orphaned children sleeping together in the living room. Notice that this transition has an intimate tone, and that the narrator is piecing together memories, emulating the fragmented recollection we have in actual life. Since memories often come to us in bits and pieces, it can work to parse out similar small bits of these recollections to create credibility.

4. ANCHORING FLASHBACKS

Transitioning into a flashback must be natural and smooth so that the reader isn't startled or lost. To signal or trigger the shift back in time, use a sensory device such as an object, smell, the sight or memory of a person, a song, or something evocative that reminds the character of the past.

After the flashback has been signaled to the readers with a line like "The scent of lilacs brought back that long-ago night on Grandma's farm, when the heady perfume seemed to permeate everything," change the verb tense to simple past perfect (*had*) in the first sentence or two to let the readers know they're in the past: "It had been a wet spring, so the lilacs were late in blooming that year." After this additional signal, you can use past tense for the rest of the flashback.

Then, when emerging from the flashback, again use a transition device to signal to the readers that they've arrived back from the past: "Startled from her reverie, she realized that the conversation at the table had switched to a new topic." Because you need to account for the time that elapsed while the flashback played out, add a device to show time has passed: "The waiter was approaching the table with their entrées. She took a last bite of her appetizer and leaned over to her date as the waiter slipped his entrée onto the table."

There are other devices you can use to end a flashback, such as a signal from the present-day environment. Perhaps a person at the character's table asks her a question, or there is a sudden noise or interruption.

5. INDICATING A CHANGE IN SETTING

The chief job of transitions is to signal change and movement. Readers are nimble, able to leap around in time and space, but you still need to provide transitions that lead them into new locales, especially when the scene change is an abrupt or surprising relocation. By "surprising" I mean something like a character walking out of a restaurant when gunmen appear and force her into a car:

> The back seat was of sumptuous creamy leather, smelling faintly of expensive cigars.

Or, leaving the restaurant, one of the diners has a heart attack on the sidewalk and must be rushed to the hospital:

> The hospital emergency room seemed lit with a thousand watts, with a hum of activity and purposeful movement that was at once frightening and comforting.

Many stories demand that the reader regularly zip into new locales, and in these cases, transitions need to accomplish much in only a few words. Transitions helpfully provide links between scenes and specify where a character is, why he is there, and how he got there.

When possible, introduce a new locale not only to inform the reader about a change of time and place, but also to provide information that will infiltrate the reader through more than one sense, as in the example of creamy leather and the scent of cigars.

Let's talk more about the problem of abrupt switcheroos in a story. If there is an abrupt or surprising switch to a new place, the reader should be caught up in the excitement of the movement, but not be disoriented by it. Often these sorts of transitions will both answer and raise questions:

> I awoke in a strange room, and the first things I noticed were a garish collection of pastel stuffed animals gathered on a shelf, and my clothes folded in a tidy pile on a white wicker chair.

Naturally the reader wants to know why the character is in the strange room, who the room belongs to, and how her clothes were removed.

When a change of locale is going to cause the character discomfort, create tension, or elicit strong emotions, signal the reader about upcoming events.

> As I walked through the heavy door into the ICU unit, I wondered if all hospitals smell the same—that underlying smell of disinfectant, rubbing alcohol, and fear.

Again, keep in mind that using sensory clues in the new locale, especially sights and smells, will help readers adjust as they move with your characters into new territory.

When a multiple-viewpoint story follows several characters, and thus is told from several locales at approximately the same time, the reader needs indications of the shift to different locales and characters. Often, shifts in locale can be accomplished in a few words, as in the infamous transition "meanwhile, back at the ranch." This well-known formula is shorthand that instantly transports the reader to the new locale.

Keep in mind, however, that readers do not need to follow characters through *every* doorway. Sometimes it's important to explain how a character arrived at a certain place, but too many writers constantly report on the mundane movements of every character, following him through rooms and streets, recording every step, wince, flexed muscle, or thought. Especially when your character is performing commonplace or normal actions, this sort of reporting is gaudy, awkward, and unnecessary. Remember to report on movement when something unusual happens or to clarify a major shift in location. It's often effective to focus on a character's physical responses with a line like "After the long flight to Sydney, Alice felt bruised and dazed." Or, "When the plane landed in Beirut after fourteen hours, I stood to release my kinked back, tortured by the too-small seat."

Be sure not to overuse a particular transitional approach. For instance, many writers always use setting details and weather to announce a change of location or scene. These sorts of announcements are a necessary part of your repertoire, but when overused they become dull. Of course, sometimes weather is important in a story, and can be used to make things happen or create a mood, but the point here is to ask yourself why you're writing like a meteorologist. Vary your techniques.

6. INDICATING A SHIFT IN MOOD, TONE, OR EMOTION

Not only do stories move around in time and place, they also trace the characters' changes in mood and emotion and the general change in tone that happens in any drama. Remember, mood and tone are not always dictated by characters, but can come from other elements, such as setting and lighting. A transition that uses setting and lighting to create mood might go like this:

> Night fell, and as the forest darkened around me, it was as if a giant, black curtain had been drawn, and it seemed that every rustle and lone bird call was echoing and thunderous in the darkness.

Shift mood, tone, and emotion as the story progresses to ensure variety in your story. If every scene plays out as light and hilarious or somber and distressing the sameness of mood and tone will flatten out the story and cause readers to become bored and restless.

Chapter four of *Crow Lake* ends with more distressing news for the orphans: Because their parents left little money, it is necessary to break up the family. Since this news is delivered in the last sentence of the chapter, it creates a cliffhanger as the reader imagines the implications of this decision. Then the author opens chapter five with this transition, indicating a shift in both mood and emotion.

You see the suffering of children all the time nowadays. Wars and famines are played out before us in our living rooms, and almost every week there are pictures of children who have been through unimaginable loss and horror. Mostly they look very calm. You see them looking into the camera, directly at the lens, and knowing what they have been through you expect to see terror or grief in the eyes, yet often there's no visible emotion at all. They look so bland it would be easy to imagine that they weren't feeling much.

And though I do not for a moment equate what I went through with the suffering of those children, I do remember feeling as they look. I remember Matt talking to me—others as well, but mostly Matt—and I remember the enormous effort required even to hear what he said. I was so swamped by unmanageable emotions that I couldn't feel a thing. It was like being at the bottom of the sea.

With this transition, ominous in tone, the reader begins to realize the full horror of the parents' deaths. Lawson is also using her chapter openings to create a consistent pattern of storytelling—most chapters open with the narrator inserting her adult presence onto the story. This serves to remind us that she's looking back on time and unraveling what has happened.

Accounting for these mood and emotional shifts is one of the trickier aspects of creating effective transitions. I suggest that you begin looking for places where your favorite authors slip in these emotional shifts, and imitate their techniques.

7. INDICATING A SHIFT IN POINT OF VIEW

Some stories must be told through more than one viewpoint because of the scope, interconnection, and depth that this structure provides. When you use more than one viewpoint, the reader has access to a wider range of information, emotions, motivations, and sensibilities.

Charles Frazier's *Cold Mountain* is an example of this type of story, and follows two distinct characters. Inman is a wounded solider deserting the Civil War and traveling home to his beloved. Ada is waiting for him and trying to cope with her new circumstances. Often, multiple-viewpoint stories are designed so the viewpoints join in the ending, bringing the main characters together in one location. Frazier uses a simple pattern in his book: The viewpoints alternate every chapter. When you use a pattern that the reader can easily recognize, the pattern, in a sense, serves as a transition.

However, even though the patterns make it easy to jump into viewpoints and locales, clues are still required at the beginning of each chapter once the pattern is established. These clues will let the readers know how much time has elapsed since they last spent time with the viewpoint character, where he is presently located, and other vital information needed to easily resume that part of the story.

8. CLARIFYING RELATIONSHIPS

Most novels contain a dozen or more characters who are somehow connected to the protagonist. It can sometimes be awkward to insert characters the reader hasn't met yet, so slipping them into a transition as they arrive on the scene can sometimes make their entry less contrived. Then, once they're in the scene, you can begin describing them or move them around.

Let's return to chapter four of Mary Lawson's *Crow Lake*. The parents' funeral is over and the following transition takes us to the next development:

> Aunt Annie arrived two days after the funeral. You need to know about Aunt Annie; she played a part in what happened. She was my father's eldest sister.

Thus, with a minimum of fuss, a character is introduced and we're told how she's related to the orphans. The transition continues:

> She was many years older than my father, short where he had been tall, fat where he had been thin, and with a behind I'm glad I didn't inherit, but she had something of him about her and she seemed familiar to me straight away. She was unmarried. My father's mother had died some years previously, not long after Great-Grandmother in fact, and since then Aunt Annie had kept house for her father and brothers.

Notice how these transitions pull double duty in the story by clarifying family relationships and introducing a character and her physical presence. When a new character enters a story, the reader must make room for him in his imagination. Thus it helps to briefly introduce the character's physicality, as in the introduction of Aunt Annie in the above example. But these introductions can be brief; don't stop the story for a biography or a chunk of detailed backstory that isn't relevant.

Devices for Delivering Transitions

Transitions need to be varied, sometimes unobtrusive, sometimes colorful, and always graceful. Don't start every scene or chapter with a character waking or reporting on a dream. If each scene starts in the same way or at the same time of day, the reader will become bored. Expand your transition repertoire and find fresh ways to indicate the passing of time and influence the mood of your story by using the following.

- **Lighting, shadows, sun, stars, moonlight, and the like.** "As the stars blinked on, one by one, she waited."

- **Weather.** "When the storm passed, we stepped out into the changed landscape."

- **Seasons, years, and eras.** "It had been five years since last she saw Jim." "Back in her grandfather's day, the small town had bustled with farmers in town every Saturday."

- **Objects.** "As the candle flickered low, shadows filled the room." "The tree that once blazed with the colors of autumn now stood naked."

- **Mundane activities.** "As she piled dirty dishes into the sink, she could hear her guests gathering their coats and preparing to leave."

- **A character's appearance and health.** "Now eight months pregnant, Mary seemed to have acquired an inner glow since last we met."

- **Specific references to time or date.** "It rained on my birthday." "Christmas dawned bright and clear." "It was the autumn equinox." "As if in a movie, the old grandfather clock struck midnight, its echoes filling the old house."

- **Indirect references to time passing or movement.** "The spring blooms were fading in the garden." "The crowd was thinning now."

- **Activities.** "As the minister intoned the familiar words, 'Dearly beloved, we are gathered here today,' the crowd grew quiet."

- **Interruptions such as a telephone or doorbell ringing, or the arrival of another character.** "Just as she found her handbag and keys, the phone rang."

291

- **Sound.** "I could hear the distant rumble of the ocean." "The ambulance roared past with its siren blaring." "As I stepped into the tearoom, the women's voices reminded me of an aviary."

- **Space breaks and chapter breaks.** These will indicate a change of some sort, including a change of mood or tone. However, while contemporary writers rely on space breaks with greater regularity, don't assume that you don't need to provide clues about place and time in the new segment.

- **Datelines.** Datelines are quick and easy signals that alert readers to viewpoint, time, and place. One method of easily informing a reader that you're moving in time is to use a dateline of some sort to head the chapter. Louise Erdrich names each of her chapters in *Love Medicine*, and also supplies the year and name of the viewpoint character. In Fannie Flagg's *Fried Green Tomatoes at the Whistle Stop Café*, each of the hundred-plus chapters is headed by a dateline.

TRANSITIONAL WORDS AND PHRASES

Simple transitions are generally, but not always, subordinate clauses placed in the beginning of a sentence or paragraph and used as an indication of change. They take the reader quickly and smoothly from one place to another, connect ideas, and add to the overall coherence of the story. They also alert readers to an unexpected shift in thought, such as a contradiction. However, while transitions can clarify relationships, they cannot correct convoluted sentences or muddled logic.

Return to the formula for writing paragraphs that you learned in grade school. The first sentence introduces the topic and is followed by supporting sentences and a conclusion. Ask yourself if your paragraphs deal with a single topic and if they need transitions to link them to the paragraphs that follow.

Place transitions at the beginning or close to the beginning of a sentence, but not exclusively. You should use a variety of sentence types. Further, always use the appropriate words to signal a contradiction or qualification. Some examples of appropriate words follow:

To illustrate results: *therefore, as a result, consequently, thus, hence, because*

To make comparisons: *similarly, likewise, in the same way, by the same token*

292

To show contrast: *but, yet, and yet, in contrast, on the contrary, on the other hand, though, still, however, nevertheless*

To show likeness: *likewise, similarly, in like manner, in the same way, also, as well*

To add or expand: *and, moreover, furthermore, further, in the second place, even more, again, also, too, besides, in addition, finally*

To show time: *now, later, this time, so far, earlier, until now, meanwhile, in the meantime, soon, since then, after that, immediately, periodically, the next day, finally, again, tomorrow, before that time, sometimes, ten years ago, last month, after, after it was all over, afterward, at the same time, formerly, hitherto, subsequently, always, never*

To show relationships in space: *above, beyond, behind, adjacent to, next to, in front of, north, south, east, west, opposite, over, within, at the top, at the bottom, nearby, along the edge, in the center, beside, on top, in the background, adjacent, nearer, near, surrounding, opposite, in the forefront, in the foreground, within sight, out of sight*

To amplify or intensify: *and again, in addition, further, furthermore, often, moreover, also, too, indeed, to repeat, in fact, surely, certainly, without doubt, undoubtedly, by all means, of course, frequently, occasionally, especially, usually*

To demonstrate sequence: *first, second, third, then, next, additionally, in addition, finally*

To indicate place: *down the road, in the middle of the block, at the site, up ahead, adjacent to, elsewhere, here, opposite to, there, near the river, above, inside the house, below, farther on*

To demonstrate results: *for this reason, because, since, as a result, thus, consequently, hence, accordingly, therefore*

To demonstrate insistence: *indeed, in fact, yes, no*

To change mood: *yet, because, despite, on the other hand, if*

To exemplify: *for example, for instance, as an illustration, in fact, thus, specifically*

293

To conclude or summarize: *in conclusion, to conclude, in sum, and so, this shows, all in all, to summarize, altogether, in brief, to sum up, finally, as a result*

Arthur Golden's *Memoirs of a Geisha* demonstrates how to write about a fairly complex topic in a style that moves along easily. In this excerpt, readers are learning about the business side of the geisha life, particularly how an apprentice is sponsored by an older geisha to learn the ropes. What is notable in this segment is how easy it is to follow the author's logic. The words that are used to smooth out and link ideas are noted in italics:

> *Of course*, no geisha keeps all her earnings, not even Mameha. The teahouse where she earned the fees takes a portion; *then* a much smaller portion goes to the geisha association; and a portion to her dresser; and right on down the line, *including* a fee she might pay to an okiya in exchange for keeping her account books and tracking her engagements. She *probably* keeps only a little more than half of what she earns. *Still*, it's an enormous sum when compared with the livelihood of an unpopular geisha, *who every day sinks deeper and deeper into a pit.*
>
> *Here's how* a geisha like Hatsumomo could make her younger sister seem more successful than she really was.
>
> *To begin with*, a popular geisha in Gion is welcome at nearly any party, and will drop in on many of them for only five minutes. Her customers will be happy to pay the fees, *even though* she is only saying hello. *They* know that the next time they visit Gion, she'll probably join them at the table for a while to give them the pleasure of her company. An apprentice, *on the other hand*, can't possibly get away with such behavior. Her role is to build relationships. *Until* she becomes a full-fledged geisha at the age of eighteen, she doesn't consider flitting from party to party. *Instead* she stays for an hour or more, and *only then* telephones her okiya to ask her older sister's whereabouts, *so* she can go to another teahouse and be introduced to a new round of guests. *While* her popular older sister might drop in on *as many as twenty parties during an evening*, an apprentice *probably* attends no more than five. *But* this isn't what Hatsumomo was doing. She was taking Pumpkin with her everywhere she went.

Grace, analysis, and logic are all evident in Golden's writing, and also belong in your writer's toolbox. Use them often and well to create a river of words a reader will not drown in, but rather sail across, with pauses to admire your craft and take in the scenery.

{ * }

Transitions aid the seamless unfolding of stories, yet it's downright shocking how often writers neglect to use them. If you're not accustomed to using transitions or you use them rarely, it might feel awkward at first when you start inserting them. But if you keep in mind that your aim is to make them inconspicuous (much like attributions for dialogue), and that they are a tool for summarizing, then the task becomes easier. Also keep in mind that transitions are a structural device, and you'll likely correct them as you edit and rewrite your final drafts.

Read like an editor, noticing how, when, and where your favorite authors use transitions and when they employ scene cuts. Emulate the ones that you find the most effective or original and then practice crafting your own varied methods.

Index

index

index

ABOUT THE AUTHOR

© EDMUND KEENE, JR.

Jessica Morrell is the author of *Writing Out the Storm* and has been teaching writers for fifteen years. She works as a writing coach, freelance editor, corporate trainer, and columnist. She is the former Writing Expert at iVillage.com. She conducts workshops throughout the Pacific Northwest and at conferences. Her Web site is at www.writing-life.com. She lives in Portland, Oregon, where she is surrounded by writers.